The American President in Popular Culture

THE AMERICAN PRESIDENT IN POPULAR CULTURE

Edited by
John W. Matviko

Greenwood Press
Westport, Connecticut • London

Library of Congress Cataloging-in-Publication Data

The American president in popular culture / edited by John W. Matviko.
   p. cm.
  Includes bibliographical references and index.
  ISBN 0-313-32705-X (alk. paper)
   1. Presidents—United States. 2. Popular culture—United States.
  I. Matviko, John W.
  E176.1.A6553 2005
  306.2'4'0973—dc22   2005006570

British Library Cataloguing in Publication Data is available.

Library of Congress Catalog Card Number: 2005006570
ISBN: 0-313-32705-X

First published in 2005

Greenwood Press, 88 Post Road West, Westport, CT 06881
An imprint of Greenwood Publishing Group, Inc.
www.greenwood.com

Printed in the United States of America

The paper used in this book complies with the
Permanent Paper Standard issued by the National
Information Standards Organization (Z39.48-1984)

10 9 8 7 6 5 4 3 2 1

This book is dedicated to my wife, Sandy,
whose encouragement and support got me through the project.

CONTENTS

INTRODUCTION

In April 2004, President George W. Bush flew to his ranch in Crawford, Texas, for a weekend of relaxation. Meeting the president there was Roland Martin, host of *Fishing with Roland Martin* on the Outdoor Life Network, along with the show's film crew. The plan was for Martin, George Bush, and the president's father, former president George H. W. Bush, to go fishing on a pond on the president's ranch that Saturday. According to Martin, the demands of foreign policy called, however, which meant that the president would have to spend that day in conferences. Luckily for Martin, the president still managed to find one hour on Friday afternoon to go fishing with the television host and his film crew. According to Martin, the president was a "very accomplished fisherman." The president also caught three fish.[1]

In this particular instance, President Bush was doing more than just relaxing for an hour with a fellow fishing enthusiast. In American culture, fishing has meaning beyond the simple act of putting a line out with the hope of catching something. Long before it became an individual sport, it was one of the major ways of sustaining human life. The symbolic value of showing President George W. Bush fishing thus communicates that the president has gotten back in touch with our preindustrial past, that he appreciates nature and the simple, basic things in life. The popularity of the sport is also important: There are over 34 million registered anglers in the United States, a number larger than the combined total of golfers and tennis players.[2] Ultimately, the headline "President Bush Goes Fishing" may be more important to the Bush reelection campaign than any environmental action of his administration.

This story illustrates one of the ways in which the president attempts to control his popular culture image. Like presidents before him, George W. Bush is aware of the important role that popular culture plays in American political culture. Early in 2004, for example, President Bush, wearing a black racing jacket, was given the honor of announcing, "Gentlemen, start your engines" at the Daytona 500, one of America's premiere NASCAR races. That NASCAR has become one of America's most popular spectator sports was not lost on Bush and his advisors. At Daytona, the culturally conservative "NASCAR dads" responded by cheering loudly for the president, changing a popular sporting event temporarily into a political one.[3]

Presidents, however, cannot always control how they will be portrayed in popular culture. In the Bush fishing example noted above, the president might have accidentally fallen in the water or made an inappropriate comment or, perhaps worse, not caught a fish. Given Roland Martin's friendship with the president, it is doubtful that the American public would have seen any of those moments, but the danger in attempting to control the popular image of the president is that it can sometimes backfire. President Gerald Ford, for example, after stumbling and falling a number of times on camera, came to became known as the "stumblebum" president. Efforts to demonstrate Ford's athleticism by inviting reporters on golf outings only made the problem worse when the president then proceeded to hit spectators with errant golf shots. Jimmy Carter, like George W. Bush, was an avid fisherman. In 1979, then-president Carter was fishing on a pond when a nearby rabbit hissed and gnashed his teeth at him. The "killer bunny," as it came to be known, was successfully repulsed when the president hit him with an oar, but the damage to Carter's image had been done as comedians, editorial cartoonists, and political opponents made certain that the moment would not be forgotten. As Carter biographer Douglas Brinkley notes: "It just played up the Carter flake factor and contributed to his public persona as something less than a commanding presence. I mean, he had to deal with Russia and the Ayatollah and here he was supposedly fighting off a rabbit."[4]

In addition to examining how the president has been able or unable to control his popular culture image, the contributors to this volume also look at how contemporary culture viewed the president. The chapters of the book are organized around mediums of communication (film, television, memorabilia, and so on). Taken together, they give us a richer understanding of the president within that era's popular culture. Space considerations have meant that some presidents will be discussed more that others. Although every president had popular images in the culture of his day, the chapter writers have done an excellent job of choosing the presidents who will most contribute to our understanding of the president in popular culture. Not surprisingly, Franklin Delano Roosevelt, one of America's most important presidents, as well as its first modern media president, can be found in every chapter. Similarly, a number of chapters devote considerable space to Andrew Jackson, our first common-man, nonelite president, and explain the sources of Old Hickory's popularity. The lesser presidents are not entirely ignored; for example, John Tyler's and Grover Cleveland's weddings are discussed in detail in the chapter on newspapers, and the not-so-flattering

President Richard Nixon meets Elvis Presley at the White House on December 21, 1970. (AP/Wide World Photos)

images of James Buchanan found in the political cartoons of the day are described in the chapter on political cartoons and comics.

Much of the text describes how American popular culture has treated the sitting president. In addition, the authors examine how that image has changed or not changed over time. The chapter on magazines, for example, documents the magazine history of a photograph of Richard Nixon and Elvis Presley taken in 1970 that did not surface until 1986. Elvis had requested a meeting with President Nixon to give him a gift of a World War II pistol and to request from him the necessary credentials to become a federal drug agent.[5] Eleven years after Nixon's resignation and nine years after Presley's death, the photograph quickly became the National Archives' most requested photo. Nixon aide Egil "Bud" Krogh would write a book about the event in 1994, and three years later Showtime would make a movie called *Elvis Meets Nixon*[6] about these two icons of midcentury America meeting for the first time. The media fascination with the photograph, along with the countless Web sites that use or discuss the photograph, are testimony to the event's continuing popularity.

Richard Nixon, who was controversial in his own time, remains a continuing object of fascination in American popular culture, but he is not the only president who transcended his own presidency. The presidencies of Washington, Jefferson, Lincoln, Franklin Roosevelt, Truman, and Kennedy all resonated in popular culture long after their terms of office. As the political and popular culture changes, we often look back to past presidents for inspiration and guidance (Washington and Lincoln) or for ways of understanding the present (Jefferson and Sally Hemings in the midst of the Clinton sex scandals). By examining how the popular culture views the president in his own era and in later times, these chapters document America's continuing fascination with the presidency as a way of understanding the nation, its culture, and ourselves.

Most of Hanna Miller's chapter on presidential memorabilia considers the image of the president in popular culture before the mass-mediated images of the twentieth century changed how we related to the president. Her section on the election of 1840, for example, demonstrates the role material culture played in making it a presidential election with one of the highest **percentages** of voter turnouts.

One of the ways in which popular culture is sometimes studied is to look at how popular culture borrows or steals from elite and folk culture. Juilee Decker's essay examines the ways in which the fine art renderings of the president, such as paintings and sculptures, are adopted by popular culture. As she demonstrates, this process lets us experience both art and the president.

Jerry Rodnitzky's introduction to his chapter on popular music notes that as presidents have changed, our popular music has "kept the beat." His chapter chronologically documents how contemporary times viewed the president.

The American stage has been fascinated with some presidents while ignoring others. Laura Pattillo's drama chapter deals with this phenomenon, as well as with how shifting popular tastes and changes in the culture create different dramatic views of the president. She documents how even very popular, prize-winning plays about a president sometimes seem dated and no longer relevant to succeeding or later generations.

Arthur Holst examines the myths, legends, stories, and jokes that have surrounded our presidents. As he notes in a number of places, studying these stories often reveals as much about popular culture as it does about the president; as the culture has changed, so have the stories.

Tony Giffone's essay on presidential homes, birthplaces, and graves asks us to consider why, when it appears that some Americans may have lost faith in the political process, these places remain such popular tourist destinations. Giffone's essay probes our fascination with the lives of our presidents, from their sometimes humble beginnings, to how they lived, to how they chose to be buried and, hopefully, remembered.

Franklin Delano Roosevelt's library, completed in 1940, was the first federal presidential library to be founded. Unlike birthplaces or homes, presidential libraries are created specifically to preserve the president in our memory. Benjamin Hufbauer, in his chapter on presidential libraries, looks at the ways in which we experience the president by visiting these libraries.

Presidents have always had a public and private side. As Elliot King discusses in his essay on newspapers, what is considered private, and thus outside what the popular culture reveals about the president, has changed considerably from the early presidents to those of today. His essay helps us better appreciate these changes as well as the role that newspapers play in our understanding of the president.

As one of the first communication mediums to achieve popularity nationally, magazines have also played an important role in how we have come to view the presidency. Katina Stapleton's chapter on magazines looks at how the president has used and been used by magazines and tabloids. Her chapter, in particular, focuses on the president as media celebrity.

Around the beginning of the nineteenth century, drawings of the president began to appear in the newspapers and magazines of the day. Within a few years, these political cartoons became quite popular, and thus important, in how we viewed the president. Sandra Czernek's chapter on political cartoons and comic strips examines how cartoonists have captured, and sometimes led, popular sentiment through humor.

The twentieth century would see the development of three mass mediums that would clearly have an effect on the presidency. Motion pictures, radio, and television, in different ways, have each changed the relationship between the president and popular culture. American popular film communicates primarily by telling a story. Scott Stoddart's chapter on film looks at how and why the stories that American film tells us about the president have changed. For the most part, film deals with previous presidents. Radio, in contrast, usually deals with the sitting president. In Timothy Kneeland's chapter on radio, he examines how the president has used the medium to connect to the culture. He also demonstrates how radio has recently become an outlet for popular criticism of the president. Finally, television both monitors the current president and tells us stories about previous presidents. Melissa Crawley's chapter on television examines both of these functions. From tours of the White House to cable talk shows devoted to the latest presidential sex scandal, television keeps the president in the cultural spotlight; by dramatizing the lives of previous presidents, it further supports the important role that the president has in our culture.

The American president has been studied in many different ways; from policies and politics to styles of leadership. By examining the connection between the American president and the popular culture, this text looks at how both the president and the culture have adapted to each other.

Notes

1. Scott Lindlaw, "Bush Catches Bass With Crew From TV Show." *The San Diego Union-Tribune*, March 25, 2005, http://www.signonsan diego.com/news/politics/20040410-1309-bush.html.

2. *Bassin' USA*, May 23, 2004, http://www.bassinusa.com/busa/company/index.asp.

3. Bryan Curtis, "NASCAR's Silent Majority," *Slate*, 23 May 2004, http://slate.msn.com/id/2095592/.

4. Buck Wolf, "Jimmy Carter's 'Killer Bunny'," *ABCNEWS.com*, March 25, 2005, http://216.239.63.104/search?q=cache:mMmXprPWkekJ:Archive.abcnews.gocom/sections/us/WolfFiles/wolffiles82.html+%22Buck+Wolf%22+and+%22Killer+Bunny%22&hl=en

5. "When Nixon Met Elvis," The National Archives, May 23, 2004, http://www.archives.gov/exhibit_hall/when_nixon_met_elvis/part_1.html.

6. *Elvis Meets Nixon*. Director, Allan Arkush. Showtime, 1997.

PRESIDENTS AND POPULAR CULTURE TIMELINE

1789	George Washington becomes president.
1791	An uprising of western Pennsylvania farmers over a tax on whiskey is put down by the federal government.
1797	John Adams becomes the second president.
1797	The Alien and Sedition Acts are passed. The Sedition Act calls for fines for those who criticize the government.
1800	The Library of Congress is established.
1801	Thomas Jefferson becomes president.
1803	The United States buys Louisiana from France for $15 million dollars.
1804	The passage of the Twelfth Amendment means that the vice president will come from the party rather than from the runner-up. The Lewis and Clark expedition begins.
1809	James Madison becomes president.
1812	John Paff publishes "Hail to the Chief."
1814	Francis Scott Key writes "The Star Spangled Banner."
1816–1824	The "Era of Good Feelings" ushers in a period of optimism and confidence for the new nation.
1817	James Monroe becomes president.
1825	John Quincy Adams becomes president.

1828	Popular political campaigning begins as John Quincy Adams and Andrew Jackson battle for the presidency. Among other charges, Adams's supporters will claim that Jackson lived with his wife before they were legally married.
1829	Andrew Jackson becomes the first "log cabin" (nonelite) president.
1830s	Inexpensive newspapers aimed at the masses appear.
1834	Nathaniel Currier begins selling prints of popular American scenes.
1836	The Battle of the Alamo is fought.
1837	Martin Van Buren assumes the presidency.
1840	The presidential election campaign features many types of presidential memorabilia. P. T. Barnum combines public relations and advertising to publicize his circus.
1841	William H. Harrison dies shortly after becoming president. John Tyler assumes the office.
1844	John Tyler becomes the first president to be married while in office. Press coverage is limited. Samuel F. B. Morse invents the telegraph. News and information will travel much quicker.
1845	James K. Polk becomes president. "Manifest Destiny" begins a period of aggressive continental expansion, culminating with war with Mexico.
1847	The first recorded baseball game is played in New York City.
1848	Gold is discovered in California.
1849	Zachary Taylor becomes president and dies in 1850. Millard Fillmore succeeds Taylor.
1852	Harriet Beecher Stowe's *Uncle Tom's Cabin* is published. The novel will strengthen Northern popular sentiment against slavery.
1853	Franklin Pierce becomes president.
1857	James Buchanan becomes president. The Dred Scott decision increases tension over the slavery issue.

1861	Abraham Lincoln becomes president. The Civil War begins.
1865	The Civil War ends. Andrew Johnson assumes the presidency after Lincoln's assassination at Ford's Theatre.
1867-68	Political cartoons fuel Johnson's impeachment proceedings.
1869	Ulysses S. Grant becomes president.
1876	The United States celebrates its centennial. Alexander Graham Bell demonstrates the telephone.
1877	Rutherford B. Hayes becomes president. Edison invents the phonograph.
1878	President Hayes adds a telephone to the White House.
1881	James Garfield becomes president, but dies on September 19 from a gunshot wound. Chester A. Arthur becomes president.
1885	Grover Cleveland becomes president. *The Adventures of Huckleberry Finn* by Mark Twain is published.
1886	Grover Cleveland becomes the second president to marry while in office. The press provides extensive coverage of the wedding and the honeymoon.
1889	Benjamin Harrison becomes president.
1891	Dr. James Naismith invents the game of basketball
1893	Grover Cleveland becomes president for a second time. Presidential buttons make their first appearance.
1897	William McKinley becomes president.
1898	At the urging of the sensational (yellow) press, the United States goes to war with Spain. Theodore Roosevelt leads the Rough Riders and garners considerable publicity for his effort.
1901	President McKinley is assassinated; Vice President Theodore Roosevelt assumes the office. Roosevelt becomes the first president to appear in motion pictures.
1905	The first nickelodeon appears in Pittsburgh.

1906	Roosevelt calls the investigative reporters of the day "muckrakers." *The Jungle*, Upton Sinclair's muckraking examination of the meat packing industry, is published.
1909	Howard Taft becomes the first president to attend a baseball game. One year later he will throw out the first pitch of the new season.
1912	The *Titanic* sinks after hitting an iceberg.
1913	Woodrow Wilson becomes president.
1915	D. W. Griffith's controversial *Birth of a Nation* premieres. President Woodrow Wilson says that it is "history writ with lightning."
1917–1918	The United States participates in World War I.
1920	KDKA in Pittsburgh becomes the first licensed radio station. Its first broadcast is the results of the Harding-Cox presidential election.
1920s	The prosperity of the "roaring twenties" increases interest in mass-mediated popular culture. Image advertising begins.
1920–1933	The Twentieth Amendment prohibits the manufacture, distribution, or sale of alcohol.
1921	Warren G. Harding becomes president.
1923	President Harding dies. New president Calvin Coolidge delivers a radio eulogy for him. Henry Luce begins *Time* magazine.
1926	RCA creates the National Broadcasting Company (NBC).
1927	Charles A. Lindbergh Jr. becomes the first person to cross the Atlantic by plane. The first successful talking picture, *The Jazz Singer*, is released. The Radio Act of 1927, the first important broadcast legislation, is passed by Congress.
1929	Herbert Hoover becomes president. The stock market crashes; the Great Depression begins.
1930s	Despite the Depression, Hollywood experiences boom times.

1932	"Happy Days Are Here Again" becomes Franklin Delano Roosevelt's popular theme song.
1933	Roosevelt takes office. His radio "Fireside Chats" will help Americans cope with the Depression and, later, World War II. *Newsweek* and *U.S. News and World Report* begin publishing.
1938	Robert E. Sherwood wins the Pulitzer Prize for his play, *Abe Lincoln in Illinois.* Orson Welles's Mercury Theater's radio broadcast of *War of the Worlds* scares the nation with a supposed Martian invasion. An actor sounding very much like President Roosevelt adds to its believability.
1939	At the New York World's Fair, President Franklin Roosevelt becomes the first president to appear on television. MGM releases *The Wizard of Oz* and *Gone with the Wind.*
1940	Franklin Roosevelt's library is completed in Hyde Park, New York. Future presidents will create their own libraries.
1941–1945	The United States participates in World War II.
1941	Mount Rushmore, with images of Washington, Jefferson, Theodore Roosevelt, and Lincoln is completed.
1945	Harry S. Truman becomes president with the death of Roosevelt. The Cold War between the United States and the Soviet Union begins.
1953	Dwight D. Eisenhower becomes president.
Mid-1950s	Rock and roll begins.
1958	Dore Schary's *Sunrise at Campobello* about Franklin Delano Roosevelt opens on Broadway. The popular play wins numerous awards and will later be made into a successful movie.
1961	John F. Kennedy becomes president.
1962	Comedian Vaughn Meader's releases the *First Family*, a highly successful comedy album that parodies the Kennedy family.
1963	Lyndon B. Johnson becomes president after the assassination of John F. Kennedy.

1964	The Gulf of Tonkin Resolution escalates United States involvement in the Vietnam conflict.
1967	A satire of President Lyndon Johnson, Barbara Garson's *MacBird*, opens off-Broadway.
1968	Candidate Richard Nixon appears on the popular *Rowan and Martin's Laugh-In* television show and uses the show's tag line "Sock it to me?"
1969	Richard M. Nixon becomes president. A play about the Founding Fathers, *1776*, opens a long run and is eventually made into a film.
1974	The Watergate scandal brings the resignation of Richard Nixon. Vice President Gerald R. Ford becomes president.
1975	James Whitmore stars in a popular one-man show, *Give 'Em Hell, Harry*. NBC's *Saturday Night* does its first Gerald Ford skit. Ford is portrayed as an incompetent bumbler.
1977	Jimmy Carter becomes president.
1981	Ronald Reagan becomes president.
1989	George H. W. Bush becomes president.
1992	Candidate William Clinton plays the saxophone on *The Arsenio Hall Show*.
1993	William Jefferson Clinton becomes president.
1998	William Clinton's sex scandal dominates popular media moving beyond tabloids and cable channels to network newscasts and major metropolitan newspapers.
2001	George W. Bush becomes president. *That's My Bush*, a satirical situation comedy about the George W. Bush presidency lasts for eight episodes. Planes hijacked by terrorists crash into the Pentagon and the World Trade Center.

References

Conlin, John. *The American Past: A Survey of American History*, 7th edition, vols. I and II. Belmont, Calif.: Thomson Learning, 2004.

Pavlik, John and Shawn McIntosh. *Converging Media: An Introduction to Mass Communication*. Boston: Pearson, 2004.

Turow, Joseph. *Media Today: An Introduction to Mass Media.* Boston: Houghton Mifflin, 1999.

Vickers, Anita. *The New Nation.* Westport, Conn.: Greenwood, 2002.

Vivian, John. *The Media of Mass Communication.* Needham Heights, Mass.: Allyn and Bacon, 1997.

CHAPTER 1

MEMORABILIA

HANNA MILLER

Highfalutin rhetoric and wonky foreign policy pronouncements don't mean much in a democracy in which the enfranchised includes the illiterate, the ill-informed, and the generally disinterested. American presidential candidates have long been forced to strip their messages of substance, translating them into alliterative slogans, eye-catching logos, and familiar everyday objects. The average voter may be mystified by the finer points of a party platform, but he or she can instantly recognize and understand log cabins and dinner pails.

The material thrust of presidential image making, which often begins before the candidate has even accepted a nomination to run and continues after his death, has produced a flood of memorabilia that reveals much about electioneering and governance in the United States. Perhaps more than any other aspect of campaigning, material objects embody the myth-making, celebration, fun, faith, and unbridled aggression that are now staples of the American election season.

With a few notable exceptions, the vast majority of president-related trinkets are produced during a campaign. This chapter explores why "stuff" was introduced to campaigning, and how it became an essential component of nearly every successful presidential candidacy for more than a century, beginning with the William Henry Harrison campaign of 1840. It also examines why it was so hard to find as much as a button for your favorite nominee in the last presidential election, let alone a ceramic pipe or silk ribbon to pin to your hat.

The First Campaigns

Americans have rarely shied away from materialism, so why didn't memorabilia play a more important role in the first presidential elections?

The answer lies in the young Republic's attitudes toward the office of the presidency. There was much hand-wringing over potential abuses of the presidential seat, which former colonists feared could easily become a throne.[1] Issuing any campaign materials, all of which boil down to the message "Vote for me!" would have smacked of a power grab.

Most of the surviving memorabilia from the earliest period of the Republic was apparently issued in conjunction with postelection events, such as inaugurations and official appearances. These items were defiantly utilitarian: It would be years before campaigns seized on the potential of tie-in puzzles and piggy banks. George Washington's inauguration was celebrated with the issue of no fewer than fifty varieties of metal garment buttons, nearly all of which honored the presidency rather than the personality assuming it. Among the most popular inscriptions affixed to these elegant brass, copper, and silver tokens were "Long live the president," "The Majesty of the People," and "Remember March Fourth, 1789."[2]

Washington's second inauguration and death inspired the release of christening cups, snuff boxes, tankards, and fawning biographies—including at least one by "Parson" Mason Locke Weems, featuring the ever-popular stump of a cherry tree—that served as models for later campaign literature. Historian Keith Melder has suggested that the inexhaustible race to insert Washington into the public memory, replete with its gewgaws and one-dimensional portrait of its central figure, represents the first real American political campaign.[3]

None of the trinkets celebrating Washington were likely designed for purchase by the average American.[2] The quality and relative rarity of these objects suggests that ownership was reserved for Washington's most loyal supporters, or at least for those whose fortunes allowed them to indulge in faddish items.

Presidential memorabilia was not at this time an arena for profiteering—at least not to Americans. But a prescient British hardware manufacturer grasped the earning potential of the new nation's quadrennial partisan brawl and in 1807 Sheffield issued a set of steel razors emblazoned "a true Jeffersonian," "a true Washingtonian," and "a true Madisonian." Presidential memorabilia scholar Roger Fischer speculates the "Madisonian" razor, offered for sale two years before Madison's election, may be the earliest American campaign artifact.[2]

The unvarnished partisanship embodied by the razor enterprise gradually became an undeniable element of presidential races. It raged throughout the first decade of the nineteenth century and briefly faded as the Democrats established an unassailable supremacy during the War of 1812's aftermath, only to reappear when long-simmering rivalries boiled over in 1824. Political parties began to emerge during Washington's first term, in defiance of the founders' wishes. Many delegates to the Constitutional Convention strongly disapproved of parties, believing they fostered disunity and fed corruption,[4] but the irreconcilable interests of rural and urban dwellers, revolutionaries and conservatives, and the rich and the less so (those without any wealth at all would have no real voice in electoral politics for years) trumped philosophy, and the nation was soon divided into two competing camps.

Animosity between the Federalists and the Republicans defined the election of 1800, in which Thomas Jefferson was finally declared the victor. His election was celebrated by jubilant partisans across the nation, including the anonymous New England supporter with an artistic streak who created a linen banner crowing over the results. The three-foot-wide banner, now in the collection of the Smithsonian Institution, features a hand-painted portrait of Jefferson believed to be based on an engraving taken from a Gilbert Stuart painting.[3] Jefferson's likeness is framed by a somewhat shaky oval, surrounded by sixteen stars and topped by an eagle-like creature with a printed banner in his mouth. All of these elements were staples of Washington memorabilia: The significance of this textile is bound up in its text. The message that swirls down the right side of the banner reads "T. Jefferson President of the United States of America/John Adams is no more." These two homespun sentences presage the exultant tone, virulent partisanship and depiction of the presidential contest as a two-man brawl that would characterize campaign memorabilia for generations.

Andrew Jackson's Contributions

While British manufacturers like the aforementioned razor maker tried mightily to foist campaign items on their democratic cousins to the west, no memorabilia was mass-produced and circulated in an effort to win an election before Andrew Jackson's arrival on the political scene in 1824.

In an article quoted by Roger Fischer, button collector Alphaeus H. Albert argues that a button with Monroe's name inscribed on its backside, probably created during James Monroe's campaigns or administrations, deserves classification as a campaign item.[5] Even by the standards of the day, however, sewing a candidate's name tightly against fabric seems unnecessarily demure. In addition, as Fischer rightly points out, Monroe was largely unopposed in 1816 and unopposed altogether in 1820; his races were highly unlikely to stimulate new developments in material tactics.[2]

The backname button typifies the bulk of pre-1840 presidential memorabilia. Like the ceramic pitchers and brass tokens before it, the button was designed for personal consumption. There is no promise—or, perhaps, prayer—that the item's buyer will somehow sway other voters. Elections, and the campaigns preceding them, were not yet the public spectacles they would become following the massive expansion of the electorate.

Obstacles barring certain white men from voting were hastily swept up in the 1820s, almost doubling the number of eligible voters. These voters were energized by new laws allowing for the selection of presidential electors by popular vote: Until 1812, that important job was left to state legislatures. One state after another modified its code to permit direct election, and by 1828, nearly the entire nation had adopted the modern practice.

Andrew Jackson was the first candidate to openly woo the new electorate. His campaign rejected the sense of civility that had restrained enthusiastic participation and emotional appeals. His supporters stormed American cities with a cavalcade of rollicking festivities modeled after Independence Day celebrations: They marched, feasted, orated, and toasted in unprecedented displays of gaiety. It was the modern student body president election writ large, with Jackson playing the role of the charming bon vivant who promises more dances and better cafeteria food. His foil was the aristocratic John Quincy Adams, representing the speech-giving, all-A student boasting every teacher's endorsement. Jackson struck voters as much more fun, winning the popular vote in 1824 and the presidency in 1828.

Jackson shrewdly rebuilt his image to exploit public sentiment, emphasizing his lack of formal education and entrepreneurial streak, while conspicuously downplaying his status as a slaveholder. His enormous wealth didn't suit the folksy Western demeanor he adopted for the campaign trail, so he ignored it. His strategy earned him a score of imitators—most recently Ronald Reagan—who won the nation's confidence astride a healthy-looking steed, and George W. Bush, a Boston Brahmin turned Texan who touted his humdrum academic performance.

Central to Jackson's carefully honed image was his military service. Jackson had decisively defeated the British at New Orleans in 1815, a heroic act that spawned songs, breathless editorials, and enough memorabilia to outfit a small army. There were snuff boxes and bandanas, plates, pitchers, crocks, and mugs. It is almost impossible to determine which of these objects were issued in conjunction with a campaign and which were the usual knickknacks associated with American celebrity.[3] The obvious point for scholars of presidential material culture is the ubiquity of military symbols among these artifacts: Even objects depicting Jackson as a dignified statesman were ostentatiously captioned "General Jackson, the Hero of New Orleans."[2]

Two 1828 sewing boxes produced in France—presidential memorabilia remained an importer's market—dramatize Jackson's use of a military image.[3] The two boxes, both held by the Smithsonian Institution, each feature a candidate's likeness on the inner lid. While the balding Adams wears a jacket and cravat, however, a rugged Jackson is clothed in military regalia, represented by his tall collar and epaulets. Most voters, unlikely to ever see either candidate, became familiar with their faces through lithographs and memorabilia. By appearing in uniform, Jackson was able to convey his strong character through these images.

Jackson had seized on one element of the Washingtonian myth and clung to it. He assumed Americans believed that the qualities that spelled success on the battlefield—bravery, persistence, and focus—guaranteed success in the White House. One-hundred seventy-eight electoral votes proved him right and sent generations of campaign managers scrambling to publicize their candidates' military exploits. It wasn't until the run of Dwight D. "Ike" Eisenhower (the candidate perhaps most deserving of accolades for military service) that kindliness emerged as a virtue as valued as courage.

One nickname wasn't enough for the Hero of New Orleans: It was Jackson's alternate moniker, Old Hickory, that added a new material dimension to American electioneering. The name was bestowed on Jackson on an 1813 military march from Natchez to Nashville. According to legend, Jackson pitied a hobbling soldier (intimations of the kindliness that invigorated Ike's fatherly smile on billboards and buttons) and insisted he ride on Jackson's horse. Jackson finished the journey on foot, walking with the aid of a hickory stick.

The hickory stick was perhaps the first everyday object transformed into a political tool. Although a branch rescued from the woods barely hardly qualifies as memorabilia in the traditional sense, its use marked a significant development in the material culture of presidential campaigning. Jackson backers met in public squares and private fields to plant hickory samplings or erect tall hickory poles. Pole-raising became the highlight of the rousing grassroots celebrations organized in Jackson's honor. Sufficiently soused partisans would whoop as the beloved hickory stick was lifted skyward. In 1832, supporters of Henry Clay co-opted the event in hopes of buoying their candidate to victory over Jackson, hoisting ash poles meant to exalt "the Sage of Ashland."[2]

When Clay's stick-waving proved futile (Jackson easily defeated Clay, and political heir Martin Van Buren in 1836 effortlessly disposed of all challengers), the nascent Whig party turned to name-calling. The Whigs, a coalition of Jackson adversaries, formally organized in 1834. They labored to link their party to the American Revolution, emblazoning party tokens with liberty caps and supplying their own nickname for Jackson: King Andrew. The Whigs churned out dozens of protest items assaulting the Democrats and their policies, including an 1834 token with a jackass marked LL.D, alluding to Harvard University's award of an honorary degree to the allegedly illiterate Jackson, and an 1837 medalet featuring a prancing jackass and the slogan "I follow in the steps of my predecessor." Although the Whigs were incessantly adversarial, they didn't harness their understanding of material culture to service a single campaign until 1840—it was a campaign not soon forgotten.

Log Cabin and Hard Cider: The Election of 1840

Historians and collectors are at odds about the presidential campaign of 1840. Historians see a boondoggle of buffoonery that demeaned the political process; collectors see a treasury of trinkets.

The race pitted William Henry Harrison, a benign Ohioan with a respectable military record, against the incumbent Van Buren. The Whigs exaggerated certain elements of Harrison's biography to make him more palatable to voters. His spread of land was reduced to a cozy log cabin; his father, a signer of the Declaration of Independence, vanished; his role in vanquishing the Indians at Tippecanoe took on gargantuan proportions; and his generosity toward war veterans became legendary.

"Old Tip" was the sort of guy who would invite you to drink hard cider with him on the porch of his cabin. "Hard cider. Cabin. Hard cider. Cabin." Every voter knew the refrain. These sentimental symbols were the touchstones of the Whigs's drive for the presidency. "Log cabin, hard cider and coon humbuggery," grumbled Andrew Jackson, who well understood the potency of a "common man" with a dazzling military record.[6]

Unencumbered by any political past to defend or future to advocate—the party refused to adopt a platform, saying it inevitably led to lies—the Whigs focused on burnishing Harrison's image as a friendly farmer. He amassed a slew of nicknames by Election Day, including "The Ohio Farmer," "The Farmer of North Bend," "The Ohio Ploughman," "The Poor Man's Friend," and "The People's Choice." These nicknames were disseminated through a carefully orchestrated campaign of material objects.

"The 'Tippecanoe and Tyler Too' campaign inspired a harvest of souvenir items seldom if ever surpassed in quantity and variety in nearly two centuries of American politics," Roger Fischer[7] writes. The race insinuated itself into every cranny of American life, as women brushed their hair with Tippecanoe hairbrushes, men leaned on Hard Cider canes, and children tugged at cardboard pull cards, in which the smile of a wine-quaffing Van Buren becomes a frown when he sips from a mug of Harrison hard cider. And everybody—*everybody*—sang. More than 120 songs declaiming the supremacy of the Whig ticket were distributed over the course of the campaign. Contemporary observers maintained Harrison was "sung into the White House,"[8] but the songs wouldn't have worked without the silver spoons, snuff boxes, ribbons, and tokens engraved "Van, Van the Used-Up Man." The Whigs did a remarkable job of "staying on message," as modern politicos would have it. Every object released or endorsed by the campaign, large or small, cheap or dear, reinforced Harrison's projected image. The Whigs inventively enlarged the stable of campaign items to include consumables such as "Tippecanoe Tobacco," "Log Cabin Bitters," and "Tippecanoe Shaving Soap," none of which could realistically be expected to outlast the administration (an expectation sadly defeated by Harrison's death just eight weeks after inauguration).[2] Unlike the keepsake items produced to honor Washington, these objects were not made to last.

The bounty of memorabilia scandalized older statesmen, who denounced the campaign as a carnival. Van Buren himself attributed his loss to the "debaucheries of a political Saturnalia, in which reason and justice had been derided."[9] Even today, it is rare to find a summation of the race that doesn't resort to the word "circus." This unabashed showmanship reached its zenith during the summer of 1840, with thousands of partisan rallies. Jackson's earlier campaign celebrations began to look like staid tea parties in contrast to the raucous parties thrown by the Whigs.

Harrison rallies sometimes stretched for days, attracting as many as one hundred thousand men. The boozy revelry that unfolded at the base of a hickory pole became the Whig parade, with miles of marchers advancing in an organized fashion. They rode on log cabin floats and rolled buckskin balls, perhaps the Whigs' most bizarre contribution to the material culture of presidential campaigning.

The balls, measuring upward of ten feet in diameter, were emblazoned with slogans and bisected by a pole long enough for ten men to get a handhold and help roll. The balls were pushed from town to town, with some traveling across state lines. These odd contraptions were perhaps the forerunner of the bumper sticker and lawn sign, intended to exhort viewers to vote a certain way.

The Whig campaign, for all its ludicrous trappings and willful blindness toward issues of substance, stirred voters like no race before or since. The contest entertained a nation starved for distraction. Voter turnout in 1840 was a whopping 80 percent, up more than 20 percent from four years earlier. The memorabilia-saturated campaign had come of age.

The Log Cabin campaign was just too good to ignore. Parties quickly instituted its innovations as ritual: Each election season brought more rallies, more banners, and more songs. The public had begun to expect a show, and they were rarely disappointed.

The Wide-Awakes: 1860–1868

The Republicans in 1860 chose Abraham Lincoln to head their ticket, hoping the lanky Illinois lawyer would succeed where John C. Fremont, who had been nominated in 1856, had failed. Although the antislavery ideology that guided Fremont's campaign dominated the memorabilia distributed in virulently abolitionist areas—"free speech, free soil, free men" was printed on scores of ribbons and medalets—many of the items circulated nationally proved that the Republicans were willing to dabble in Whig-style personality politics. Lincoln was styled "The Rail Splitter of the West," capitalizing on Americans' fascination with the rural frontier.[2] The campaign hailed wooden axes and thousands of rails, each allegedly split by Lincoln himself, on a public electrified by the coming vote.

The legend of Honest Abe, Prince of Rails, was disseminated by the Wide-Awakes, a national coalition of partisan marching clubs. Nearly half a million men counted themselves among the Wide-Awake ranks in 1860. These members were schooled in complicated marching formations, sometimes marching in orderly groups numbering ten thousand participants. An entirely new collection of material culture was introduced in conjunction with the Wide-Awake movement, including the military-style regalia worn for marching and campaign torches. The Wide-Awakes literally blazed its way into the American consciousness, waving symbolically shaped torch lights and captioned transparencies lit from within. Melder quotes the *New York Times* reporting that, "the Wide-Awake torch-light procession is undoubtedly the largest and most imposing thing of the kind ever witnessed in Chicago."[10]

The rise of the Wide-Awakes marked the apex of what historian Richard Jensen has described as the army-style campaign.[11] Its parades and trappings intentionally mimicked the military. Although this approach perhaps helped to mentally prepare citizens for the upcoming Civil War, its popularity grew toward the close of the century.

Novelties: 1868–1892

Victorian America was awash in trinkets. A new mania for material objects fueled fiendish accumulation of everything decorative, from dried flowers to china plates. There wasn't a single intangible virtue that couldn't be translated into some *thing*: Americans wishing to express their piety invested in great family Bibles; teetotalers purchased gilded lemonade sets.

Campaigns fed the hunger for bric-a-brac by producing ornate novelties, including lapel pins with moving parts, toys, figural cologne bottles, and an array of textiles. The partisan ribbon received an ostentatious makeover, with James Blaine and Grover Cleveland in 1884 both issuing heavy fringed versions embossed with golden threads.[12]

Bandannas played a prominent role in the 1888 campaign, which paired Grover Cleveland with an aging Allen Thurman, perhaps best known for his devotion to snuff. Thurman's habit meant he was never without a bandanna, leading one critic to comment: "you have nominated a pocket handkerchief!" The campaign embraced the charge, releasing dozens of varieties of bandannas. The symbol stood in for Cleveland in hundreds of political cartoons, demonstrating the import of memorabilia.[2] Cleveland's opponent, Benjamin Henry Harrison, tried to resurrect elements of his grandfather's legendary campaign, rolling oversized balls and chattering about log cabins, but even Harrison acknowledged the Victorian passion for stuff by distributing bandannas and broom lapel pins, implying that his administration would clean up the government.[3]

Politics was a great game to the fun-loving Victorians. Elections so thoroughly captivated voters—most of whom were untainted by the cynicism familiar to latter-day Americans—that advertisers appealed to potential buyers by picturing candidates. Dr. W. W. Watson in 1888 hawked his "quick cure liniment" for "complaints of all nature" with cards fronted by portraits of Harrison and Benjamin Morton.[12] Similar commercial items constitute much of the political memorabilia produced during the Victorian era.

The Celluloid Button—1896

Nineteenth-century campaigns had bells and whistles—as well as badges, hats, jigsaw puzzles, and buttons—but at least one manifestation of material culture was conspicuously absent from pre-1896 races. The patent for the celluloid button, perfected in 1893 by a Boston dressmaker, was acquired by Whitehead and Hoag Company of Newark, New Jersey, which rushed to make the technology available to those vying for office.[2]

Buttons, which rapidly elbowed pin-on tokens and ribbons into obscurity, soon became the dominant form of presidential memorabilia. Tens of thousands of buttons have been produced since 1896, each offering a different combination of words and pictures intended to stir the voter's emotions. Some of the first celluloids, issued in conjunction with the hard-fought standards battle of 1896, featured gold bugs (a reference to the Republican's support of the gold standard) and clocks set at 12:44 (alluding to the Democrats support of a 16:1 silver coinage ratio). Although collectors refer to the pin-back button's first two decades as its golden age, the design, color, humor, and creative wordplay that still surface on campaign buttons is astounding. Many slogans deemed unworthy of wider circulation are consigned to buttons, leaving collectors a fascinating record of discarded and ineffective campaign strategies. There are punning buttons ("Dewey or Don't We"), rhyming buttons ("Click with Dick"), negative buttons ("Better a Third Termer than a Third Rater," distributed by Franklin D. Roosevelt's campaign), symbol buttons (Morse code spelling "Ike"; "AuH20" for Barry Goldwater), and buttons drawing on popular culture (Reagan's "Fritz Busters" buttons of 1984). There are portrait buttons and cartoon buttons (a smiling peanut labeled "The grin will win" was sported by Carter fans in 1976), buttons smaller than a pinky finger's nail, and buttons bigger than a dinner plate.[12] The story of twentieth-century campaigning is written in buttons.

The Decline of the Spectacular: 1900–Present

It is difficult to go a day during a modern presidential campaign without seeing at least one of the major candidates. They appear on early-morning and late-night television, hold town meetings across the country, and grant endless interviews.

Until 1880, however, it was almost impossible to lasso either candidate for a public appearance. The tradition of "mute campaigning" dictated that the candidate should disappear from the public eye, offering no comment on political issues or the campaign itself until Inauguration Day. It wasn't until a slew of bad publicity forced James Blaine on the campaign trail in 1884, delivering more than four hundred speeches in six weeks, that candidates and voters began to soften their stance on silent campaigns.[3] Blaine, who according to rumor was a secret Catholic; a dying leper and a sexual scoundrel who'd slept with his wife before marriage, apparently felt he had little to lose by defying convention and speaking on his own behalf.

The emergence of the candidate allowed parties to forge more personal campaigns, based on the character of the nominee. Teddy Roosevelt perfected this approach, using his massive charisma to appeal directly to voters. But his progressive stance on certain issues alienated others, inciting the ugly use of bigotry in campaigning. Roosevelt in 1901 invited black educator Booker T. Washington to dine at the White House, outraging racists throughout the nation. But Charles Thomas, a white Chicago Republican, was certain the event could aid the party by relaying a message of openness to ambivalent black voters. He commissioned a lithograph print and matching button of the two men at a dinner table, flanking a portrait of Lincoln, with the word "Equality" inscribed across the tablecloth. Roger Fischer quotes a 1903 report by the *Cincinnati Enquirer*: "thousands of buttons are being worn by colored men in Chicago, and the demand throughout the country is growing." Republican leaders apparently tried to quell the anger of white supremacists in their ranks by issuing benign multicultural buttons believed more palatable to racist sensibilities: These buttons depicted Roosevelt leading a charge of black soldiers up San Juan Hill. Democrats weren't so subtle: Some proudly pinned one of a raft of mean-spirited imitation buttons to their lapels. These buttons showed the same dinner scene, but with Washington pictured in the foreground, his face blacker and lips larger, and the formal dinnerware featured in the original was changed into tall bottles of liquor. If these revised buttons weren't clear enough, Southern Democrats could consult their "The Election of Roosevelt Means Booker Niggerism" postcard, or their button portraying Democrat Alton Parker alongside a white wedding couple and Roosevelt accompanying a white bride and black groom.[2]

Three-dimensional objects assumed less importance as candidates spoke more for themselves, however.[3] Although his campaign issued teddy bears and whistles shaped like Roosevelt's well-known grin, his speeches mattered more. The institutional partisan campaign, with its unquestioning exuberant parades and fireworks, fell into ruin.

Twentieth-century candidates were quick to incorporate new technologies into their campaigns, starting with Calvin Coolidge's 1920 release of his orations on phonograph records,[3] and in 1928, Democrat Al Smith barraged the nation with license plates and car decals.

Despite a general decline in memorabilia production over the last one hundred years, the twentieth century produced its share of memorable slogans and even witnessed a few brief resurgences of interest in old-style campaign stuff.

Befitting a generation bewitched by wordplay, slogans twisting candidates' names became a staple of electioneering in the 1920s. In 1924 (the same year the *New York World* launched a crossword puzzle craze by publishing a collection of its puzzles in book form), Republicans issued paper fans, urging supporters to "Keep Cool-idge." Four years later, the party released buttons with an owl asking "Hoo but Hoover?" A willingness to toy with a candidate's name remains a central component of campaign shtick.

The memorabilia market limped along throughout the Depression, when few voters could afford to add a "campaign trinket" line to their household budgets. Durable campaign items were elbowed out by an array of paper goods, including posters, postcards, stamps, and stickers.

After two warm-up campaigns, Franklin Delano Roosevelt in 1940 unleashed a memorabilia storm in hopes of capturing the White House for an unprecedented third term. The Republicans—led by Wendell Willkie—refused to fold, ordering thity-three million buttons to the Democrats' twenty-one million.[2] But buttons were just the beginning in a year that shamed even some of the most exuberant nineteenth-century campaigns: bandannas were back, as were hats, pocket knives, paperweights, and cigars. A recovering economy and real outrage surrounding Roosevelt's bid for reelection fueled the frenzy. Republicans responded to Democrats' banners and fobs reading "Carry on with Roosevelt," with buttons correlating a third term to the Third Reich and window stickers proclaiming "Exterminate Third Termites" and "Force Franklin out at Third."[2]

The next election cycle again deviated from the twentieth-century norm, producing one of the poorest crops of material culture in American history. Both campaigns were hamstrung by wartime shortages limiting the use of plastic and metal. Republicans, still reeling from Willkie's loss, may have understandably wondered whether gadgets did any good at all.

The national mood had lifted by 1948, when Harry Truman upset Thomas E. Dewey in what turned out to be the last of the back-slapping, baby-kissing, memorabilia-making presidential campaigns. By 1952, television had emerged—a candidate's successful use of new media would forever after trump material culture.

Memorabilia production, dealt a serious blow by the changing nature of politics and media, was further stung by seemingly trivial cultural changes: As smoking and drinking became less acceptable pastimes, cigars, cigarette cases, matchbooks, and beer steins were no longer viable campaign items. Americans also began wearing synthetic fabrics, which, when pierced by pinback buttons, retained the two telltale holes.

The sloganeering on memorabilia didn't stop, however: Dwight Eisenhower's catchy "I Like Ike," supposedly created by the Abilene High School marching band for a 1947 routine, reverberated with the American public and inspired a raft of imitators.[2] Campaigns relied on knock-off rhymes well into the 1970s, reminding voters "We Need Adlai Badly," "Let's Back Jack," "All the Way with LBJ," "You're Absurd, Bird," "Click with Dick," and "I Love McGov."

Campaigns continued to churn out novelty items, but in the new television-dominated culture, voters were often more likely to be exposed to coverage of memorabilia than the memorabilia itself. Very few voters actually drank either Johnson Juice or Gold Water, but the soda battle attracted media attention.

Buttons slumped badly in 1976, when campaign finance laws and post-Watergate disaffection combined to severely reduce button orders. Jimmy Carter's campaign planned to forego the whole button-and-bumper-sticker show until angry volunteers forced the campaign to reconsider.[2]

Whereas Carter's proposed abandonment of the pin-back button provoked outrage, political parties and campaigns today have largely backed away from the memorabilia market. The political trinkets with which most Americans are familiar—the bobble-head dolls, Halloween costumes, and decks of cards—are usually produced by independent entrepreneurs once the candidate is ensconced in office, much as they were in the Federalists' day. Electioneering materials haven't vanished entirely, however: As interest in a campaign intensifies, collectors have noticed a spike in memorabilia production. "We got a bumper crop," Akron, Ohio–based collector Avi Greenbaum told the Columbus Dispatch in the wake of Election Day, 2000. Greenbaum scored a button reading "Inauguration Day/January 20, 2001/This button will show the picture of the new team when they are known."[13]

Technology has allowed memorabilia makers to produce items more quickly than ever, enhancing the timeliness of their message. Youforgotpoland .com, a Web site lampooning President George W. Bush's debate reprimand of Senator John Kerry for failing to credit Poland's contributions to the military operation in Iraq, debuted soon after the event with a full array of "You Forgot Poland" T-shirts, stainless steel travel mugs, and mouse pads.[14]

New and unique forms of memorabilia have continued to spring up in the post-Vietnam era, a period usually characterized by disaffection for the electoral process. In 2004, some Latino communities created ofrendas, or altars, for Day of the Dead observances, that incorporated references to the next day's election.[15] Halloween retailers every four years stock their shelves with plastic masks featuring likenesses of the presidential candidates; perhaps as a sign of the enduring importance of memorabilia, the best-selling mask has accurately predicted the winner of every election since 1980.[16]

Most memorabilia today is found at nominating conventions, which most faithfully imitate the military model developed in the nineteenth century. Campaigns make sure supporters at these made-for-television spectacles are bedecked in T-shirts, hats, and pin-back buttons. In contrast, contemporary campaigns have otherwise placed a low priority on memorabilia, largely because of the changing nature of elections. The skyrocketing cost of campaigning has shifted the electoral battle to the bank. Rather than woo individual voters with throwaway items, campaigns now concentrate on producing luxury goods for their wealthiest contributors. In 2004, Kerry's campaign rewarded its most generous givers with silk ties and golden brooches that spelled out "Kerry 2004" in faux diamonds.[17]

Although memorabilia no longer plays the pivotal role it once did, the number of bumper stickers affixed to cars every four years indicates that the nation hasn't entirely shrugged off material culture when it comes to choosing their leader. It is likely that campaign memorabilia will continue to mirror the American relationship with other material goods—a relationship that shows every sign of lasting.

Notes

1. M. J. Heale, *The Presidential Quest: Candidates and Images in American Political Culture, 1789–1852* (London; Longman Group, 1982).

2. Roger A. Fischer, *Tippecanoe and Trinkets Too: The Material Culture of American Presidential Campaigns, 1828–1984* (Urbana: University of Illinois Press, 1988).

3. Keith Melder, *Hail to the Candidate: Presidential Campaigns from Banners to Broadcasts* (Washington, D.C.: Smithsonian Institution Press, 1992).

4. Roger Hofstadter, *Idea of a Party System: The Rise of Legitimate Opposition in the United States, 1780–1840* (Berkeley: University of California Press, 1969).

5. Alphaeus H. Albert, "Backname Buttons," *The APIC Keynoter* 80 (Summer 1980):21.

6. Robert Gray Gunderson, *The Log-Cabin Campaign* (Lexington: University of Kentucky Press, 1957).

7. Fischer, *Tippecanoe*, 33.

8. Melder, *Hail to the Candidate*, 87.

9. Heale, *Presidential Quest*, 107.

10. Melder, *Hail to the Candidate*, 104.

11. Richard Jensen, "Armies, Admen, and Crusaders: Types of Presidential Campaigns," *History Teacher* 2 (1969):33–59.

12. Ted Hake, *Hake's Guide to Presidential Campaign Collectibles: An Illustrated Price Guide to Artifacts from 1789–1988* (Radnor, Pa.: Wallace-Homestead, 1992).

13. Eileen Dempsey, "Electoral Collage," *Columbus Dispatch*, January 17, 2001, F1.

14. Rob Hiaasen, "Are We Having Fun Yet?" *Baltimore Sun*, October 31, 2004, 6E.

15. Cindy Gonzalez, "Latinos Getting Geared Up for Holiday," *Omaha World-Herald*, November 2, 2004, 2B.

16. Mary Vallis, "This Survey Comes with a String Attached: Anyone Want to Buy a Pile of Leftover Al Gore Masks?" *The Vancouver Sun*, September 29, 2004, A1.

17. Anne Marie O'Connor, "Kerry's California Coddling," *Los Angeles Times*, October 26, 2004, A1.

CHAPTER 2

PAINTINGS AND SCULPTURES

JUILEE DECKER

Art is not static. Paintings, sculptures, and other forms of art take meanings from their contexts, which may be mutilated, modified, or destroyed over time. By activating a public space or privatizing one's experience, these art forms inspire ongoing conversations with their viewers—be they children or adults, immigrants or citizens, residents of the nation or tourists from foreign lands. This essay examines the ways in which American presidents have been portrayed in formal portraiture such as the Gilbert Stuart portrait of George Washington[1] or the monumental façade of Mount Rushmore. In addition to considering these celebrated works that are part of our cultural memory, folk art and mass-produced imagery, which bring presidential likenesses literally into the hands of the viewer, will also be examined. These less formal but equally important art forms include works on paper and new media including photography and mass-produced reproductions.

The first section considers who is portrayed in these works of art by examining presidential likenesses as they appear in individual and group compositions. The second section explores what activities are commemorated (e.g., inaugurations, pre- and postpresidential activities, and death). The third section considers several examples of where physical likenesses of presidents have been translated into other media. Throughout the essay, emphasis is given to examining how sculptures, paintings, and other works of art are given new, reinvented meanings in other contexts.

Individual and Group Compositions

Presidential portraits come in a variety of forms including individual or group portraits. Because paintings are often displayed in a fixed position

George Graham's mezzotint print of the Lansdowne portrait of George Washington. (National Gallery, Smithsonian Institution/Art Resource, NY)

these works are often granted more formal status than sculptures. Mounted on a wall, paintings command a particular visual and aesthetic distance from the viewer. This distance is clearly important in Gilbert Stuart's paintings of George Washington, which promote the image of the president as military hero. Washington stands in his formal black outfit; he grasps a sword that is sheathed, and a quill and ink, papers, and books lie on the table beside him.

In contrast to paintings, sculptures are easily approachable because they can be viewed from all sides and easily negotiated by the viewer. One sculpture of George Washington, created by Horatio Greenough, connotes the classical heroism that embodied Washington's presidency. His torso is partially draped, and his arms are extended (one up and one out) in a classical pose, seated on a throne. These classical ideals were first connected with Washington's presidency during the eighteenth century, when the French sculptor, Jean-Antoine Houdon, carved and cast several busts and a heroic full-length portrait.[2] Houdon portrayed Washington draped in an antique Roman costume—a pleated tunic and toga—which give him a timelessness that connects his role as president to that of ancient Roman rulers. These attributes were adopted to suggest a shared sympathy with classical ideals of democracy, freedom, and knowledge. Perhaps more familiar, however, are the pieces in which Washington is shown in contemporary costume. Houdon's statue of Washington in the Capitol Building conveys the dignity and poise of the classically styled sculpture equally as well; however, here traditional clothing and a full-length pose are used instead. Henry Kirke Brown cast an equestrian portrait of Washington in 1856. Situated at Union Square, one of New York City's bustling urban green spaces, the work is the oldest public monument in the city. Although these variations in Washington's clothing seem to suggest different meanings, the works actually share a concern for promoting American ideals and the solemnity, poise, and wisdom of George Washington, the nation's first leader.

Life-sized sculptures may offer singular representations of heroic individuals, as in the case of the Washington sculptures. Monuments to presidents may also incorporate their surroundings, as in the case of the monument to Abraham Lincoln. The Lincoln Memorial, dedicated in 1922, was built to resemble a Greek temple, with thirty-six columns surrounding the rectangular building in Washington, D.C. Inside the memorial, Abraham Lincoln is seated and surrounded by words and images relating to his presidency and his quest for democracy and freedom for all citizens. A sculpture created under the supervision of master carver Daniel Chester French stands nineteen feet tall and weighs more than 175 tons. The memorial serves to commemorate Lincoln's presidency by quoting his Second Inaugural Address and the Gettysburg Address and reaffirms the potency of Lincoln's identity as both the Great Emancipator and the Savior of the Union.

Our nation's third president, Thomas Jefferson, is featured in portraiture less often than Washington or Lincoln. Notably, Jefferson's physical likeness and intellectual prowess are captured at the bicentennial memorial of his birth located near the Potomac River tidal basin in Washington, D.C. The memorial consists of two parts: the sculpture of Jefferson and the building that houses it. The memorial was designed by John Russell Pope, who was inspired by Roman-inspired Jeffersonian buildings such as Monticello and the Rotunda. Inside the memorial stands a nineteen-foot-tall bronze sculpture of Jefferson designed by Rudolph Evans. The walls surrounding the sculpture are engraved with Jefferson's writings, including verses from the Declaration of Independence, speeches, and letters. Comprising architecture, sculpture, and engraving, the Jefferson Memorial marks a transition from singular monuments to all-encompassing memorials. Although not commemorating a particular event, the Jefferson memorial captures the essence of Jefferson: The still pose, peaceful surroundings, and contemplative writings pay tribute to this prolific public and private author, founding father, and enlightened president.

Once they had been granted status as a presidential portraitist, artists were invited to create likenesses of subsequent presidents. On successful acceptance of his full-size Washington sculpture, Houdon, for example, carved a bust of Thomas Jefferson.[3] Sculptor Hiram Powers carved Martin Van Buren's bust in 1840 and then carved a likeness of Washington two decades later. Both of these works call to mind Greenough's classically styled pose—complete with Roman toga—though Powers reduces the image to a bust form only. Nonetheless, the adaptation of the republican legacy remains.

The artist George Peter Alexander Healy was commissioned by Congress in 1857 to paint several portraits of presidents. Perhaps most interesting among these is Healy's depiction of John Tyler, who became the first vice president to succeed on the death of a president. In the portrait, Tyler's left hand crumbles a newspaper, whose title, *National Intelligencer*, is just visible, suggesting Tyler's displeasure with the paper's report. All of this points to the importance of closely observing presidential portraits not only for their realistic detail but also for their allegorical meaning.[4]

In addition to singular treatments of individual presidents in painted or sculpted form, the portrayal of more than one figure in one setting enabled viewers to draw parallels among American leaders. A nineteenth-century lithograph attempted to trace the lineage of the presidency from George Washington to Zachary Taylor, the twelfth president. Taylor was prominently featured in the center of this print, which was published by Nathaniel Currier in 1848. A dozen oval, bust-length portraits of presidents and the presidential candidate nominee Taylor are shown among four flags. From the top, center, position, the ovals provide illustrations of the eleven presidential predecessors to Taylor.[5] In our modern contexts, this type of imagery recalls the practice of hanging an individual's annual school picture from grades one through twelve, with the large, center oval reserved for the senior photo. Whereas the modern context of the dozen portraits trace a student's life in likeness, the presidential oval traces, instead, the presidential lineage from George Washington to Zachary Taylor, billed as "the people's choice for 12th President."[6]

Whereas the Healy portraits and the printed works discussed here are intimate compositions that invite closer viewing, public sculpture offers impressive examples of presidential portraiture as well. Sculptures of presidents are sometimes clustered to commemorate leaders and their home states. These works are distinct from birthplace monuments, which will be discussed later in this chapter. Here, the sculptures celebrate statehood first and foremost. Among the individuals celebrated, presidents are featured, along with other historic individuals (inventors, military heroes, and civil servants). Celebrating collected achievements of several individuals, the monuments often decorate state capitol buildings, as in North Carolina and Ohio statuary.

At the North Carolina State Capitol, three presidents are depicted in bronze: Andrew Jackson, James Polk, and Andrew Johnson. Jackson's status as national hero, beginning with his defeat of the British at the Battle of New Orleans in 1815, is commemorated through his elevated position on a horse, which signifies his military role. Polk, the nation's eleventh president, was hailed as the leader who extended the nation's boundaries to the Pacific, signified by the map he holds in his hand. Andrew Johnson, shown holding the Constitution, was known for his commitment to the supremacy of states' rights during Reconstruction. Because of this, Johnson was sanctioned with eleven articles of impeachment against him, challenging the Constitution and calling into play the balance of powers between the three branches of government.

Levi Tucker Scofield's sculpture *These are My Jewels* (1893) was created for the Columbian Exposition and Worlds Fair and later moved to the Ohio State Capitol building in Columbus. Portraits of seven men surround both a column and a robed female figure who symbolizes not only the state of Ohio but also the Roman allegorical figure of Cornelia, who prized her children more than material possessions. Cornelia stands above the men, boasting of their importance to her—they are her jewels, as the title of the sculpture proclaims. Among the men standing beneath Cornelia, are three presidents: Ulysses S. Grant, Rutherford B. Hayes, and James A. Garfield. These celebrations of statehood in North Carolina and Ohio, among others, herald the individuals who claim these states as their homeland.

By contrast, Mount Rushmore, an impressive memorial nestled in the Black Hills of South Dakota, pays tribute to four of our nation's presidents—Washington, Jefferson, Theodore Roosevelt, and Lincoln—more so than statehood. More than two million people each year visit the sixty-foot tall granite portraits in tribute to the presidents and the craftsmen who created the sculpture: Gutzon Borglum, his son Lincoln, and a cadre of more than four hundred workers who carved the impressive physical likenesses from 1927 to 1941.[7]

Because of the monument's status as a national treasure and because of its popularity, the sculpture and, by extension, the facial likenesses of these presidents have been translated into many other media including postcards, decorative plates, stamps, decanters, jewelry, and other items.[8] These items are reproduced and replicated for the public and serve as "surrogates" for the original work. Viewers at any time and in any place can engage in one-to-one dialogues with part of the nation's past, present, and future. These works and many other examples of presidential imagery remind viewers of the past while also providing a historical prism through which to view our present.

Activities

In addition to painting and sculpture, related media such as fine art prints and sculpted medals were produced to commemorate presidential inaugurations. Other key moments were depicted as well, extending our knowledge of presidents as people in addition to knowing them in their role in the executive branch of the government. Subjects of these works have included the birth, life, postpresidential activities, and death of the men who have held the office of the president.

Traditional two-dimension media, such as paintings and prints, and three-dimensional cast works were issued to commemorate presidential inaugurations. The tradition of making medals to commemorate presidential inaugurations began with Washington's administration and continues today. Although these medals were once used as tokens of peace between governmental agents and Native Americans, today they are symbolic of historic moments in the nation's past.

Inaugurations have been celebrated in print media as well. William Henry Harrison's inauguration, for example, was commemorated with a print taken on March 4, 1841. As the only president to have served two terms that were nonconsecutive, Grover Cleveland's return to the White House was marked with Fromhart and Benson's issue of a commemorative print. In the center of the print, a large emblem features the words "Home Again" and portraits of President Cleveland and his wife, Frances. Underneath sits a picture of the White House (1894).[9]

In addition to the inaugural festivities, memorials celebrating the president's birth, presidency, and postpresidential activities have been treated as popular subjects. Because of their varying formats, some of these works are highly visible and become tourist sites, whereas others may go unnoticed. Images of Lincoln, for example, can be found in such popular sites as his memorial in Washington, D.C., and such lesser-known places as his birthplace in Kentucky, as well as his residence in Illinois.

Another Illinoisan, Ronald Reagan, was commemorated during his presidential tenure with a bronze sculpture paying tribute to him and his home state. Located in Dixon, Illinois, the bronze sculpture shows Reagan bedecked in a suit and tie. He looks down at kernels of corn while pointing to them with his right hand. A plaque accompanying the sculpture reads: "Illinois is famous for its production of agricultural products; so it seems appropriate for him to be admiring the kernels of corn in his hand." A sculpture commemorating Bill Clinton's birth in Hope, Arkansas, was dedicated in 1993. Carved by Albert Smith, the work associates the president with his home state by placing his hand and shoulders in a circular medallion between the flags of the United States and his home state.

Washington, D.C.'s Lincoln Park boasts a moving sculptural group titled *The Emancipation Monument* (1876) by Thomas Ball, which features a life-sized Lincoln next to a recently freed slave, identified as such by the symbols of slavery beside him including a whipping post, chains, fetters, and a frayed whip. Lincoln rests his arm on a column decorated with a bust of George Washington. Although the forms are certainly emotive themselves, the meaning of the sculpture and circumstances of its commission are even more powerful because the work was purchased through donations contributed by emancipated slaves. Charlotte Scott, a freed woman of Virginia, put five dollars toward the commission price, thus making the first payment toward this monument, which symbolized the rise to freedom abolitionists championed.[10]

Less traditional public works have featured presidential likenesses as a way to provide a historical context for the viewer. Grover Cleveland is featured in a cast bronze fountain by Ruth Asawa on the grounds of the Beringer Winery in St. Helena, California. This sculptural fountain depicts the history of wine, with a large bronze urn depicting events of the wine culture in California's Napa Valley region. Among the images, Michael Moone, president of the winery, looks over the shoulder of the president. In another panel, singer Marvin Gaye cups his ear against a grapevine, thus performing the motions of his soulful 1960s song, "Heard It Through the Grapevine." The president's role here, however, is marginalized and seems to serve only as a historical indicator.

Traditional and folk media have also captured the essence of the presidency and American identity in the form of two totem poles. The Gerald Ford Totem Pole,[11] for example, shows the president in his pre-presidential fame and also in contemporary politics. The top image portrays Ford bedecked in his University of Michigan football uniform. The next image features the U.S. Capitol, thus illustrating Ford's political career. The remaining three images are stylized faces of Vice President Nelson Rockefeller; Secretary of State Henry Kissinger, with his hallmark black-rimmed glasses; and former President Richard Nixon, whose lips are sealed with a safety pin, perhaps lampooning his Watergate troubles. In contrast to the specific nature of Ford's totem, the Americana Totem Pole[12] serves as a general reminder of American ideals. The mixed-media column features familiar symbols of American democracy including a bald eagle, the Liberty Bell, and the Constitution. Below this scroll, George Washington sits atop an original flag of the United States and a white pillar of justice. Carved in 1994, this sculpture is a visual as much as a cultural history of our nation.

Just as inaugurations and life activities were commemorated through fine art illustration, totems, paintings, and cartoons, so too was the death of a president. Lincoln's death was commemorated by an oil painting by Alonzo Chappel, and numerous engravings were published after Lincoln's death. One of these featured an ancient Greek philosopher with a lantern above a medallion portrait. The inscription reads: "Diogenes his lantern needs no more; An honest man is found; the work is o'er." This print revived Lincoln's political slogan of "Honest Abe" even after his death, thus firmly associating him with this attribute.

James A. Garfield's memorial in Lake View Cemetery—dedicated in Cleveland, Ohio, in 1890—serves an impressive example of presidential imagery on the site of a memorial. Five terra-cotta panels by Casper Buberl portray Garfield as a teacher, a soldier in the Union Army, a statesman in Congress, a president, and in death. Inside, a memorial hall provides information about Garfield's life, brief presidency, and death. Beneath the hall is a crypt featuring Garfield and his wife, Lucretia. Although the monument took several years to construct, the immediacy of Garfield's death was commemorated through the issue of prints. Many of these focused on the president's military career. One, in fact, was titled "Death of General James A. Garfield," for this was the capacity in which most Americans knew him, as Garfield had only served four months of his presidential term when he was assassinated in 1881.

The Lincoln Tomb State Historic Site in Oak Ridge Cemetery in Springfield, Illinois, boasts an evocative sculpture that has become a defining ritual for visitors: a bronze bust of Lincoln designed by Larkin Mead. The face bears the mark of visitors to the site who have stopped to rub the nose of Lincoln for good luck. By stopping to rub the nose, visitors directly experience the sculpture. They bring the work literally into their hands and thus remove any barriers of propriety and decorum. In contrast, viewers of the Stuart's portraits of George Washington are invited to experience the work in a formal, museum context, in which rubbing the president's nose would be highly inappropriate. Likewise, scaling Mount Rushmore to touch the nose of any of the four presidents would be difficult and dangerous. Yet the Lincoln bust in Springfield beckons visitors to interact with the work.

Portrayals of the birth, life, and death of presidents have expanded the number of sites available for commemoration and, at the same time, broadened the appeal of presidential imagery. Although the meaning and making of every example of presidential portraiture are beyond the scope of this essay, it can be argued that these works allow a level of appreciation that many other forms of physical likeness do not. Art—from painting to photography, sculpture to totem pole—is a part of the national cultural fabric. By virtue of their public ownership, these works serve as emblems of the past as well as markers of the present and future.

Translation into another Art Form

Marking the past, present, and future, these images have served to document the likeness of presidential figures from Washington's time to the present. Whether large-scale public works or small, intimate works, paintings, sculptures, and other art forms, works created by an artist have often served as artistic inspiration for another composition. The most common examples of this "translation" into another art form result from a painting's copy by an artist. Gilbert Stuart, for example, made more than one version of his "Lansdowne" portrait—at least four known renderings exist today—but the work served as inspiration for other painted and printed renditions. In this way, the Stuart painting has become a "standard" in Washington iconography. It served as aesthetic inspiration for subsequent portrayals of Washington, including John Vanderlyn's 1834 painting—a work that shares visual and compositional elements, such as the formal clothing and pose; the busy, paper-filled desk; and the open view in the back left corner.[13] In our modern times, mechanical means have enabled the Lansdowne painting to be easily reproduced in print form. A full-color replica print only one-fourth the size of the original is a modern commercial product that takes its inspiration from Stuart and allows modern viewers to own a substitute for the original painting.[14]

Whereas Stuart suggests an interior, framed, setting for Washington, John Trumbull moves the setting from indoors to out. His 1780 painting of Washington features the general in his full military uniform, standing on the bank of the Hudson River. Barely visible, to the right, a young servant holds his horse at bay. The painting was translated from large-scale canvas to small, intimate print form by Valentine Green the following year. Working out of London, Green served as purveyor of Washington's image to the European public. Green's adaptation of Trumbull's painting served not only as a presidential portrait but provided visual evidence of the decline of the British rule in the American colonies.

The monumental carvings on Mount Rushmore, as mentioned earlier, are well known through their transfer into other art forms. Discussion of translation brings to mind multiplicity, or the multiple replication of an image. During the last century, collecting and preserving these historical "documents"—including photographs and memorabilia of presidents—changed emphases, shifting from an avocation into an industry. In terms of

The Lincoln Tomb State Historic Site, Oak Ridge Cemetery, Springfield, Illinois. (Illinois Historic Preservation)

the number of reproductions, of course modern presidents (post-1945) have seen more widespread reproduction of their physical likeness, as now it is easier to reproduce a photograph or transfer an image from a painting into a cover of a magazine.

Washington and Lincoln, however, are known today from historical as well as modern reproductions. Lincoln, for example, garnered much more fame after his death than during his life. This is because the market for collectibles associated with him and his presidency is limited.[15] The widespread fascination with memorabilia and fine arts of American presidents, over time, has become the foundation of the phenomena known as "Washingtoniana" or "Lincolniana." Accordingly, prints and photos as well as paintings and sculptures of American presidents may be found in private homes as well as local or regional collections, in addition to our nation's treasures found in the White House and Smithsonian Museums.

New Interpretations

Posthumously, Abraham Lincoln became an emblem of freedom and civil rights. Printed in 1919, "Emancipation Day," a color print by F. G. Renesch, included Lincoln, Paul Laurence Dunbar, and the African-American educator Frederick Douglass.[16] Lincoln holds verses from the Declaration of Independence in which the American colonies embraced the idea of rights and individual freedoms for all mankind. Though penned by Thomas Jefferson, these verses became a weapon to use in support of the abolition of slavery and, later, in civil rights struggles. In addition, excerpts or complete transcriptions of Lincoln's Gettysburg Address are often included as part of the "physical likeness" of the president, just as Washington's antique Roman costume or his contemporary costume, including a uniform and walking stick, commemorate his presidency. One of many occasions in which verses from the Gettysburg Address were featured as part of the "presidential image" include the larger-than-life-size bronze sculpture of Lincoln that was commissioned in 1927 in Cleveland, Ohio. To pay for this sculpture, Cleveland school children began saving their pennies—coins embellished with Lincoln's profile—in 1924. The old adage that "pennies make dollars" is evidenced here, as the funds collected amounted to more than $35,000, which was a significant sum for an artist to receive for completing a sculpture. Kalish's sculpture of the colossal Lincoln was placed near the west entrance of the Board of Education as a reminder of the sculpture's sponsors.[17] Recently, the sculpture became a rallying point for Cleveland teachers and their union. In labor disputes over the past several years, and most recently in 2001, teachers came to Lincoln's side to demand better wages from the administrative officers who work in the building to Abe's back. The Lincoln sculpture was originally intended to call to mind the Gettysburg Address; individuals and groups, however, continue to endow the work with a new meaning—one that is dependent on current political, economic, and social concerns. Likewise, the Lincoln Memorial in Washington, D.C., has served as a site for civil rights demonstrations for the last two generations. In 1963, Martin Luther King Jr., for example, delivered his famous "I Have a Dream" speech to a crowd gathered near the memorial.

Portraits of presidents need not be limited to one sculpture or painting. A thematic approach can encompass several broad aims or themes, as in the case of the Franklin Delano Roosevelt memorial in Washington, D.C. In 1974, Lawrence Halperin was selected to design a memorial that would encompass more than seven acres of a park-like structure in the nation's capital. Four rooms were part of this initial design, signifying the four terms of Roosevelt's presidency. The designer worked with six sculptors to capture the essence of Roosevelt's presidential career from 1933 to 1945. Robert Graham, George Segal, Tom Hardy, Neil Estern, Leonard Baskin, and John Benson designed sculptures that together make up the four galleries of the outdoor monument.

In this and other monuments to Roosevelt, the presence or absence of the president's wheelchair, which serves as a visual reminder of his polio affliction, has been a source of contention. The question of whether to include the wheelchair in plain sight or in a more concealed manner has created controversy and, moreover, led to an array of portrayals, even within the same memorial. For example, Neil Estern's sculpture of Roosevelt and his pet dog conceals the president's wheelchair beneath his flowing cloak. An additional sculpture, by Robert Graham, of Roosevelt added to the memorial in 2001 prominently featured the president's wheelchair. Other portraits, however, separate his presidential status from his advocacy for polio research. Edmond Amateis's sculpture entitled *The Battle Fought—The Victory Won* (1958) commemorates the lives of seventeen prominent individuals— mostly scientists—who aided in the fight against polio. Roosevelt is included in this grouping because of his role as founder of the Georgia Warm Springs Foundation and the National Foundation for Infantile Paralysis. In this way, Roosevelt's polio is associated visually and ideally with overcoming obstacles—be they disability, the Great Depression, or World War II.

Another example of new interpretations of public sculptures is evidenced by the creation of impromptu sites of mourning after the terrorist attacks on the United States on September 11, 2001. In Union Square in New York City, for example, the bronze equestrian statue of George Washington by Henry Kirke Brown and John Quincy Adams Ward was heralded because of its original purpose (a symbol of democracy) and its renewed importance in light of the atrocious attacks on America and its ideals. This sculpture and many other sites related to the presidency and American identity were charged with another purpose as candles, graffiti, signs, and stuffed animals were left by mourners to symbolize both affection and loss.

Conclusion

Recent works by art and cultural historians have created exhibitions that celebrate the commemoration of presidents through portraiture.

During the renovation of the National Portrait Gallery in Washington, D.C., two major exhibitions concerning presidential imagery have allowed viewers to come face-to-face with our nation's leaders without traveling to the capital. One of these, "George Washington: A National Treasure," focused on Washington's physical likeness, as captured by Gilbert Stuart and translated by numerous others. A second exhibition, "Portraits of the Presidents from the National Portrait Gallery," featured more than sixty paintings, sculptures, photographs, and medals that celebrated the physical likenesses of our nation's leaders.

In many of these paintings, the artists employed full-length poses, formal clothing, and settings that bestow formalism on the works. Such formalism celebrates achievement and destiny, and the accessories—such as papers, legal books, columns, or pillars of justice—call to mind the importance of the president's role as leader of the nation. These portraits thus serve primarily as historical documents as well as evocations of humble beginnings, personal activities, or private lives. Therefore, viewers interact with the works not only because of their historical significance but also because of the shared sense of community that viewers experience when looking on a portrait of Washington or the façade of Mount Rushmore. The works are, at once, emblems of the past, present, and future and also biographical reminders of the lives of individuals.

Considering the range of presidential portraiture, we can see the increasingly open portrayals of these men enabling viewers to engage with the works on much less formal manner. The different levels of engagement that visitors to presidential sites or viewers of presidential portraiture experience reflect the changing perception of the role of the president. Portrayals of Abraham Lincoln and Franklin Roosevelt have often evoked a human quality that beckons the viewer to touch, hold, and experience the painting or sculpture. Lincoln, a champion for civil rights in the nineteenth century, became a beacon for freedoms in the twentieth–be they racial freedoms or labor disputes. Roosevelt seems approachable because we are aware of his association with polio and disability, which made him a champion for those causes. Although he was certainly an influential president, he looms also as an interesting, and more human, individual. Lincoln and Roosevelt are often portrayed in very human, real terms, and thus viewers have come to relate to them in this way. George Washington's portraits and sculptures have tended to be formal and seemingly impenetrable. The nation's first president and emblem of the United States, Washington was less a figure draped in Roman costume and formal portraiture and more a representation of classical heroism that embodied the first presidency and current twenty-first century ideals. While the sculptures of Washington had not been permanently altered, the works were transformed into one of the many rallying points in the aftermath of September 11. The heroism and classical ideals that Houdon, Greenough, and other artists bestowed on

Washington were exactly the qualities desired by Americans in a post–September 11 quest for democracy.

Presidential public art blends notions of culture, memory, and tradition. The examples discussed throughout this essay are historical documents of our nation's history. They stand as symbols of our heritage and our government, and most important, they recall the lives of individuals who have held the office of the president. Images of presidents have recalled the lives of individuals, but they have also commemorated activities and important beliefs that these individuals have upheld. As such, a "presidential portrait" can be more than mere ink on a page or paint on a canvas. The individuals who have been commemorated have, in word and deed, characteristically stood as emblems of our democracy. Moreover, they have become present in activities of everyday life.

The range of presidential portraiture discussed throughout this chapter has shown to what extent our culture is constantly in a state of change, emerging out of the dynamism of popular culture and everyday life. Individuals are encouraged to make connections rather than draw distinctions between the local and the national, between the national and the global, and between the everyday and the extraordinary. Visiting a site of national importance (such as Mount Rushmore or the Capitol building), with its numerous examples of presidential portraits and other symbols of democracy, enables viewers to make connections between our nation's past and the present. Because such works have become part of our cultural dictionary, we can associate the same significance to the examples of pop culture that take their cues from the notorious and formal art forms. In this way, viewers are encouraged to connect the high art forms with the low forms and thus embrace a fuller conception of art that thrives in a multitude of contexts.

Notes

1. Likely inspired (compositionally at least) by a portrait of Jacques-Benigne Bossuet by Hyacinthe Rigaud, Gilbert Stuart painted Washington at least four times from 1796 to 1797. The four paintings are referred to as the "Lansdowne" portraits because one had been gifted to the Lord Lansdowne, an English supporter of American independence. At least three copies of the original painting were produced; for the last two centuries, the identity of the "original" and the "copies" has remained elusive. Despite recent questions of authenticity, the painting, which is on display in the East Room of the White House, has been held in high esteem since its placement there in 1800. The image was often reproduced, as demonstrated

by the 1801 mezzotint print by George Graham that accompanies this chapter.

2. Anne L. Poulet, *Jean-Antoine Houdon: Sculptor of the Enlightenment* (Washington, D.C.: National Gallery of Art, 2003), 263–268.

3. Houdon's portraits of Washington and Jefferson were translated into unglazed porcelain busts in the early twentieth century by the National Porcelain Factory of Sèvres. Gifts of the French nation, these busts reside in the White House, along with nonpresidential figures such as Benjamin Franklin and the Marquis de Lafayette.

4. William Kloss, Doreen Bolger, William Floss, John Wilmerding, David Park Curry, and Betty C. Monkman, *Art in the White House: A Nation's Pride*. (Washington, D.C.: The National Geographic Society in cooperation with The White House Historical Association, 1992), 141, 143.

5. Clockwise from the top of this print, the bust portraits included George Washington, Thomas Jefferson, James Monroe, Andrew Jackson, William Henry Harrison, James K. Polk, John Tyler, Martin Van Buren, John Quincy Adams, James Madison, and John Adams.

6. *Zachary Taylor, The People's Choice of 12th President*, Lithograph on wove paper printed by Nathaniel Currier, 1848.

7. National Park Service, http://www.nps.gov (accessed June 15, 2003).

8. Many of these translations are related to the tourist industry. Postcards, jewelry, and plates were available for purchase on visiting Mount Rushmore, thus enabling visitors to bring a piece of their tourist experience home with them. Charms for ladies' bracelets and decorative pendants permitted the wearer the opportunity to wear their patriotism on their sleeve or over their lapel. Decorative plates celebrated the national character of Mount Rushmore through the literary description of the monument, hailing its status as "the shrine of democracy." Through both word and image, viewers are reminded of Rushmore's significance as a historical monument as well as a benchmark against which to measure future progress. In this way, the portraits of these four presidents have been transformed from individual works into a thread of representations that become part of our cultural fabric. Mount Rushmore was also featured among the "Greetings from America" postage stamp series issued by the U.S. Postal Service in October 2002. The stamp for South Dakota, the only one in the series to feature presidential likenesses, celebrates its state with a depiction of Mount Rushmore and a roaming buffalo. Details about the stamps may be obtained from the Travel Industry Association at http://www.tia.org/Press/greetingsfacts.PDF or from the U.S. Postal Service.

9. This print was issued in 1894 after Cleveland's second inauguration.

10. This sculpture was so popular that a copy was commissioned by the city of Boston in 1877.

11. Created in 1974 by Edward A. Kay, the carved and painted monument includes turned wood, modeling composition, printed paper, wishbone, and metal. The work is in the permanent collection of the American Art Museum of the Smithsonian Institution.

12. Mark S. Wilson carved the red pine totem in 1990, for display at his Yankee Doodle Country Store in Canastota, New York. The sculpture was listed in the most recent survey of inventory of American sculpture coordinated by the Smithsonian Institution. See www.siris.org.

13. Vanderlyn's painting is on view at the U.S. House of Representatives in Washington, D.C.

14. The original painting measures 59" × 93", and the full color print measures 15" × 22". The print is available for purchase at the Smithsonian Institution's online gift shop at http://www.smithsonianstore.com.

15. In 1886, for example, a "Lincoln Memorial Collection" was shown in Chicago and Milwaukee, and the World's Fair in 1893 held a similar exhibit. These shows included books, furniture, and letters in addition to works of artistic merit. In New York in the same year, coin collector Andrew Zabriskie organized an outstanding exhibition of Lincoln medals. Items celebrating Lincoln's role as Emancipator appeared after his death and thus began to garner attention from numismatics, political historians, and collectors alike. In fact, Zabriskie's essay, "A Descriptive Catalogue of the Political and Memorial Medals Struck in Honor of Abraham Lincoln," (New York: for the author,1873) became the foundation of the phenomenon known as "Lincolniana."

16. Color photogravure by F. G. Renesch owned by The Lincoln Museum, Fort Wayne, Indiana.

17. Grace Kelly, "Lincoln Statue Accepted; Site on Mall is Urged," *Cleveland Press,* December 18, 1928. According to the *Plain Dealer* article "Kalish Named to do Statue of Abe" (April 7, 1927), Polish immigrant Max Kalish was selected among a pool of candidates to create this sculpture. Information on the Kalish sculpture and many outdoor sculptures in Cleveland may be found in Helen Lybarger's *A Survey of Public Monuments in Cleveland* (Cleveland: Early Settlers Association of the Western Reserve, 1979).

Further Readings

Please note that Web sites and search engines are helpful tools for finding information about painted or sculpted likenesses of presidents. Art inventories such as the Smithsonian American Art Museum (http://www.siris.si.edu), may be searched and filtered to retrieve information for works relating to all U.S. presidents. The online search provides data about the work (artist, title, date, medium, and owner), and images can be ordered from the Smithsonian. Another helpful site is the National Park Service (http://www.nps.gov), which maintains history, statistics, and visitor information for presidential sites such as the Jefferson and Lincoln Memorials, as well as Mount Rushmore, among others. Regional databases such as The Sculpture Center (http://www.sculpturecenter.org) include detailed information about outdoor sculptures in a particular region. Again, a simple subject search (such as "United States—President") yields records and, in most cases, images of sculpted likenesses of the presidents. To bring children into the discovery of physical likeness of our nation's leaders, coloring book images of all forty-three presidents are available at http://www.whitehousekids.gov. These simple illustrations are often derived from celebrated likenesses of the presidents. For example, the Lansdowne Portrait of Washington served as the inspiration for the children's version of our nation's first president. The list below contains further readings on painted or sculpted likenesses of presidents:

The American President, http://www.americanpresident.org (accessed April 15, 2003).

The Garfield Memorial Committee. *James A. Garfield: The Man and the Mausoleum.* Cleveland, Ohio: Garfield Monument Committee, 1890.

Greetings from America Stamp Facts, http://www.tia.org/Press/greetingsfacts. PDF (accessed May 15, 2003).

Hartigan, Lynda Roscoe. *Made with Passion: The Hemphill Folk Art Collection in the National Museum of American Art.* Washington, D.C.: Smithsonian Institution Press, 1990.

Johnston, Norman. *Washington's Audacious State Capitol and Its Builders.* Seattle: University of Washington Press, 1988.

"Kalish Named to do Statue of Abe," *Plain Dealer*, April 7, 1927, 27.

Larner, Jesse. *Mount Rushmore: An Icon Reconsidered.* New York: Nation's Books, 2002.

Peterson, Merrill D. *Lincoln in American Memory.* Oxford: Oxford University Press, 1994.

The Sculpture Center, http://www.sculpturecenter.org (accessed June 2, 2003).

Smithsonian American Art Museum, http://www.siris.si.edu (accessed June 15, 2003).

Smithsonian Store, http://www.smithosonianstore.com (accessed November 1, 2004).

Taliaferro, John. *Great White Fathers: The Story of the Obsessive Quest to Create Mount Rushmore.* New York: Public Affairs, 2002.

U.S. Department of Treasury, http://www.treasury.gov/topics/currency/index.html (accessed June 18, 2003).

Virga, Vincent. *Eyes of the Nation: A Visual History of the United States.* New York: Knopf, 1997.

Voss, Frederick S. *Portraits of the Presidents: The National Portrait Gallery.* Washington, D.C.: The National Portrait Gallery, 2000.

Weinstein, Randy F. *Against the Tide: Commentaries on a Collection of African Americana, 1711–1987.* New York: Glenn Horowitz Bookseller, 1996.

The White House, http://www.whitehouse.gov/history/presidents/ (accessed March 1, 2003).

CHAPTER 3

POPULAR MUSIC

JERRY RODNITZKY

Although the presidency has changed over the last two hundred years, American popular music has kept the beat. Music cuts across ideologies and erases time boundaries. One era's songs are sometimes tailored for a later time. Music can also overcome class and regional distinctions or emphasize the differences between the present and the past. This is especially true of American music, which has been more classless and specific to time periods than European music. This has made American popular music a natural and effective tool for promoting political ideas and specific presidents.[1]

Practical American pioneers chose simple folk tunes for their music. Folk songs told a direct story and encouraged simple emotions. They were musical equivalents of graphic American art and Longfellow's simple story poems. From the beginning, Americans sang about politics, wars, heroes, and hard times. They also sang about specific presidents, mostly with election songs. Political songs give particularly important insights, as America's political system has changed relatively little. From George Washington to George W. Bush, the presidency and party system have been relative anchors in a sea of change. Yet each president has dealt with unique stormy issues that divided Americans. Thus presidential actions inevitably made presidents heroes to some and villains to others.

Songs about presidents reflected their personal strengths and weaknesses as well as policy decisions. Election songs ran the gamut from hero worship to satiric disdain and either supported a president or ridiculed his opponent. These songs were particularly important from 1789 through World War II, because political media and advertising were largely absent. With the steady rise of political media after 1945, election songs were replaced by protest songs in the 1960s and satiric songs after 1980. Protest songs attacked presidential policies, whereas satiric songs often ridiculed presidents personally.

George Washington was our most venerated president. As the primary hero of the Revolutionary War, Washington was featured in patriotic songs long before his presidency. A good example is "Cornwallis's Surrender," which celebrated Washington's victory at Yorktown in 1781. It noted: "Here's a health to General Washington and his brave army too." These songs celebrated America's victory over the leading superpower and made Washington a superhero.[2] Long before his presidency Washington was the subject of songs such as "A Toast to Washington" (1778), "Washington's March" (1784), and in 1786, "God Save Great Washington." Ironically, the latter song was sung to the tune of "God Save the King."[3] In 1788, just before the first presidential election, Eli Lewis wrote the words for "A New Federal Song." One verse noted:

> Great Washington shall rule the land,
> While Franklin's council aids his hand.[4]

These songs were not really election songs, as Washington did not need election help. They were patriotic songs that used Washington as a heroic symbol. The contemporary "nutty George" February sales and flip Washington television ads are in marked contrast to the early idolatry popular culture accorded Washington.

During Washington's presidency, two future presidents prepared for the 1796 election. John Adams and Thomas Jefferson had been friends during the Revolutionary War, but now Jefferson had formed a new political party to challenge the party that supported John Adams. Both Adams and the Federalist party leader, Alexander Hamilton, thought election songs below their dignity. Likewise, they frowned on banners, slogans, and buttons. In contrast, the first modern political party, Jefferson's Republicans, had few qualms about using anything that stirred mass emotions. Adams won the 1796 election by three electoral votes over Jefferson, who became the vice president under a Constitution that did not recognize parties. Adams supporters tried to enhance Adams's image with songs depicting Adams as a resolute war leader in America's undeclared 1798 sea war against France. Adams was inserted into a parody of "Yankee Doodle," which was now directed against France rather than Britain. Then, in 1798, Robert Paine, the most active Federalist songwriter, wrote several songs highlighting Adams's virtues. The most famous was "Adams and Liberty," a song sung to the tune of "Anaecreon in Heaven," which eventually became "The Star Spangled Banner"—the national anthem.

Jefferson supporters struck back with songs such as "Watching O'er Your Freedom" and a singing Jefferson biography, "The Son of Liberty." The most successful Jefferson song was "Jefferson and Liberty," a post-election song that Republicans sang for the next twelve years. Ironically it was written by Robert Paine, who switched parties in 1800. The song warned of a political dictatorship if the Federalists ever regained power. It was used in Jefferson's reelection campaign and also in James Madison's two successful elections, as these contests all featured Federalist opponents.[4–6]

The rousing chorus exclaimed:

> Rejoice Columbia's Sons rejoice
> To Tyrants never bend your knee
> But join with soul and heart and voice
> For Jefferson and Liberty

The song "Madison, Union, and Liberty" in 1808 talked about Jefferson as much as Madison, and likewise "Monroe is the Man" in 1816 passed the Jefferson mantle on to yet another Jeffersonian friend from Virginia.[2] Jefferson had handpicked both Madison and Monroe to follow him—Monroe was the last of the so-called Virginia Dynasty.

In 1812, during yet another war with Britain, John Paff published "Hail to the Chief." The words were from Sir Walter Scott's *The Lady of the Lake*, and the music was by James Sanderson. The tune became more important than the words, as it has often been played to honor presidents. We do not know when the practice started, but do know it was played at James Polk's Inauguration on March 4, 1845.[7] "Hail to the Chief" has often been overshadowed, as The War of 1812 also produced the national anthem, "The Star Spangled Banner," written by Francis Scott Key.

Andrew Jackson's move into national politics in the 1824 election opened a new era of songs about presidents. Jackson was the first "common man" to run for president. Jefferson might have been for the people, but Jackson was of the people—and he was a victorious general to boot. Americans identified more personally with Jackson. They called him "Old Hickory" or Andy. They did not call Washington, Georgie, nor Jefferson, Tommy. In 1815 Jackson had become a national hero at the battle of New Orleans, and Samuel Woodworth, perhaps the first serious and gifted American popular songwriter, wrote "The Hunters of Kentucky" to celebrate the New Orleans victory.[6,7] This witty, whimsical song featured Jackson as the leader of Kentucky and other state militiamen. Jackson later used it for his campaign song in 1824, 1828, and 1832. It was particularly effective in 1832 when Jackson, the Democrat, ran against Henry Clay, the Whig. Clay was a U.S. Senator from Kentucky, but in 1815, Jackson had led the Kentucky militia. Jackson lost the 1824 presidential election to John Quincy Adams even though Jackson won the popular vote handily and also led the electoral count. Clay, also a presidential candidate, threw his electoral votes to Adams in the House. Adams thus became president under a cloud of suspicion and made Clay his Secretary of State.

In 1828 Adams supporters used a song titled "Adams and Clay"—sung to the tune of "The Star Spangled Banner"—that was just a parody of "Adams and Liberty," which John Adams used in 1796. In contrast, Jackson's "Hunters of Kentucky," sung to a popular tune, "The Unfortunate Miss Bailey," was vibrant and popular. It noted that Jackson "was not scared at trifles" and that Jackson's troops were "half a horse and half an alligator." The song was filled with Western idioms and enhanced Jackson's image as the first Western president. Another song, "The Hickory Tree," traded on Jackson's nickname—Old Hickory—whereas "Jackson Toast" toasted him.[4]

In 1836, Jackson handpicked Vice President Martin Van Buren for the presidency. Van Buren won easily against four regional Whig candidates. William Henry Harrison led the other three Whig candidates and emerged as the Whig presidential candidate in 1840. Harrison's father had signed the Declaration of Independence, and Harrison himself had been the victorious general at the Battle of Tippecanoe during the War of 1812. Harrison had been born rich and had managed to work his way down in life since his war exploits. However, he now resided in the West (Indiana) and was an ex-general. In a brilliant campaign, Whigs put down New Yorker Van Buren, an actual self-made man, as a pompous Eastern aristocrat. Harrison was skillfully presented as much more Jacksonian than Van Buren. In the 1840 election, songs played their most effective political role yet. Whigs used many songs to pump up Harrison's reputation or tear down Van Buren's image. Van Buren was depicted as Jackson's mere apprentice. Their most popular song was "Tyler and Tippecanoe," with the punch line, "to run the ship, we'll try old Tip." The title referred to John Tyler, who was Harrison's running mate, and Tippecanoe, which conjured up immediate visions of Harrison as the Western Indian fighter. Other pro-Harrison songs were "Old Tippecanoe" and "Harrison," sung to the tune of "Yankee Doodle." They noted that Harrison lived in a log cabin and drank hard cider, whereas Van Buren drank wine from goblets. Also effective were clever anti–Van Buren songs such as "Van Buren" and "Little Vanny."[3]

"Van Buren" might be the most caustic political song ever written. It posed several questions such as "Who wants to bring the poor man down?" and "Who never had an honest thought?" And finally:

> Who rules us with an iron rod?
> Who moves at Satan's beck and nod?
> Who heeds not man, who heeds not God?
> Who would his friend, his country sell?
> Do other deeds too base to tell,
> Deserves the lowest place in Hell?

The song's answer to all these questions was, of course, "Van Buren."[4,6] Harrison won handily.

In 1844 the Whigs again nominated Henry Clay—a much-defeated candidate. The Democrats had learned their lesson and nominated a candidate as close to Jackson's image as possible. This was James Polk, governor of Tennessee, who was nicknamed Young Hickory and was a Jackson protégé. Whig songwriters valiantly tried to make Clay into a common man like Jackson and Harrison with songs such as "Farmer Clay" and "Harry of the West." Both Whigs and Democrats livened up the campaign with songs written to a popular minstrel tune about Negro life called "Old Dan Tucker," Whigs sang their ticket song "Clay and Frelinghuysen," and Democrats copied with "Polk, Dallas and Texas."[4,7]

Throughout the nineteenth century, songs about presidents were almost always election songs. It was considered disrespectful to bandy about a president's name in popular or theatrical songs, and it could also harm a singer's career. Election songs were increasingly imitative parodies of older songs, using new words. Songs for a given president differed in number and passion, rather than type. If the issues or candidate created a lot of passion, there would be more songs. The Civil War era would also bring more passionate songs in its wake.

Polk was a one-term president who guided America in and out of the Mexican War. In 1848, the Whigs chose a Mexican War general, Zachary Taylor, as their candidate. Taylor's signature campaign songs were "Old Zack upon the Track," sung to "Old Dan Tucker," and "Rough and Ready" (Taylor's nickname), sung to "Yankee Doodle." Taylor won a close election but died suddenly in 1850 and was replaced by Vice President Millard Fillmore. Few people took Fillmore seriously enough to write songs about him, yet in 1856, when Fillmore ran for president for a new third party, the American Party (or "Know Nothings"), his song was "The Union Wagon," sung to the tune of the folk song, "Wait for the Wagon."[4,6,7] Fillmore was such a presidential lightweight that in 1964, *Life* magazine satirically titled their presidential campaign song album *Sing Along with Millard Fillmore*.

In 1852, the Democrats ran a different lightweight candidate, Franklin Pierce. The Whigs countered with yet another Mexican War general, Winfield Scott. The Whigs sang several songs poking fun at Pierce, such as "The Fainting General," which pointed to Pierce's inglorious Mexican War service. The Democrats settled for slogans such as "we Polked them in 44, we'll Pierce them in 52." The Whigs had better songs, but Pierce won easily. In their final election, the Whigs nominated a general for the third time. Their other two generals, Harrison and Taylor, had both been elected, but died in office. This time their general lived, but the Whig party died—unable to bridge the North–South split over the slavery issue.[4]

Democrats continued to compromise over slavery in 1856 by electing James Buchanan, a Northerner who had been friendly to territorial expansion of slavery. Buchanan was a so-called "doughface"—a Northerner with Southern sentiments. In their first presidential election, the new Republican Party sang the stirring song "Fremont and Freedom" for their candidate, John Fremont. Democrats countered with several tepid Buchanan songs such as "The President's Chair" and the ticket song, "Buchanan and Breckenridge."[3,4]

The 1860 election brought Abraham Lincoln to the national scene amid the passions that brought the Civil War. Lincoln's campaign included typical songs to the tune of "Yankee Doodle" and "Old Dan Tucker," as well as "Lincoln and Liberty" to the tune of "Rosin the Beau." The 1860 Republican Songster[8] included fifty Lincoln songs alone. In 1864, "Union Coming" helped Lincoln's reelection. The song, written in fake slave dialect, noted that "Mac" (opponent McClellan) was "smart, but 'Lincum's' smarter." Perhaps the most stirring song about Lincoln was the Civil War marching song, "We Are Coming Father Abraham."[3–5,7] Lincoln's assassination also produced a flood of songs and some forty funeral marches, which have all been overshadowed by the tragic event and forgotten.

Ulysses Grant was the next of five Republican presidents, from 1868 to 1900, who served in the Union Army during the Civil War. Rutherford Hayes, elected in 1876; James Garfield, elected in 1880; and Benjamin Harrison, elected in 1888, like Grant, all rose to the rank of general. William McKinley, elected in 1896 and the last of this quintet, had enlisted at age eighteen years and only rose to the rank of major. Grover Cleveland, who was elected in 1884 and again in 1892, was the only Democratic president in this period. Cleveland had paid a substitute to take his place in the Civil War so he could continue to support his widowed mother and younger siblings.

Many of the all-male electorate were Union veterans, and pensions for veterans was a constant issue. Not surprisingly, most Republican election songs during this era were written to the tunes of Union Army marching songs such as "The Battle Cry of Freedom," "Tramp, Tramp, Tramp," "Hold the Fort," and "When Johnny Comes Marching Home."[4] From election songs such as "General Grant's the Man" in 1868, to "His Name is General G" in 1880 for James Garfield, to "Shout McKinley" in 1896, Republican presidents are seen as Civil War leaders as much as national leaders: They made it clear that they represented the party that won the Civil War.[3] Only Cleveland was able to break the mold by focusing on government integrity and North–South reunification. Cleveland was helped by songs such as "Let's Have a Change" and "Good Democrats," sung to the tune of "Maryland, My Maryland." Republicans always waved "the bloody shirt" of Civil War: Some lines from "Good Democrat" said Cleveland would "get the blue and get the gray," for there was no "stains" on fair

Cleveland's shirt" and "they'll wave no more the bloody shirt." One of the only election songs that crossed over to the popular stage was Monroe Rosenfeld's anti-Cleveland song, "Ma! Ma! Where's My Pa?" which satirized Cleveland for being the confessed father of an illegitimate child. The song's rejoinder was "up in the White House dear, making the laws."[4,7]

William McKinley, the last Republican Civil War president, was elected easily in 1896. After the Spanish-American War in 1898, McKinley decided to ensure reelection in 1900 by choosing war hero Theodore Roosevelt as his vice president. His advisers also tried to liven up McKinley's stodgy image with lively music. His 1900 campaign song, "Hooray for Bill McKinley," was the first ragtime election song. Its tag line was "hooray for Bill McKinley and that great Rough Rider Ted." Ragtime had come up the Mississippi River from New Orleans throughout the 1890s. Some adults saw it as barbaric as some would later view early rock music in the 1950s.

That "great Rough Rider Ted" fell into the presidency after McKinley's assassination in 1901. Mark Hanna, a McKinley political advisor, had cautioned against putting Roosevelt on the ticket, as that would leave only one heartbeat between the president and "that damn cowboy," but "Teddy" was no mere cowboy—indeed, he wanted no part of ragtime. Roosevelt personally chose a dignified, dirge-like election song, "Roosevelt the Cry." This was ironic, as the forty-three year old, hot-tempered, emotional Roosevelt seemed better suited to hot ragtime music than any politician of his era. Roosevelt supporters, however, did use popular music in Roosevelt's 1904 and 1912 campaigns. The most controversial song was the ragtime march, "A Hot Time in the Old Town Tonight," originally linked to a St. Louis brothel, but also associated with Roosevelt's charge up San Juan Hill with his Rough Riders.[4,6,7]

Ragtime broke down all remaining barriers between election songs and popular music. From 1900 on, politicians were increasingly impressed with popular music's hold on voters and were eager to tie presidents to popular genres and songs. Yet songwriters were reticent about throwing a president's name into a lyric.

In 1908, William Taft, Roosevelt's hefty, handpicked successor, won easily, but songwriter backers took no chances and tried to liven his image with a near copy of George Cohan's hit, "Harrigan," titled "B-I-Double L-Bill," and another song, "Get on the Raft with Taft." Taft and Roosevelt later split politically. In 1912, Roosevelt formed a new Progressive Party, whose symbol was a Bull Moose. The Democratic candidate, Woodrow Wilson, won the spirited election. Whereas Roosevelt supporters sang songs such as "We're Ready for Teddy Again" and "The Moose is Loose," Wilson backers worked on changing his stiff image. They used the lively ragtime ditty, "Wilson, That's All," and the zany "We Think We Have Another Washington and Wilson is His Name."[4,6,7]

Wilson won a close election over Republican Charles Evans Hughes in 1916 on the slogan, "He Kept Us Out of War" as was celebrated as a peacemaker in a song titled, "We're Going to Celebrate the End of the War in Ragtime," which included the line: "And be sure that Woodrow Wilson leads the band." Once engaged in World War I, Wilson was hailed as war leader in "Go Right Along Mr. Wilson" ("and we'll all stand by you"). President Wilson paid tribute to songwriters by sending an autographed photo and message to George Cohan, who had received the Congressional Medal in 1918 for his song, "Over There." Wilson called the song "a genuine inspiration to all American manhood." On the flip side, California songwriter, Robert Keiser, reminded Wilson that California's electoral votes gave him the election with a song, "Be Good to California, Mr. Wilson" ("California was good to you").[3,4]

The 1920s brought three colorless Republican presidents—Warren Harding, Calvin Coolidge, and Herbert Hoover. Yet, the twenties were culturally radical and chaotic. If contemporary America is now postmodern, clearly the modern period began in the 1920s. This era brought a sexual revolution, a youth revolt, the pervasive mass media of film and radio, a sports-crazy public, widespread auto ownership, and newly enfranchised women voters. Popular music ignored the three boring presidents but added to the cultural chaos by popularizing jazz and zany novelty songs. As usual, political parties tried to use the new music to liven up their candidates, who otherwise appeared as relics in the new cultural era. In 1920, Harding backers got Al Jolson, the famous vaudeville singer-songwriter to write "Harding You're the Man for Us." In 1924, Republicans turned their campaign slogan, "Keep Cool and Keep Coolidge," into a song with prosaic verses, but a punchy chorus and jazz beat. In 1928, Republicans used the hero–aviator Charles Lindbergh's support of Hoover in another jazz-beat song, "If He's Good Enough for Lindy, He's Good Enough for Me." The song linked Lindbergh and former engineer Hoover with "good American know-how."[4,9]

Franklin Delano Roosevelt won a record four presidential elections and dominated politics from 1932 through 1945. However, the somber Depression-era America he governed offered little to sing about, and World War II songs focused on soldiers and separation from loved ones. Franklin Roosevelt was perhaps the first president since Jackson, Lincoln, and Teddy Roosevelt whose real strength lay in emotionally connecting to the common American, but his hold on workers developed gradually, and songs about him were not, at first, very personal. His chief 1932 campaign song was "Row Row Row with Roosevelt" ("on the good ship USA"). The song rather woodenly suggested that everybody must work together to beat the Depression. However, by 1934 Roosevelt adopted "Happy Days Are Here Again" as his recovery theme song. It was a happy choice that caught the public's imagination and emphasized Roosevelt's trademark, upbeat optimism. This song, originally written for a 1929 MGM movie musical, remained the song most identified with him. After his crushing 1936 reelection victory, Roosevelt had clearly become a folk hero to most Americans and an economic savior to many. Bill Cox, a country singer, caught the national mood with his joyous song, "Franklin D. Roosevelt's Back Again." The song also celebrated Prohibition's end with the lines: "You can laugh and tell a joke, you can dance and drink and smoke." In 1939, Jay Gorney, who had written the music for "Brother Can You Spare a Dime," collaborated with Henry Myers on a musical plea for a third term, titled, "Mister Roosevelt, Won't You Please Run Again."[3,4,7]

The postwar years witnessed the steady decline of campaign songs, as radio and television became the dominant election vehicles. When Vice President Harry Truman became president after Roosevelt's death, he continued to use "Happy Days Are Here Again" to depict himself as the new Roosevelt. However, the song did not work as well in the new media environment. Truman's most successful 1948 campaign song was "I'm Just Wild About Harry," a parody of a 1921 ragtime hit with the same title. However, Truman opponents sang a counter parody, with the title, "I'm Just Mild About Harry." Truman won a surprising election victory in 1948, but Korean War woes convinced him to pass by the 1952 election. Republican Dwight Eisenhower won election easily in 1952, but his success was based more on his dignity and great grin than on songs. His campaign did feature the song, "I Like Ike," but the simple "I Like Ike" slogan on buttons and ads was much more effective.[3,7,9] Likewise, when John F. Kennedy was elected in 1960, election songs were irrelevant: Americans fastened on Kennedy's charismatic television manner and his television debate with opponent Richard Nixon, instead.

The 1960s opened up a new era of protest songs that often mentioned sitting American presidents. John Kennedy's assassination also brought mourning songs such as Phil Ochs's melodramatic "That Was the President," and later in the decade the still popular Dion hit, "Abraham, Martin, and John," was published. The latter song linked Abraham Lincoln, Martin Luther King Jr., and John Kennedy forever as America's primary political martyrs. However, most rock music that has mentioned presidents since 1960 simply throws in "president" in flip, irrelevant ways. A good example is Credence Clearwater Revival's "Fortunate Son."[10–12] Lyndon B. Johnson, Kennedy's vice president and successor, did not fare as well as Kennedy. In 1964, Johnson's campaign tried, with little success, to turn the Broadway hit, "Hello Dolly" into a song parody titled "Hello Lyndon." As the Vietnam War escalated, Johnson became the target of several protest songs. One famous anti-Johnson song was Tom Paxton's "Lyndon Johnson Told the Nation" ("have no fear of escalation, I am trying everyone to please"), which pictured Johnson as a crafty war hawk, masquerading as a dove. Also noteworthy was Pete Seeger's anti-Vietnam song, "Waist Deep in the Big

Muddy." Seeger eventually performed it on the Smothers Brothers television show. The song does not mention President Johnson by name, but the refrain, "and the big fool says to push on" is clearly referring to Johnson as the "big fool."[13-15]

Another sixties trend had some popular singers supporting presidents by traveling with the candidate. Thus, Frank Sinatra stumped for John Kennedy in 1960, and in the 1968 election, Phil Ochs and Peter, Paul, and Mary stumped for Eugene McCarthy, while several country singers, including Ernest Tubbs and Merle Haggard, helped Richard Nixon. This limited practice has continued.

In general, country singers have been more conservative and supported Republicans, whereas liberal, urban singers such as Barbra Streisand and Bette Midler have supported Democrats. However, there are exceptions, as shown by The Dixie Chicks' denunciation of President George W. Bush at a 2003 concert in England, and the subsequent campaign to boycott the country trio's records. The incident showed how much political activism can damage a singer's career, especially when one's views run counter to the sentiments of one's fan base. Not surprisingly, most popular singers have steered clear of politics.

Tom Lehrer, a master satirist, wrote many songs in the 1960s about national foreign policy but drew the traditional line at satirizing presidents. The 1970s saw President Richard Nixon implicated in the depressing Watergate scandal and later witnessed President Jimmy Carter plagued by the Iran Hostage Crisis. This era saw the virtual elimination of election songs or mention of presidents in popular music, except for some protest songs against Nixon by Phil Ochs and other antiwar singers.[10,16] However, Ronald Reagan's 1980 election opened a new era of satiric music that concentrated on politicians and presidents. It was fueled by the general political disillusionment following Vietnam and Watergate.

Leading the charge in popular music from the 1980s through the present were the path-breaking Capitol Steps. This satiric group originally included sixteen younger Washington staffers, both male and female. They included both Republicans and Democrats, and starting in 1981, they poked fun at everything political (but especially presidents) with clever, wicked satire. They usually used popular rock music and standard tunes for political parody. Thus, Dolly Parton's hit, "Workin' 9 to 5," became a song satirizing President Reagan's poor work habits, titled "Workin' 9 to 10." And "Puff the Magic Dragon" became "Dutch the Magic Reagan" (about Reagan's personal political magic).

The Capitol Steps soon released a record each year and taunted George H. W. Bush with songs such as "If I Weren't a Rich Man," "Georgie's Kind and Gentle Land," and an entire 1990 album, Georgie on My Mind.[17-21] President Bill Clinton also got special attention, with songs about his "wishy washy" politics, such as "I've Taken Stands on Both Sides Now," and

"Return to Center." His long speeches were mocked with "Don't Stop Talkin' Until Tomorrow," and his rich White House guests were roasted with "White House Hotel" to the tune of "Heartbreak Hotel."[22–24] The Capitol Steps took special delight in satirizing President Clinton's sexual affairs, from "Sneakin Flowers through the Wall" about his prepresidential mistress, Gennifer Flowers, to "Happy Monica," "The Bimbo Collection," and "You'd Better Sleep Around," about the Monica Lewinsky affair.[25,26]

George W. Bush is getting the same rough treatment. Most of the Steps satire centers on Bush's trading on his father's name and ex-staff. Typical are songs such as "Son of a Bush" and "My Staff Belongs to Daddy." Other songs such as "Don't Go Faking You're Smart" question Bush's knowledge and intelligence.[27]

The long tradition of limiting songs about presidents to election songs, out of respect for the office or because presidents were too boring or dangerous as popular music subjects, might be ending. Popular song-writers may increasingly take their best shots for or against presidents, just as cartoonists, political writers, and election song composers always have.

Conventional wisdom suggests that music unites people in a common humanity. That view conveniently ignores hate groups such as the Nazis and Ku Klux Klan, who used songs to spread their message and inspire followers. Another myth suggests that protest songs are always on the political left, but conservatives ask why liberals and radicals should have all the good tunes. Every political group has used songs to inspire supporters or criticize their opposition: American popular music is a universal political tool, open to all players.

Notes

1. Jerry Rodnitzky, *Minstrels of the Dawn: The Folk-Protest Singer as a Cultural Hero* (Chicago: Nelson-Hall, 1976).

2. Jim Burroughs, *Songs of Rebellion*, Audio Fidelity Records, 1976.

3. Sigmund Spaeth, *A History of Popular Music in America* (New York: Random House, 1948).

4. Irwin Silber, *Songs America Voted By* (Harrisburg, Pa.: Stackpole Books, 1971), 20.

5. Peter Janovsky, *Winners and Losers: Campaign Songs, Vol I, to 1876 (with Notes)*, FolkwayRecords, 1978.

6. Oscar Brand, *Election Songs of the United States*, Folkway Records, 1960.

7. David Ewen, *All the Years of American Popular Music* (Englewood Cliffs, N.J.: Prentice-Hall, 1977).

8. *Hutchinson's Republican Songster*, edited by John W. Hutchinson, (New York: 1860).

9. *Sing Along with Millard Fillmore: The Life Album of Presidential Songs*, Time, Inc. Records, 1964.

10. Phil Ochs, *I Ain't Marching Anymore*, Elektra Records, 1965.

11. Dion, *Sanctuary*, Warner Brothers Records, 1971.

12. Credence Clearwater Revival, *Willy and the Poor Boys*, Fantasy Records, 1968.

13. Tom Paxton, *Ain't that News*, Electra Records, 298 (1965).

14. Pete Seeger, *Waist Deep in the Big Muddy and Other Love Songs*, Columbia Records, CS 9505, 1967.

15. David King Dunaway, *How Can I Keep From Singing: Pete Seeger*, (New York: McGraw Hill,1981, pp. 262–264).

16. Tom Lehrer, *An Evening Wasted With Tom Lehrer*, Reprise, 1959.

17. The Capitol Steps, *Workin' 9 to 10*, Capitol Steps Records, 1988.

18. The Capitol Steps, *We Arm the World*, Capitol Steps Records, 1986.

19. The Capitol Steps, *Fools On the Hill*, CSCD, 1992.

20. The Capitol Steps, *Danny's First Noel*, CSCD, 1989.

21. The Capitol Steps, *Georgie on My Mind*, CSCD, 1990.

22. The Capitol Steps, *Sixteen Scandals*, CSCD, 1997.

23. The Capitol Steps, *A Whole Newt World*, CSCD, 1995.

24. The Capitol Steps, *The Joy of Sax*, CSCD, 1993.

25. The Capitol Steps, *Lord of the Fries*, CSCD, 1994.

26. The Capitol Steps, *Unzippin' My Doodah*, CSCD, 1998.

27. The Capitol Steps, *One Bush, Two Bush, Old Bush, New Bush*, CSCD, 2001.

CHAPTER 4

Drama

Laura G. Pattillo

In Shakespeare's day, audiences flocked to play after play about the kings of England and the history of their nation. The American theater has similarly staged many plays about its presidents, both past and present, but most of the plays have achieved neither the artistic stature nor the literary longevity of a *Henry V* or *Richard III*. Sometimes the plays revere the presidents, sometimes they seek to understand them as human beings instead of figureheads, and sometimes they hold them up to ridicule. In many cases, the plays are as reflective of the times in which they were written and performed as they are of the leaders they depict. Of course, the presidents with the most box office clout and name recognition are the most frequently portrayed, for the American theater is driven to a great extent by ticket sales, even in its not-for-profit incarnations. It also seems that, unless the president is being castigated for politically unpopular actions, passage of time is also a factor. Presidents, particularly those of the television age, are too familiar to be accepted as "characters" in plays unless they are distant figures; in fact, more recent presidents are more likely to be portrayed in tour-de-force one-man shows than as characters in full-fledged dramas with larger casts. In recent years, perhaps the television movie or miniseries has often done the work once done by long-running plays, as fewer and fewer stage offerings take the presidents for their subject matter.

George Washington

George Washington commands significant attention as the first president and "father of the country," but he appears in surprisingly few stage works meant for professional production and adult audiences. There are dozens of simple scripts meant for use by schoolchildren or church and community pageants, but only a scant offering of major works. Perhaps this situation results from reverence for Washington; his function as a figurehead is too important for audiences or playwrights to see him as a fully rounded character with flaws and struggles, as they do Lincoln, the most written-about president in the American theater.

Washington appears in a handful of plays from the eighteenth and nineteenth centuries—his first appearance in a play was in 1776, but the play, *The Fall of British Tyranny; or, American Triumphant* by John Leacock,[1] though published, was never performed. In 1803, William Dunlap's Revolutionary War musical, *Glory of Columbia*,[2] portrays Washington as a revered, almost mythic figure; he remained so for decades to come. In October 1903, *Captain Barrington* by Victor Mapes,[3] debuted to critical and audience acclaim at Boston's Globe Theatre. The story revolves around a plot to capture George Washington, though the president is not a central character.

In the twentieth century, Washington was the symbolic focus of Percy MacKaye's *Wakefield*,[4] first produced in Constitution Hall in Washington, D.C., on February 21, 1932. The play takes its name from Washington's birthplace and was commissioned by the federal government, along with several musical works, to commemorate the bicentennial of the first president's birth. The characters are all allegorical figures: George Washington becomes "The Presence of Washington," a cloaked figure, who appears periodically and speaks words written by Washington at the climax of the piece. The script, including some patriotic songs, was published as a government document with instructions as to how it might be presented by groups nationwide.

In 1934, Maxwell Anderson created *Valley Forge*,[5] a play about Washington's struggle to unite the people and the Congress against the British in the difficult winter of 1777–1778. Anderson's scripting of a scene in which Washington is consoled by a supposed childhood sweetheart was controversial among critics, but the play was otherwise mostly well received. Critic Brooks Atkinson points out that Washington has never been a favorite on the stage—perhaps American audiences are more self-conscious about how plays portray our own leaders that those that showcase, for example, English monarchs. He notes, "If this is not a literal Washington, it is what Washington represented in the agonizing labor of a nation a-borning," and declares the play a "declaration of faith in America."[6]

In the latter half of the century, Washington saw less serious attention from major playwrights. He makes a sort of deus ex machina appearance in a 1950 musical called *Arms and the Girl* by Herbert Fields, Dorothy Fields, and Rouben Mamoulian, a reworking of the nonmusical play *The Pursuit of Happiness*. It garnered lukewarm reviews, nearly all of which mention Washington's climactic scene, and some of which lament his absence from the rest of the play. In the turbulent 1960s, Washington faded even more from the scene, appearing only in 1962 in a brief play by Kenneth Koch called

George Washington Crossing the Delaware,[7] which was part of a short-lived bill of three short comedies; in 1969 in the form only of letters read aloud in the musical *1776*;[8] and in passing in some revues that encompass many presidents. Washington's value on stage is primarily symbolic: Never do we get an insightful character study of the man, but every time a playwright puts him in a play, it seems to have an effect on critics and audiences alike. Only after Washington does the theater begin to look at presidents as more fully human, flawed, and psychologically complex.

John Adams

The nation's second president, John Adams, is featured only a few times on the stage. His two most prominent appearances both happened in 1969. In March of that year, Sherman Edwards and Peter Stone's musical *1776*[8] opened at the 46th Street Theater in New York. It does not have a conventional plot for a musical—rather, it focuses on the drama and delay involved in drafting the Declaration of Independence—and it shows Adams as a key, but unpopular, player in the events. Critics credited much of the show's success to William Daniels's performance as Adams, whom many saw as the most compelling figure in the play because it revealed his complexity, depth, austerity, and courage in his political life, as well as his private devotion to his wife Abigail. The year 1969 was a difficult time for America and for its faith in itself as a nation, so *1776*'s popularity may have been in part because it reminded the country of the noble ideas on which it was founded, while at the same time allowing the flaws of its founders to be more honestly portrayed than they had been in the past. The play continues to be revived frequently at smaller theaters throughout the country, perhaps because contemporary audiences appreciate that admitting that democracy is a messy endeavor does not preclude patriotic feeling.

Adams's devotion to his wife is central to his other major stage appearance, *American Primitive*,[9] which is a dramatic presentation of the letters of John and Abigail Adams by William Gibson; the play premiered in a Circle in the Square production at Ford's Theater in Washington, D.C., in January of 1971. The letters are from the years 1774–1777, during which the Adamses were forced to spend a good deal of time apart, as Abigail stayed at home in Braintree, Massachusetts, while John was embroiled in the business of revolution and nation-shaping in Philadelphia (a process examined in *1776*). The letters reveal the personal hardship of being separated through family illnesses and deaths of parents, siblings, and even their own child, with only letters from the other for support. They also show the trials of war from the side of both home front and headquarters and talk of the great issues at hand in the formation of the new government, with Abigail pointedly reminding John to "remember the ladies" in the new laws or they will "foment a rebellion."[10] Many of the letters contain now-famous statements by Adams; for example, "I was born to be in such times, but not made for them," and "You will never know what your freedom cost this generation.... Make the most of it."[11] Perhaps this sentiment connected in a unique way with troubled American audiences in 1971, who saw in their own generation's time the quagmire of the Vietnam War and the protests at home, the upheaval of the civil rights movement, the assassinations of Martin Luther King Jr. and the Kennedys, the emergence of the women's movement, and major changes in American culture as the baby boomers came of age and rejected old conventions and beliefs. The play continues to be produced regularly, probably because each new generation relates in its own way to both the love story and the history of the piece.

Thomas Jefferson

Thomas Jefferson was frequently away from his home at Monticello in service to the government, and his longing for his rural home is central to Sidney Kingsley's *The Patriots*,[12] which premiered in January 1943 and was widely anthologized. The play focuses on Jefferson's years in the cabinet and his conflict with Alexander Hamilton over the nation's future direction and closes with Jefferson's 1801 inaugural address. Wilella Waldorf notes that the play "uses Jefferson as a symbol of Democratic government in its most enlightened form."[13] Many critics see it as a play of its moment as well as history, drawing parallels between the founding fathers' efforts to establish the ideals of democracy in America and the nation's contemporary engagement in what critic Lewis Nichols called "the second year of a desperate war to preserve the doctrines [Jefferson] summed up in the Declaration of Independence," a comparison heightened by the fact that Kingsley was serving in the army at the time.[14] Others, however, cautioned against looking for answers to current struggles in the play and against, in the words of critic Burton Rascoe, making "the mistake of identifying Mr. Roosevelt with Jefferson."[15]

The musical *1776* portrays Jefferson as a reluctant statesman and author of the Declaration of Independence who is so consumed with pining for his new bride that only a conjugal visit arranged by a wise Ben Franklin finally gets him focused on the work of the revolution. The musical reflects the cultural changes that evolved during the 1960s, because it is unlikely that before 1969, Broadway theatergoers would have been so receptive to portrayals of the founding fathers as fully human beings with all their characters flaws and with frankly expressed sex lives.

An interesting recent footnote to Jefferson's stage history came in 1988 with the Philadelphia production of a new play by Granville Burgess, called *Dusky Sally*.[16] The play deals frankly with the then-less-well-known story of Jefferson's supposed relationship with a slave named Sally Hemings, which made historical headlines a decade after the play as descendants of Hemmings demanded to be acknowledged and allowed burial in the Jefferson family cemetery. The play was based on the Barbara Chase-Ribaud novel *Sally Hemings*,[17] which was reissued in the late 1990s as the nation became ready to finally examine the difficult issue of Jefferson's personal life. By 1998, DNA technology had progressed far enough to make the speculation more than just hearsay; tests showed that some of Hemings's descendants were genetically linked to the Jefferson family, though they could neither prove nor disprove that Jefferson himself was their direct ancestor. That was also the year in which the country had to confront unpleasant details about the personal life of President Bill Clinton, so the public may well have been less resistant to unsavory revelations about the private failings of past presidents in the aftermath of the Lewinsky scandal.

Andrew Jackson

Aside from several different plays named *Young Hickory* about his boyhood, all written since the late 1960s, the most prominent appearance made on the stage by seventh president Andrew Jackson was Maxwell Anderson and Lawrence Stallings's *First Flight*,[18] which made its New York premiere in September 1925. The play deals with the 1788 backwoods adventures of then–Captain Andy Jackson as he makes his way to Nashville across a rebellious section of North Carolina that calls itself the "Free State of Franklin." Jackson was the first president to represent popular, rather than elite, American culture. This depiction, as well as later ones, characterized him as a folk hero rather than a revered statesman.

Abraham Lincoln

Most of the other presidents between the revolutionary period and the Civil War, with the exception of James Buchanan in John Updike's little-known *Buchanan Dying*,[19] do not appear in plays at all. Abraham Lincoln, in contrast, has graced the stage more times than any other president. In 1919, John Drinkwater's play *Abraham Lincoln*[20] arrived in New York after a successful run in England. The play was popular, even though some critics disparaged it for its lack of depth and historical accuracy. In 1938, E. P. Conkle ventured to tell the story of young Lincoln's years in Illinois in *Prologue to Glory*.[21] The sentimental play closed with the death of Lincoln's young love, Ann Rutledge, who was played by her great-grandniece, the actress Ann Rutledge. American audiences seemed ready to see Lincoln onstage, as in the twentieth century he assumed the symbolic role of the hero of the previous century and an icon of American ideals, though no playwright had yet captured the complexity of the man or his quintessentially American journey from log cabin to White House.

The Lincoln play that achieves that end is Robert E. Sherwood's Pulitzer Prize winner, *Abe Lincoln in Illinois*.[22] Critic Brooks Atkinson declared it Sherwood's "finest play" and rated it better than any previous efforts to tell Lincoln's story because it furthers "the principles of American liberty" throughout while looking honestly at events, the man and the facts of his story. He declares it above the level of the box office success it would soon become because "Sherwood has looked down with compassion into the lonely blackness of Lincoln's heart and seen some of the fateful things that lived there. As a craftsman he has had the humility to tell the story quietly."[23] Raymond Massey's performance in the lead role was widely praised, and both he and the play garnered numerous honors. When the play was revived with Sam Waterston in the lead in 1993, however, many critics said that the play was too long and outdated. What had once been deemed ground-breaking and complex in 1938 did not connect well with the America of 1993. Although some critics praised the grand sweep of the production and Waterston's performance, many, like critic David Richards, found it too "didactic or melodramatic" for contemporary audiences.[24] Some, like Linda Winer, observed that the television miniseries had, since the 1970s, become the best venue for such an epic historical tale[25]; the absence of epic presidential dramas from the stage in the decades since seems to bear out her theory, perhaps in part because the American tastes now run more to seeing the lives of ordinary people and antiheroes, rather than heroic historical figures, as worthy of such treatment on the stage.

From 1938 on, Lincoln was an important character on the American stage. With the perhaps surprising exception of the turbulent 1960s, seldom did the New York stage go more than five years without some sort of Lincoln play, though some later plays focused more on Mary Todd Lincoln or on John Wilkes Booth rather than on Lincoln's presidency itself. Lincoln has retained his stature as a powerful patriotic icon and symbol of American ideals perhaps better than any other president portrayed on the stage. As recently as 1994, playwright Suzan-Lori Parks used Lincoln to powerful symbolic purpose in examining the struggle of African-Americans and their place in history in *The America Play*,[26] and again, more obliquely, in her 2002 Pulitzer Prize–winning play *Topdog/Underdog*.[27] Lincoln not only embodies the ideal journey from his lowly origins to the presidency but also stands as a martyr to American ideals who brought the country through a terrible war, faced up to the dark underside of the society of a supposedly free country that relied on slavery, took direct action to correct the injustice, and solidified the nation as a federal entity, not just a collection of states. He was a crucial player in a defining moment in the nation's history and also a remarkable and complex human being to which American audiences feel drawn as a compelling character in his own right.

From Lincoln to Franklin Delano Roosevelt

Several subsequent nineteenth- and early-twentieth-century presidents appear only briefly on the national stage, most likely because they are less inspiring figures than Lincoln and other high-profile presidents. Twentieth-century audiences, who have become less idealistic about the presidency, have little interest in seeing any but the most conflicted or compelling presidents examined in the theater. Ulysses S. Grant makes minor appearances in a few of the Lincoln plays, and also in two Romulus Linney plays. He is peripheral to "Yankee Doodle," part of a 1986 bill of thematically related short plays called *Pops*,[28] but central to Linney's longer play, *Democracy: A Comedy Based on Two Novels by Henry Adams and the Administration of Ulysses S. Grant*,[29] which was adapted from two Henry Adams novels and expands Grant's role from that of an unnamed president in the satirical novel *Democracy*.[30] Grover Cleveland is the subject of an 1890 play entitled *Grover the First*,[31] republished in microprint in 1970. Warren G. Harding also appears in two plays of importance: Jerome Lawrence and Robert E. Lee's 1959 play *The Gang's All Here*,[32] and Mark St. Germain's 1995 play, *Camping With Henry and Tom*,[33] which speculates about a 1921 camping trip made by Henry Ford, Thomas Edison, and President Harding.

The two most important presidents between Lincoln and Franklin Delano Roosevelt—Theodore Roosevelt and Woodrow Wilson—make some significant stage appearances. Theodore Roosevelt is featured in a one-man show entitled *Bully*,[34] by Jerome Alden, that starred James Whitmore in its 1977 Delaware and New York productions. The play makes extensive use of Roosevelt's own words as he reviews the events of his life for the audience, including the death of his son and the famed charge up San Juan Hill. Wilson is the focus of two plays—1970's *Wilson in the Promise Land*[35] by Roland Van Zandt, and 1974's *President Wilson in Paris*[36] by Ron Blair. Van Zandt, a professional historian, tries to examine Wilson's life in the context of all of America's history, in the process incorporating a number of other presidents and a large group of hippies in its cast of characters. The play's examination of how to fulfill the American Dream was reviewed as thought-provoking and at times quite good. Blair's *President Wilson in Paris*[37] is set in the Hotel Murat in Paris and focuses on the president's meetings with various heads of states as he promotes a League of Nations in 1919.

Franklin Delano Roosevelt

Franklin Delano Roosevelt makes a number of important stage appearances, the first while he was still in office. George M. Cohan played Roosevelt in the 1937 Broadway musical *I'd Rather be Right*[38] by George S. Kaufman and Moss Hart, with music by Richard Rogers and lyrics by Lorenz Hart. Brooks Atkinson's opening night review praises the entertaining production but seems to express some disappointment that the "playful," "pleasant," and "affectionate treatment" of the sitting president did not deliver more: "[I]t is not the keen and brilliant political satire most of us have been fondly expecting."[39]

In 1958, Dore Schary's *Sunrise at Campobello*[40] made its Broadway premiere in January, with Ralph Bellamy in the lead, and went on to win many of that year's Tony Awards, including Best Play, Best Actor, Best Supporting Actor, Best Author, Best Director, and Best Producers. The play covered the years between 1921, when Roosevelt contracted polio, and 1924, when he went forward and stood, with the help of crutches, to nominate Al Smith for president at the Democratic National Convention in Madison Square Garden. Richard Watts Jr. of the *New York Post* calls the 1958 production a "tremendously moving drama" and "a stirring and heroic portrait of a great political figure in the heartbreaking days of desperate personal crisis, but it is also considerably more than that."[41] Many critics praise the play for telling a private story about the human spirit, family, and the force of will, but most also acknowledge that it is made all the more powerful because of the public man at its center. Roosevelt was a popular president who had led the country out of the Great Depression and, like Lincoln, led America into a difficult major war that ultimately united and defined it as a nation. The times in which Roosevelt served and his personal struggle with polio make him a complex and interesting dramatic character, and his untimely death in office, although not the overt martyrdom of Lincoln's demise, perhaps served to secure for him a place of reverence and iconic status on the American stage thirteen years later.

The 1977 musical *Annie*,[42] based on the "Little Orphan Annie" comic strip, uses Roosevelt to a much more light-hearted purpose. Clive Barnes of the *New York Times* notes that, rather than keep *Annie* as shallow as a comic strip, "the authors have taken her as a symbol—a symbol of the end of the Great Depression and Franklin D. Roosevelt's New Deal."[43] Roosevelts's predecessor, Herbert Hoover, gets skewered in a musical number called "We'd Like to Thank You," sung by people forced by circumstance to live in a "Hooverville" under the 59th Street Bridge. Barnes described Raymond Thorne as "urbanity personified as F.D.R.,"[44] DouglasWatt of the *New York Daily News* called the portrayal of Roosevelt "a tasteless caricature,"[45] and Jack Kroll of *Newsweek* describes the character as an "amiable boob of a President" who is inspired by Annie's saccharine song "Tomorrow" to create the New Deal.[46] This mockery of a long-revered president is not surprising when one considers that in the post-Watergate, recession-plagued America of 1977, such optimism surely must have seemed naïve and laughable to many theatergoers.

Harry S. Truman

Roosevelt's successor, Harry S. Truman, was famously portrayed by James Whitmore in a 1975 one-man show called *Give 'Em Hell, Harry* by Samuel Gallu.[47] The play was first performed in Hershey, Pennsylvania, in March, then given a gala premiere at Ford's Theatre in Washington, D.C., which was attended by President Ford, members of the cabinet and other dignitaries, and members of the Truman family. Perhaps the renewed interest in Truman, both for audiences and for the nation's capital itself, derived in part from his reputation for being a man of principle who spoke the truth and made tough decisions for what he felt were the right reasons rather than for political gain; the play helped post-Watergate America recall a time when the presidency was more easily respected.

John F. Kennedy

John F. Kennedy is one of America's most charismatic presidential figures, but he makes surprisingly few appearances in plays, perhaps because the nation's memories of the real man are so vivid. Kennedy is among several politicians mentioned as inspirations for President Stephen Decatur Henderson in the 1962 musical *Mr. President*,[48] written by Irving Berlin, Howard Lindsay, and Russell Crouse, but the first true portrayal of Kennedy comes only after his assassination. Jean-Claude Van Itallie's controversial experimental play *The Serpent*[49] premiered in Rome in 1968 and was staged by Joseph Chaikin's Open Theatre in New York in 1970. It originally bore the subtitle "A Ceremony," and it draws parallels between the book of Genesis and contemporary American life, including the assassinations of John F. Kennedy, Martin Luther King Jr., and Robert Kennedy. More often, Kennedy haunts the landscape of American plays, as characters give voice to the effect his assassination had on them, particularly those who were just coming of age at the time. Robert Patrick's *Kennedy's Children*[50] made its New York debut in 1975 and makes the loss of innocence tied to the event a central theme; a number of other plays about the baby boom generation include obligatory "Where were you when Kennedy was shot?" scenes. In Tony Kushner and Jeanine Tesori's 2003 musical theater piece, *Caroline, or Change*,[51] the Kennedy assassination is depicted as a tipping point in the changes facing America, and the South in particular, in 1963; the news of Kennedy's death is delivered in a dramatic dirge sung by an actor representing a sad, slow-moving bus awaited by two African-American maids.

Lyndon B. Johnson

One of the most historically significant plays to feature a Kennedy character is also the most significant to feature his vice president and successor, Lyndon Baines Johnson. Barbara Garson's *MacBird*[52] was an underground phenomenon in 1967. The playwright was only twenty-five years old, had spent two weeks in jail after a free speech rally at the University of California at Berkeley in 1964, and originally planned the play as a skit for an anti–Vietnam War rally in 1965. Instead, she wound up with a New York production that turned a profit and was later denounced by Federal Bureau of Investigation Director J. Edgar Hoover. The play takes Shakespeare's MacBeth as its model, retaining the verse format, and replaces the principal characters with President MacBird and his wife Lady MacBird, thinly disguised versions of the Johnsons, who are implicated in the murder of MacBird's predecessor John Ken O'Dunc, a Kennedy figure. The play had trouble finding a press willing to print its programs, and *The New Yorker* refused to run advertising for it on the grounds that it was in poor taste. The production spawned many angry letters to the editor and outraged opinion pieces, but it was also hailed as "the most powerful piece of pro-American theater in a long time" by famed director Peter Brook.[53] In response to Walter Kerr's charge that it was not so much a play as a vulgar lampoon, critic Martin Esslin declared it a "brilliant vulgar lampoon" that ought not to be taken so seriously.[54] In *The New Republic*, literary critic and director Robert Brustein called it "an exhilarating experience" and "a genuine happening."[55] He asserts, as do others, that Garson's point is not to literally accuse Johnson of murder but, "rather to name the unnamable and speak the unspeakable. If we are living in a world of anguish, frustration, and senseless violence—a world which only the mad continue to find sane and reasonable—then *MacBird* helps destroy anxieties merely by making our nightmares tangible and manifest."[56] The play was very much a work of its moment, reflecting not only the rebellious questioning of the government by young people all over America, not just young artists in the theater during the Vietnam War era, but also the growth of experimental, edgy, often political work in the American theater at the time.

Johnson's life was given a more historically accurate and even-handed treatment in *Lyndon*,[57] a 1991 one-man show written by James Prideaux, which starred Laurence Luckenbill in its New York premiere. In an odd turn of events, this play about a president dogged by the quagmire of Vietnam opened the night after the first Gulf War began.

Richard Nixon

If the nation's anxiety was high during the Johnson administration, the anxiety surrounding the presidency became even greater during the Watergate era. Richard Nixon has been the subject, either directly or indirectly, of so many plays and films that an entire volume, Thomas Monsell's 1998 *Nixon on Stage and Screen: The Thirty-Seventh President as Depicted in Films, Television, Plays and Opera*,[58] is devoted to the subject. Nixon may have ultimately been an unpopular president, but his flawed character and darkly complex story made him a popular figure for playwrights and audiences alike. Even as a candidate, Nixon helped inspire the character of presidential candidate Joseph Cantwell in Gore Vidal's *The Best Man*,[59] which made its Broadway premiere during the 1960 campaign. Another fictional candidate strikingly similar to Nixon, Senator George W. Mason, appeared in the musical *The Selling of the President* by Jack O'Brien, Stuart Hample, and Bob James,[60] which staged a tale of a 1976 election in 1972.

Published Watergate era plays featuring Nixon seemed to echo *MacBird*'s twist on a classic drama. *The Devil and Dr. Noxin*,[61] by B. H. Wolfe, was based on Marlowe's *Doctor Faustus*; *The Tragedy of Richard II*,[62] by Robert J. Myers was based on Shakespeare's *Richard III*; and *The Tragedy of King Richard: Shakespearean Watergate*[63] by Dana Glenn Bramwell borrows from Shakespeare's tragedy—none, however, duplicated Garson's success. A comic musical based on *Richard III* called *Dick Deterred*[64] by David Edgar spoofed Nixon on the London stage in 1974, and many American theaters and comedy troupes staged satirical productions about Nixon during these years.

In 1987, Nixon returned to the stage in the opera *Nixon in China*,[65] written by John Adams with a libretto by poet Alice Goodman, and perhaps the fullest and most complex stage portrait of Nixon to date arrives in 1996 in Russell Lees's *Nixon's Nixon*.[66] The play depicts a meeting between Nixon and Kissinger late at night on August 7, 1974, the night before Nixon's resignation. Reviews were somewhat mixed but were positive enough that the play went on to a healthy life in regional theaters after its New York run. Just as the American stage has continued to examine Lincoln as perhaps our quintessential noble president, it also remains fascinated with Nixon as his polar opposite: a man whose personal struggles led not to moral victory and the unification of a divided nation but, instead, to the ultimate undermining of the country's already diminished faith in the integrity of its federal leadership at the end of the Vietnam era.

Presidents after Nixon

More recent presidents have seen far less attention than their infamous predecessor. Ronald Reagan is an offstage force, talked about and struggled with, in several plays, but never seen. Tony Kushner's 1993 *Angels in America*[67] is set during the Reagan years, and the characters curse him. Arje Shaw's *The Gathering*[68] focuses on Reagan's trip to Bitburg and the efforts of the Holocaust-survivor father of one of his speechwriters to protest the event. It premiered in 1999 off-Broadway at the Jewish Repertory theater, starring Theodore Bikel, and then was restaged on Broadway with Hal Linden in the lead.

The only play focused exclusively on Bill Clinton, aside from many comedy revues that did sketches about the President, also keeps him offstage. *Snatches*[69] by Laura Strausfeld debuted off-Broadway in 2001 and was also staged at the renowned Edinburgh Festival in 2002. The play is a one-act comedy pieced together from actual bits of dialogue from the recorded telephone conversations between Monica Lewinsky and Linda Tripp.

A number of plays over the years have taken the presidency as a whole, not just a single president, as their subject. The most notable of these, Anna Deavere Smith's play *House Arrest: A Search for the American Character in and Around the White House, Past and Present*[70] was performed in several different versions at major regional theaters in Washington, D.C.; Los Angeles; Chicago; and Seattle in the late 1990s before opening in New York in 2000. The play, which was published in 2003, uses Smith's trademark journalistic style, often drawing on the actual words of its subjects to explore the role of the presidency in American culture throughout the country's history; many presidents are discussed, but only Jefferson, Lincoln, Clinton, and George H. W. Bush appear as characters.

Clearly, America's fascination with its presidents as dramatic figures continues, so perhaps new scripts, which seem always to be appearing, will give attention to those presidents previously neglected by playwrights. For example, an organization called The History Project is currently engaged in a long-term effort to develop historically worthwhile biographical one-act plays about each of the American presidents. According to their Web site, http://www.uspresidents.com, they have so far completed plays about Washington, Adams, Jefferson, Madison, Monroe, John Quincy Adams, Jackson, Van Buren, and Tyler and have more in the works. As creative artists gain distance from and new perspective on recent presidencies or, conversely, if world events inspire the sort of examination of sitting presidents that occurred in the late 1960s and early 1970s, the playwrights of the twenty-first century may offer new, more inspired, portraits of the people who have held and will hold the nation's highest office.

Notes

1. John Leacock, *The Fall of British Tyrrany: or, American Triumphant* (Philadelphia: Styner and Cist, 1776).

2. William Dunlap, *The Glory of Columbia; Her Yeomanry* (New York: Longworth, 1803).

3. Victor Mapes, *Captain Barrington, an American drama in four acts* (New York: Samuel French, 1931).

4. Percy MacKaye, *Wakefield: a folk-masque* (Washington, D.C.: George Washington Bicentennial Commission, 1932).

5. Maxwell Anderson, *Valley Forge: Eleven Verse Plays* (New York: Harcourt Brace, 1939), 1–166.

6. Brooks Atkinson, "Washington at Valley Forge," *New York Times*, December 23, 1934, IX 1.

7. Kenneth Koch, "George Washington Crossing the Delaware," in *A Change of Hearts: Plays, Films and other Dramatic Works, 1951–1971*, ed. Kenneth Koch (New York: Random House, 1973), 62–86.

8. Peter Stone and Sherman Edwards, *1776: A Musical Play* (New York: Viking, 1970).

9. William Gibson, *American Primitive* (New York: Dramatists, 1972).

10. Ibid., 32.

11. Ibid., 40, 57.

12. Sidney Kingsley, *The Patriots: a play in a prologue and three acts* (New York: Random House, 1943).

13. Wilella Waldorf, "Sidney Kingsley's 'The Patriots' Produced at the National Theatre." *New York Post*, January 30, 1943. Reprinted in *New York Theatre Critics' Reviews*, February 8, 1943, 386.

14. Lewis Nichols, "The Play in Review: 'The Patriots,'" *New York Times*, January 30, 1943. Reprinted in *New York Theatre Critics' Reviews*, February 8, 1943, 387.

15. Burton Rascoe, "The Patriots Opens at the National," *New York World-Telegram*, January 30, 1943. Reprinted in *New York Theatre Critics' Reviews*, February 8, 1943, 388.

16. Granville Wyche Burgess, *Dusky Sally* (New York: Broadway Play Publishing, 1987).

17. Barbara Chase-Riboud, *Sally Hemings: A Novel* (New York: Viking, 1979).

18. Maxwell Anderson and Laurence Stallings, *First Flight. Three American Plays* (New York: Harcourt, Brace, 1926), 91–179.

19. John Updike, *Buchanan Dying; a play* (New York: Knopf, 1974).

20. John Drinkwater, *Abraham Lincoln* (Boston: Houghton Mifflin, 1927).

21. E. P. Conkle, *Prologue to Glory: a play in eight scenes based on the New Salem years of Abraham Lincoln* (New York: Samuel French, 1938).

22. Robert E. Sherwood, *Abe Lincoln in Illinois* (New York: Dramatists, 1939).

23. Brooks Atkinson, "Raymond Massey Appearing in Robert E. Sherwood's 'Abe Lincoln in Illinois,'" *New York Times*, October 17, 1938, 12.

24. David Richards, "Lincoln as Metaphor for a Big Job Ahead, in 1939 and Today," *New York Times*, November 30, 1993. Reprinted in *Theatre Critics' Reviews* 54 (1993):406–407.

25. Linda Winer, "Sherwood's Passionless '38 'Lincoln,'" *New York Newsday*, November 30, 1993. Reprinted in *Theatre Critics' Reviews* 54 (1993):404.

26. Suzan-Lori Parks, *The America Play* (New York: Dramatists, 1995).

27. Suzan-Lori Parks, *Topdog/Underdog* (New York: Theatre Communications Group, 2002).

28. Romulus Linney, "Yankee Doodle," in *Pops* (New York: Dramatists, 1987), 40–48.

29. Romulus Linney, *Democracy: A Comedy Based on Two Novels by Henry Adams and the Administration of Ulysses S. Grant* (New York: Dramatists, 1976).

30. Mel Gussow, "Theatre in review: Timely political satire from two Henry Adams novels via Romulus Linney." *New York Times*, October 7, 1992, C 16:3.

31. *Grover the First: a drama in three acts.* 1890. New York: Readex Microprint, 1970.

32. Jerome Lawrence and Robert E. Lee, *The Gang's All Here* (Topanga, Calif.: Boulevard Books, 1960).

33. Mark St. Germain, *Camping with Henry and Tom: a play in two acts* (New York: Samuel French, 1995).

34. Jerome Alden, *Bully: an adventure with Teddy Roosevelt* (New York: Crown, 1979).

35. Roland Van Zandt, *Wilson in the Promise Land* (New York: Samuel French, 1970).

36. Ron Blair, *President Wilson in Paris, a play* (Sydney: Currency Press; London: Eyre Methuen, 1974).

37. Ibid.

38. George S. Kaufman, Moss Hart, Lorenz Hart, and Richard Rodgers, *I'd Rather Be Right* (New York: Random House, 1937).

39. Brooks Atkinson, "George M. Cohan as the United States President in 'I'd Rather Be Right,'" *New York Times*, November 3, 1937, 28.

40. Dore Schary, *Sunrise at Campobello* (New York: Dramatists, 1961).

41. Richard Watts Jr., "The Drama of Franklin D. Roosevelt," *New York Post*, January 31, 1958. Reprinted in *New York Theatre Critics' Reviews*, February 3, 1958, 378.

42. Charles Strouse, Martin Charnin, and Thomas Meehan, *Annie: a new Broadway musical* (New York: E. H. Morris, 1977).

43. Clive Barnes, "Stage: 'Annie' Finds a Home," *New York Times*, April 22, 1977. Reprinted in *New York Theatre Critics' Reviews*, May 16, 1977, 258.

44. Ibid.

45. Douglas Watt, "'Annie' finds a home on B'way," *Daily News* April 22, 1977. Reprinted in *New York Theatre Critics' Reviews* May 16, 1977, 259.

46. Jack Kroll, "Annie Takes Broadway," *Newsweek*, May 2, 1977. Reprinted in *New York Theatre Critics' Reviews*, May 16, 1977, 262.

47. Samuel Gallu, *Give 'em Hell Harry: reminiscences* (New York: Viking, 1975).

48. Irving Berlin, Howard Lindsay, and Russell Crouse, *Mr. President*, 1962.

49. Jean Claude Van Itallie and Joseph Chaikin, *The Serpent; a ceremony* (New York: Atheneum, 1969).

50. Robert Patrick, *Kennedy's Children* (New York: Samuel French, 1976).

51. Tony Kushner and Jeanine Tesori, *Caroline, or Change: a musical.* (New York: Theatre Communications Group, 2004).

52. Barbara Garson, *MacBird* (New York: Grove, 1967).

53. Peter Brook, "Is 'MacBird' Pro-American?" *New York Times*, March 19, 1967, II 1.

54. Martin Esslin, "London Broils 'MacBird,'" *New York Times*, April 16, 1967, II 3.

55. Robert Brustein, "*MacBird* on Stage," *New Republic*, March 11, 1967, 30.

56. Ibid.

57. James Prideaux, *Lyndon*, 1991.

58. Thomas Monsell, *Nixon on Stage and Screen: The Thirty-Seventh President as Depicted in Films, Television, Plays and Opera* (Jefferson, N.C.: McFarland, 1998).

59. Gore Vidal, *The Best Man* (New York: Dramatists, 2001).

60. Bob James, Stuart E. Hample, and Jack O'Brien, *The Selling of the President* (San Francisco: Geary Theatre/Studio Duplicating Service, 1972).

61. Burton H. Wolfe and Christopher Marlowe, *The Devil and Dr. Noxin* (San Francisco: Wild West Publishing, 1973).

62. Robert J. Myers, *The Tragedy of Richard II* (Washington, D.C.: Acropolis Books, 1973).

63. Dana Glenn Bramwell, *The Tragedy of King Richard: Shakespearean Watergate* (Salina, Kans.: Survey Publishers, 1974).

64. David Edgar, *Dick Deterred; a play in two acts* (New York: Monthly Review Press, 1974).

65. John Adams and Alice Goodman, *Nixon in China: an opera in two acts.* [s.l.: s.n.] Hart Graphics, Morin Division, 1987.

66. Russell Lees, *Nixon's Nixon* (New York: Dramatists, 1996).

67. Tony Kushner, *Angels in America: A Gay Fantasia on National Themes* (New York: Theatre Communications Group, 2003).

68. Arje Shaw, *The Gathering*, 1999.

69. Laura Strausfeld, *Snatches*, 2001.

70. Anna Deavere Smith, *House Arrest: A Search for American Character In and Around the White House, Past and Present* (New York: Dramatists, 2003).

CHAPTER 5

MYTHS, LEGENDS, STORIES, AND JOKES

ARTHUR HOLST

Stories, legends, jokes, and anecdotes about American presidents complement their executive actions by letting the average citizen catch a glimpse of these larger-than-life individuals. From childhood legends surrounding our first president to Campaign 2000 mock debates on comedy shows, personal stories, jokes, and humor have shaped the personas of the presidents.

George Washington

Early in the nation's history, stories of George Washington's physical feats circulated, giving him what many today would call "superhero" status. Stories about the life of George Washington are enhanced by myths of his youthful honesty and his physical prowess. For example, the young George Washington supposedly cut down a cherry tree on his father's land. When his father demanded to know who chopped down the tree, Washington, unable to lie, admitted to the deed. This endearing story is a myth, originally created by Parson Mason Weems—an early biographer of Washington—who wanted to portray Washington's honesty.

As an adolescent, Washington spent time at his family's farm in Fredericksburg, Virginia. One day, a friend challenged Washington to throw a rock across the Rappahannock River. His success led to another myth in which the rock became a silver dollar and the Rappahannock became the Potomac River. The Potomac is over a mile wide in most areas near Mount Vernon, where the newer myth placed Washington's feat. Although Washington was athletic, his contemporaries exalted his superhuman persona to an almost unbelievable extent, not only posthumously but during his lifetime as well.

The story of George Washington's "wooden" teeth is another popular myth. Washington did wear false teeth, but they certainly were not made from wood, and they were not made for him by the famous craftsman Paul Revere. With the lack of preventative dentistry during his time, Washington had only one remaining tooth by the time of his first term. When colonial dentist John Greenwood crafted one of Washington's first sets of dentures, he carved a hole through the lower ivory section of the teeth to use Washington's last tooth as an anchoring base for the dentures. The final set was crafted using fragments of cow and human teeth, elephant ivory, lead, and metal springs. Soon after he started wearing the set, Washington's final tooth came loose, was extracted, and is now in a golden case, which can be seen at the New York Academy of Medicine.

Washington was extremely self-conscious of his teeth. He believed that they were always too loose-fitting, causing him great difficulty when he tried to make the "s" sound. Surprising many who knew him well, Washington ended his inaugural speech at the start of his second term with the difficult phrase, "witnesses of the present solemn ceremony."[1]

Washington's difficulty with teeth did not stop there. While Washington was posing for his portrait, famous artist Gilbert Stuart asked Washington to stuff cotton into his mouth to support his lips. On completion, Washington and his wife, Martha, both were very critical of the portrait, yet to this day, Stuart's work is seen on the U.S. one dollar bill. Washington did not allow his sensitivity toward his teeth keep him from fulfilling any of his duties, including the less important one of sitting for a painting.[2] Washington is still popular and revered today: He personifies the American sense of duty to country.

John Adams and Thomas Jefferson

Two contemporaries of Washington were John Adams, Washington's vice president and later the second president of the United States, and Thomas Jefferson, Adams's vice president and successor as the third American president. Before election procedures and outcomes were modified in the Constitution, the two presidential candidates with the highest number of votes became president and vice president. Consequently, Adams, a member of the Federalist Party, and Jefferson, a member of the Democratic-Republican Party, became president and vice president, respectively, in 1797, even though they were serious political adversaries.

Both Adams and Jefferson died on July 4, 1826, the fiftieth anniversary of the Declaration of Independence. Before their deaths, both men had continued to correspond. Adams often stated that he wished to outlive Jefferson, who was seven years younger. At the time of his death on July 4, 1826, John Adams's last words were "Thomas Jefferson still lives." A messenger was supposedly dispatched at the time of Adams's death, but

Adams's statement did not prove true. In fact, Jefferson had died a few hours before Adams.[3]

One story that has outlasted Jefferson's death is his relationship with his slave, Sally Hemings. Most recently during President Clinton's scandals, many people drew parallels between Clinton and Jefferson. As a consequence, the Sally Hemings debate became even more politicized when it reemerged in the middle of the political controversy and impeachment trials surrounding Clinton.

The answer to the question of whether Thomas Jefferson fathered some of Sally Hemings's children is, according to scholars, anywhere from "remote" to "certain." Recently, DNA evidence has proven that there is a link between ancestors of Thomas Jefferson and Sally Hemings.[4] However, the DNA data leaves the possibility that one of Jefferson's close relatives fathered Hemings's children. Interestingly, the scandal about Jefferson and Hemings was first published in a Richmond newspaper in 1802 by a spurned political ally of Jefferson, James T. Callender, although he did not present any conclusive evidence to back up his accusation. Jefferson's "secret" relationship with Sally Hemings still fascinates many today, especially considering its significance as a relationship between a master and a slave and considering the more recent improprieties of Bill Clinton.

Andrew Jackson

The myths and stories surrounding Andrew Jackson developed early in his life. During the American Revolution, when Jackson was just thirteen years old, he was captured by the British. During his captivity, Jackson refused to obey the orders of a British officer. When Jackson disobeyed a command to clean a British officer's boots, he was hit across his face with the side of a saber, leaving him with a large scar on his forehead. Jackson was able to take his revenge on the British some years later, however, while commanding the defense of the New Orleans during the War of 1812. The battles with the superior British force from December 1814 to January 1815 ultimately resulted in an unexpected victory for the United States and ensured Jackson's status as a national hero.

Once he became a part of the national scene, earlier stories of Jackson's notoriously short temper resurfaced. In 1805, one of Jackson's close friends made insulting comments about the way in which Captain Joseph Ervin handled his horse racing bets with Jackson. Ervin's son-in-law, Charles Dickinson, who heard the comments, became enraged and denounced Jackson as a "worthless scoundrel, a poltroon, and a coward," in an issue of the *Nashville Review* in May 1806. Jackson challenged Dickinson to a duel and allowed him to choose the weapons, even though Dickinson was regarded as one of the best marksmen in Tennessee. Dickinson fired the first shot, which lodged in Jackson's ribs, very close to his heart. Holding his bleeding chest, Jackson was permitted to take his shot at Dickinson while he stood at mark according to dueling practices. Jackson took his time aiming, shot, and mortally wounded Dickinson.[5]

After his military victories, Jackson, despite little formal education, became a successful Tennessee lawyer and entered politics. Campaigning as a successful war hero, Jackson was elected president in 1828. As many candidates still try to present themselves today, Jackson ran as an outsider candidate, far removed from the politics and bureaucracy of Washington, D.C.

As president, Jackson faced more challenges when John C. Calhoun, a senator from South Carolina, sought to get rid of the United States' high protective tariffs. When Calhoun's efforts failed to sway Jackson and the rest of Congress, South Carolina attempted to nullify the tariff and act independently of the national government in Washington, D.C. Taking quick action, Jackson dealt with the insurrection by sending in U.S. military troops and threatening Calhoun by saying in private that he would personally hang Calhoun. A compromise was negotiated, and South Carolina dropped nullification.[6] Jackson is credited with strengthening the presidency. He left office in 1837, still a very popular leader and an advocate for the common man.

Abraham Lincoln

Myths surrounding Abraham Lincoln began long before his assassination at Ford's Theatre. Like Andrew Jackson, Lincoln's frontier childhood was idealized as something very American. Another similarity with Jackson was Lincoln's image as a plainspoken man. In addition, he had amazing physical attributes, such as his height and his ability to outrun others. He could chop wood quickly, wrestle well, and carry the heaviest logs. In truth, Lincoln was athletic, but more than likely not to the exaggerated extent of the legends. Americans like not only a physically strong president, but also one who is morally strong. They feel there is a morality to American democracy and have a firm belief in the victory of right over wrong. The image of Lincoln as a rail-splitter serves to enhance the image of the American president as a strong, noble person physically ready for any battle that may lie ahead.

Lincoln was always known for his honesty. One story, widely accepted as true, deals with a store he was managing in New Salem, Illinois. One day a store customer purchased some items but forgot to take his change. Lincoln, feeling somewhat responsible for the mistake, walked more than a few miles to return the change to the customer's home quite a distance away.

Another famous myth is that Abraham Lincoln wrote his famous "Gettysburg Address" on the back of an envelope while riding on the train to Gettysburg from Washington, D.C. Lincoln actually wrote the speech during stops on the train trip and at the home of David Willis, not during the ride, which would have been much too bumpy to allow for legible writing. When he returned from Gettysburg, Lincoln contracted a mild form of smallpox. Lincoln, who was always hounded by other politicians for never acceding to their demands, asked that all office seekers be allowed to visit him. When his doctors advised against visitors, Lincoln complained that he finally had "something that I can give to everybody."[7]

Lincoln received the news of Lee's surrender at Appomattox while at an event at the White House, during which a band performed. When Lincoln was asked for the song he most wanted to hear, he requested the song "Dixie." Band members were obviously confused as to why the President would select a song that was clearly identified with the (now-former) Confederacy. Admitting that "Dixie" was one of his favorite songs, Lincoln said "I have always thought 'Dixie' one of the best tunes I have ever heard. Our adversaries over the way attempted to appropriate it, but I insisted yesterday that we fairly captured it. I now request that the band favor me with its performance."[8] Soon after this event, Lincoln was assassinated. Possibly the most storied American politician of all time, he received even more fanfare for his accomplishments following his death. Though Lincoln was disliked by some and misunderstood by others, citizens were still shocked by his assassination, which has lead to the preservation of his memory and myth.

Theodore Roosevelt

Theodore "Teddy" Roosevelt has often been given godlike status by historians. From his actions with the Rough Riders during the Spanish-American War to his nickname, which would be carried by "teddy" bears throughout the world, Roosevelt, like his persona, made a larger-than-life impression on American history.

The teddy bear legend is important to understanding the Roosevelt myth. During one of his hunting trips, Roosevelt searched for grizzly bears in Mississippi. Unable to come across any bears, he and his party finally saw an old, tired bear walking slowly through the forest. The dogs accompanying the party attacked and injured the nearly helpless bear. The other party members told the president that they had found a bear he could shoot in the forest. Seeing the bear, Roosevelt refused to shoot the poor, wounded creature for sport. Soon after, Clifford Berryman, a political cartoonist for the *Washington Post*, heard of the story and composed a cartoon that popularized the tale. A Brooklyn-based toy-maker, Morris Mitchom, created a stuffed animal, to which he gave the President's nickname, "Teddy." As the story of Roosevelt's actions on the hunt spread, people identified Roosevelt as a figure who was sharp and determined when necessary, yet also caring and noble when necessary.

Roosevelt's presidency was one filled with many presidential firsts: He was the first president to ride in an airplane and a submarine, to own a car, and to travel outside the United States, going by battleship to Panama in 1906. Roosevelt also coined a phrase that many people hear daily. While visiting the home of another influential former president, Andrew Jackson's Hermitage home in Tennessee, he drank coffee from the Maxwell House Hotel in Nashville. After quickly drinking the cup, he said that the brew was "good to the last drop."[9] Later, the local brand of coffee from the hotel, marketed by the Cheek family, was sold to the General Foods Company of New York. In the 1920s, the company used the president's words as a slogan to market Maxwell House coffee.

William H. Taft

William H. Taft started a tradition during his presidency that still continues today. While at a baseball game between the Washington Senators and the Philadelphia Athletics on April 14, 1910, the umpire handed the baseball to Taft after the competing teams' managers were introduced. Taft went to the pitcher's mound and threw it to home plate. Since then, every President except for Jimmy Carter has opened a baseball season with a "presidential" pitch.

Taft also may be responsible for another baseball tradition. At the same game at which he pitched the first ball, Taft, who weighed around three hundred pounds, became uncomfortable in the stadium's small seats. In the middle of the seventh inning, he rose from his seat. When the crowd saw the president stand, they believed that he was about to leave, so they rose to show their respect. Somewhat embarrassed by making everyone stand, Taft sat back down after he stretched a little. Thus, the tradition of the seventh-inning stretch was born.[10]

Calvin Coolidge

Calvin Coolidge became president in 1923. Coolidge, nicknamed "Silent Cal," maintained a very quiet demeanor. Many of Coolidge's contemporaries believed that his true talent as president was effectively doing nothing—refusing new spending plans, preferring smaller government and freer trade. He held few public conferences, once saying, "The American

President William Howard Taft throws out the first ball on the opening day of the 1912 baseball season. (AP/Wide World Photos)

public wants a solemn ass as president and I think I'll go along with them."[11] He was frugal not only with government money but also with his own speech. He would sit through interviews for hours at a time, only answering "yes" or "no." His shortness of speech became famous. A young woman sitting near the president whispered to her friend, claiming that she could get the president to say at least three words. Overhearing the conversation, Coolidge turned to the young woman and simply said, "You lose."[12]

Franklin Delano Roosevelt

With the onset of the Depression, the citizens of the United States turned to Franklin D. Roosevelt to guide the nation through troubled times. Roosevelt had an incredible ability to endear himself to people. One of Roosevelt's most powerful actions when he was president may not have even included words. While visiting an army hospital for the wounded, many of whom were enduring excruciating pain, Roosevelt removed the blanket he had over his legs and revealed his crippled limbs. This display of physical pain and weakness, coupled with Roosevelt's mental fortitude, awed all the wounded men at the camp as Roosevelt passed by in his wheelchair.[7]

Harry S. Truman

Roosevelt's successor, Harry S. Truman, never let the trappings and the prestige of the presidency allow him to forget his upbringing on a farm in rural Missouri. He was not afraid to be direct, even if it didn't always agree with presidential norms. For example, Truman's daughter, Margaret, was pursuing a singing career during her father's presidency. When Truman saw a critical review of his daughter's singing in the newspaper, he wrote back to the music critic, calling him names and threatening to break his nose.[7] When the letter was first published, Truman looked foolish, considering his position as president. With time, however, the letter was seen as an example of Truman's family loyalty. Truman stood up and defended his daughter's ill-fated career move, and Americans have always admired this type of personal loyalty.

John F. Kennedy

In 1960, John F. Kennedy was elected president. Kennedy was admired greatly for his intelligence, wit, and love of reading. Kennedy said, "I'm reading more and enjoying it less," while complaining about the recent lack of quality publications. Although he too was very bright, Kennedy paid respect to those who exhibited remarkable intelligence. Speaking at a reception for the Nobel Prize winners, Kennedy told the group that he thought "this is the most extraordinary collection of human knowledge that has ever been gathered at the White House, with the possible exception of when Thomas Jefferson dined alone."[13]

Before his time in the White House, Kennedy had already established an honorable and courageous reputation while with the navy during World War II. When Kennedy was only twenty-six, he skippered PT-109, a small patrol craft operating in waters of the Solomon Islands. Heir to a massive fortune, Kennedy had chosen service over the easy life. One night, a Japanese destroyer appeared out of the darkness and smashed through his vessel, killing two members of his crew. With the help of his fellow crew members, Kennedy was able to swim his crew to safety on an uninhabited island several hours away. Kennedy had the task of towing a seriously injured member of his crew, which he did with his teeth. Then, he and his crew courageously held out for six days on the island before relief arrived. Later asked about his actions, Kennedy simply replied, "It was easy, they sunk my boat."[14]

Kennedy knew how to use his wit to endear himself and connect with citizens. In one particular instance, Kennedy was giving a speech in Wisconsin on an autumn Sunday. Recognizing that it was the middle of football season, Kennedy said, "I was warned to be out here in plenty of time to permit those who are going to the Green Bay Packers game to leave. I don't mind running against Mr. Nixon, but I have the good sense not to run against the Green Bay Packers." Also while on campaign, Kennedy was often attacked for his financial ties with his father and was accused of buying votes. In response, Kennedy once said, "I have just received the following telegram from my generous Daddy. It says, 'Dear Jack: Don't buy a single vote more than is necessary. I'll be damned if I'm going to pay for a landslide.'"[15]

Kennedy was also known for his active White House—one filled with a young, active, and attractive family. Behind the Camelot façade, however, Kennedy was rumored to have had many extramarital romances, including with movie stars and women connected to the mafia.[16] Although recent biographers have brought to light many of these affairs, they have not tarnished Kennedy's image as a young, handsome, and strong president.

Lyndon Baines Johnson

Lyndon Baines Johnson assumed the presidency after Kennedy's death. Often, Johnson was impatient with those who had never experienced rural living. Once, when reporters from a northern city came to the ranch, Johnson harassed them, somewhat excessively, about types of cattle and other rural ranch knowledge. Johnson used his direct approach while dealing with fellow politicians. One time, Johnson asked Idaho Senator Frank Church, who was against the Vietnam War, "Where do you get your ideas on Vietnam?" Church answered that he got them from "Walter Lippmann," a popular syndicated columnist at that time. In response, Johnson quipped, "next time you need a dam in Idaho, you just go ask Walter Lippmann."[17]

Richard Nixon

Richard Nixon appeared more somber and serious than his immediate predecessors. A number of Nixon's contemporaries considered him a slick liar, often attacking his integrity in the media. One of the first major attacks on Nixon's honesty came in 1952, when political opponents claimed that Nixon used campaign contributions by wealthy California businessmen for personal use. Eisenhower, who was running for president at the time, wanted to drop Nixon from his ticket as a result, but Nixon soon appeared on television to offer a defense. Nixon claimed that, after thinking about it long and hard, he accepted a cocker spaniel from businessmen after the nomination and had given it to daughter. He said his daughter loved the dog, which had been named Checkers, and that giving the dog up was not an option.[18]

The "Checkers Speech," as it is now known, offers an example of what some people consider to be Nixon's questionable integrity. In response to his speech, many supporters sent letters to President Eisenhower's offices praising Nixon's heartfelt openness about the situation, while others were aghast that Nixon would use his daughter and a cocker spaniel for an alibi. After Watergate, Nixon's reputation for dishonesty became, at least for some, his alibi. On Halloween, "Nixon" appears everywhere—his mock Halloween mask has become a best-seller.[19]

Ronald Reagan

Ronald Reagan certainly used humor to his advantage, easing tension in situations and endearing himself to others. His comments during his assassination attempt, in which he was wounded, put the nation at ease during a difficult situation. He told his wife that "he forgot to duck." He asked his staff, "Who's minding the store?" and most famously, he told his doctors he hoped they were "all good Republicans." He also said "All in all, I'd rather be in Philadelphia," referring to a famous statement by W. C. Fields.[20]

Reagan was also able to use humor in political situations. During his campaign for a second term, Reagan was able to quiet democratic opponent Walter Mondale and his followers, who believed that Reagan was too old to be an effective president, by saying "I'm not going to exploit my opponent's youth and inexperience" on a televised debate.[17] At times, however, Reagan's humor went just a little too far. While appearing on a radio show one time, he jokingly said that he had ordered the launch of a massive nuclear strike against Russia, not knowing that the microphone was on already. The report circulated, and Soviet troops and nuclear arsenals were put on high alert.[17]

William Jefferson Clinton

President William Jefferson Clinton's two terms in office provided ample material for political humorists. Comics lampooned Clinton for just about everything, whether it was his supposed sexual adventures, his three hundred dollar haircut, the quality of his golf game, or his love of fast food. Clinton, however, was also good at using humor against his adversaries. Nonetheless, his opponents continue to make jokes about him. A search for Clinton jokes on the internet quickly gathers results that range from slightly risqué to obscene. Still, Clinton's reaction to this humor strengthened his standing with at least some of the American public. Clinton reacted coolly to charges leveled against him during his presidency.

However, he was not beyond poking fun at himself. Before departing the presidency, Clinton appeared in a video shown at the White House Correspondent's Dinner in which he wandered the empty halls of the White House and engaged in humorous activities serving to illustrate the lack of activity in a "lame duck" administration.

The Election of 2000

Political humor and the importance of its use by candidates reached new levels during the presidential campaign in 2000. At the Al Smith Dinner in New York, which benefits Catholic health charities, both George W. Bush and Al Gore used a lot of self-deprecating humor, as well as taking a few shots at each other. Bush opened by saying that he enjoyed being with the "distinguished dais, better known as the top one percent," in direct response to Gore's attacks on his tax-cut scheme, which benefited wealthy citizens. Then, Bush commented on a fellow Yale graduate in the crowd, William F. Buckley Jr., Bush said that Buckley and he shared a lot in common, stating "Bill wrote a book at Yale. I read one. He started the Conservative Party, I started a few parties myself."[21] Bush's ultimate influence on popular culture is yet to be determined, but jokes and even entire books have surfaced—filled with his famous slips of the tongue.

For Bush and his predecessors, stories, myths, and jokes have greatly influenced popular culture and have allowed citizens to decide their fates and their legacies. Time has served to enhance the legends of some, transforming them into noble men of great character and strength, whereas for others it has, perhaps, diminished their stature. In the future, some legends may change, mistakes may be forgotten, and the legacies of past presidents may transform some of them into leaders of mythic proportion.

Notes

1. *George Washington Myths, Mount Vernon,* http://www.mountvernon.org/learn/meet_george/index.cfm/pid/382 (accessed June 2, 2003).

2. Scott E. Casper, "George Washington: The Man Behind the Myths," *Journal of the Early Republic* 20 (Summer 2000):328.

3. *Requiem for an American President,* http://www.homeofheroes.com/profiles/profiles_jeffadams.html (accessed June 18, 2003).

4. In 1998, the scientific magazine *Nature* published results from extensive DNA tests. The results, widely accepted by scientists and scholars, find that Jefferson fathered at least one of Sally Hemings's children, and possibly all six of her children. However, the article has been contested by many, including the Thomas Jefferson Foundation, which states that "the precise nature of the relationship that existed between Thomas Jefferson and Sally Hemings" is not based upon "definitive information" [Thomas Jefferson Foundation, "Thomas Jefferson and Sally Hemings: A Brief Account," 4 Jan 2004, http://www.monticello.org/plantation/hemingscontro/hemings-jefferson_contro.html (accessed May 27, 2005)].

5. *The History of Dueling in America,* "The American Experience," http://www.pbs.org/wgbh/amex/duel/sfeature/dueling.html (accessed January 3, 2004).

6. *The White House,* "Andrew Jackson," http://www.whitehouse.gov/history/presidents/aj7.html (accessed December 30, 2002).

7. *Presidential Stories.* The Presidential Expert, http://www.presidentialexpert.com/stories.htm (accessed June 9, 2003).

8. *Stories, Legends, and Myths,* The Lincoln Museum, http://www.thelincolnmuseum.org/new/research/stories.html (accessed December 31, 2002).

9. *Myths, Legends & Trivia.* Theodore Roosevelt Association, http://www.theodoreroosevelt.org/life/mythleg.htm (accessed July 2, 2003).

10. David Emery, *The Seventh-Inning Stretch: Origin (Or Not) of a Baseball Tradition, Urban Legends and Folklore,* http://urbanlegends.miningco.com/library/weekly/aa102500a.htm (accessed December 31, 2002).

11. Joseph R. Conlin, *The American Past*, 5th edition, vol. 2 (Ft. Worth, Tex.: Harcourt Press, 1997), 716.

12. *The White House*, "Calvin Coolidge," http://www.whitehouse .gov/history/presidents/cc30.html (accessed December 18, 2002).

13. *Quotations about the U.S. Presidency*, The Quote Garden, http:// www.quotegarden.com/presidents-about.html (accessed August 19, 2004).

14. *JFK's Naval Service*, The Naval Historical Center, http://www .history.navy.mil/faqs/faq60-2.htm (accessed January 4, 2004).

15. JFK's Wonderful Humor, http://www.americanpresident.org/ history/johnfkennedy/biography/resources/Articles/KunhardtKennedyBio .printable.html (accessed May 27, 2005).

16. In her 1977 autobiography, *My Story* (New York: Grove Press), Judith Campbell-Exner claimed she had been the mistress of John F. Kennedy. Exner was, at the same time, a friend of Mafia don Sam Giancana. Exner's story was revealed in 1975 when the Senate Intelligence Committee, headed by Idaho senator Frank Church, was investigating the government's role in espionage and Mafia links to assassination attempts on Cuban leader Fidel Castro. In 1988, Exner told Kitty Kelley in a *People* magazine interview that while she was Kennedy's lover, she served as a courier between Kennedy and Giancana.

17. John Bussey, "U.S. Presidents Are Very Funny Fellows, Often on Purpose," *Wall Street Journal*, September 17, 1986, A1.

18. *Checkered History*, Anecdotage.com: Famous People, Funny Stories, http://www.anecdotage.com/index.php?aid=13905 (accessed January 4, 2004).

19. *Harpers Index for October 2002*, October 1, 2002, http://harpers .org/HarpersIndex2002-10.html (accessed February 23, 2004).

20. Paul A. Gigot, "The Capital Captures a President," *Wall Street Journal*, October 26, 1990, A14.

21. Ronald G. Shafer, "D.C. Dinner Shocker: Jeb in the Buff, W. in the Tub," *Wall Street Journal*, April 30, 2001, A16.

CHAPTER 6

Homes, Birthplaces, and Graves

Tony Giffone

Although historians debate the merit of various presidential administrations and the achievement of their historical record, the preservation of houses where presidents were born, lived, died, and are buried is a fascinating chapter in the transformation of history into popular tourist destinations. These houses are owned and operated by various agencies including the National Trust, the National Park Services, various state associations, and private organizations such as the Mt. Vernon Ladies Association, the Pierce Brigade, the Daughters of the American Revolution, and the Daughters of the Confederacy. The preservation of these houses runs the gamut from those with numerous authentic objects that belonged to the presidents to those relying mostly on period recreations; those with tour guides who are students in history ready to discuss recent scholarship to those with tour guides dressed in period costumes; those in which you may wait on long lines to get in to those in which you may be the only visitor.

In visiting presidential houses, one is interested in what the houses reveal about the man; the houses themselves are not necessarily of any architectural interest, but the man that the house is meant to commemorate may also be of dubious merit. Unlike visiting the houses of authors, whose status is based on a presumed literary excellence, the houses of presidents are preserved on the simple basis that the person was president, no matter how briefly, no matter what the merits of his presidency. Some curators deal honestly with controversial aspects of the individual or the shortcomings of his policies, whereas others go out of their way to make excuses for the president and whitewash his record. The Franklin Pierce Manse in Concord, New Hampshire, deals forthrightly with Pierce's pro-Confederate sympathies. In contrast, the display in the museum that is part of the Warren Harding home portrays the Harding administration as a victim of the liberal media and muckraking journalists, contending that "there was corruption in the Harding presidency, but history has exaggerated it."

Visiting presidential sites is often seen as patriotic—as fostering a sense of national identity—but it is also a means of bolstering local tourism and state pride. Virginia and Ohio vie for having produced more presidents than any other state: Both boast of having eight presidents come from their state, though both count William Henry Harrison as one of their own. Virginia boasts that eight presidents were born in Virginia—even if some of them left shortly after (Zachary Taylor left when he was eight months old) or ran as presidential candidates from other states. Ohio boasts that it, too, is a "state of eight," for although only seven presidents were born in Ohio, Harrison spent most of his adult life there. That both states count Harrison as one of their own gives him an importance that his administration never had, as he died after only a little more than a month in office.

Although Virginia and Ohio are proud of their eight presidents, curators at presidential houses in states that have sent only one president to the White House go out of their way to suggest that their state and their president should not be overlooked. This is especially true of states such as New Hampshire, whose small percentage of electoral collage votes makes it likely that Franklin Pierce may indeed be their only president. The Amtrak railroad station in Independence, Missouri, proclaims the town as the "Home of Harry Truman." Though Harry Truman is one of our most popular presidents, he is nowhere more popular than in his native state, where he adds to the aura of local pride that "even a country boy from Missouri" can become president.

Great Estates and Homes

The most impressive of the presidential homes date from before the Civil War. Though the term "New England" refers to the states of the northeast, it was actually the antebellum South that replicated the "great house" traditions of England. Seven of the fifteen presidents before the Civil War—almost 50 percent—were from Virginia, and many lived on slave plantations: Washington at Mt. Vernon, Jefferson at Monticello, Madison at Montpelier, Monroe at Ash Lawn, Harrison at Berkeley, and Tyler at Sherwood Forest. Of these, the houses of Washington and Jefferson are far and away the most popular as presidential tourist destinations, not only because of the popularity of both Washington and Jefferson as presidents but also because of the beauty of their estates.

Washington was born in Westmoreland, Virginia, forty miles south of Mt. Vernon, in 1732. Originally owned by his father and then his half-brother, the plantation was acquired by Washington in 1761. Though he thought of Mt. Vernon as home for nearly the next forty years, Washington spent little time there, as he was often away from home as commander of the Continental Army. Washington returned to Mt. Vernon after two terms in office and lived there until his death. Embodying the architectural principles of eighteenth-century Georgian design, rather than palatial opulence, Mt. Vernon stands in stark contrast to more ornate European royal houses of the period. Just as Washington had no desire to become a new monarch, his home has no aspirations to be a royal palace.

Even more than Mt. Vernon reflects the sensibility of Washington, Monticello reflects the sensibility of Jefferson because he designed it. Located on the outskirts of Charlottesville, Virginia, at the foothills of the Blue Ridge Mountains, Monticello shares with Jefferson's other architectural projects (the state capital building in Richmond and the University of Virginia in Charlottesville) an adherence to the Palladian style of architecture that he witnessed in Europe, as well as his fondness for domes. Monticello is among the most iconic of presidential homes, given its place on the nickel. More than a house, it was Jefferson's retreat away from the world of government duty. Madison and Monroe were frequent guests at Monticello; Madison lived in adjacent Orange County at his estate, Montpelier, and Monroe was almost literally Jefferson's neighbor at his estate, Ash Lawn, only two miles away.

The homes of pre–Civil War presidents from northern states were sometimes also working farms, but they contained servant's quarters, not slave quarters. The most impressive of the northern presidential homes are the Adams Family Homestead in Quincy, Massachusetts and the Martin Van Buren estate in Kinderhook, New York. The family home of both John and John Quincy Adams not far from the much smaller homes in which they were born, was purchased in 1788 when John Adams returned from Europe, where he had served as ambassador to England. The house remained in the family for the next three generations and until very recently was unique in being the only house in which two presidents had lived. Martin Van Buren retired to his thirty-six-room estate, Lindenwald, in Kinderhook, New York, in 1840. Though he was widowed, the house was filled with children, grandchildren, and frequent guests, as Van Buren remained active in politics, running unsuccessfully for president several more times after the end of his term. Van Buren took an active role in remodeling the house, originally built in 1797, adding both a flush toilet and an indoor bathtub—both rare in the 1840s and among the house's most unique features.

The first president not from one of the original thirteen colonies, Andrew Jackson, is in many ways the first "Western president." His mansion, the Hermitage, is one of the most fascinating of presidential homes. Although he was born and educated in the Carolina colonies, he left in 1788 and settled in Tennessee. His image as a "backwoodsman" (and thereby uncouth by Eastern standards) would define him. Jackson's personal life would also conspire to suggest that he had different manners than previous presidents; as, for example, it was revealed that he had married his wife before she was legally divorced from her previous husband. In the 1824 election, Jackson won the popular vote, but no candidate received a majority of the electoral college vote. The election was then thrown into the House of Representatives, where John Quincy Adams was chosen. The two were essential opposites: The aristocratic son of a former president versus the backwoodsman/populist. Jackson's reputation as a backwoodsman is belied by his Tennessee plantation, the Hermitage, which is, in many ways, modeled on the Virginia plantations and is most certainly a much more aristocratic estate than the Adams Family Homestead. Jackson purchased the vast acres of the Hermitage, on the outskirts of Nashville, in 1804 and moved there with his wife and several slaves. By the time Jackson was elected President, he owned ninety-five slaves at the Hermitage. The house was destroyed by fire in 1834 and rebuilt, new and improved, two years later, with a "fake facade" of Greek revival columns that was inspired by both Mt. Vernon and the White House—making it look even more aristocratic.

The Hermitage is not the only Virginia-style presidential plantation transposed to "Indian territories." Although the Whig party was formed in opposition to Jackson, its 1840 presidential candidate (and victor) was William Henry Harrison. Like Jackson, Harrison was a transplanted Easterner who made his name as an "Indian fighter." Unlike Jackson, who was of humble origins, Harrison was the son of a signer of the Declaration of Independence. Harrison was appointed governor of the "Indiana territories" in 1800 and built a Virginia-style plantation in Vincennes, Indiana, named Grouseland, where he lived from 1803 to 1813. Unlike the Hermitage, which was an appropriation of a Virginia-style plantation to disguise Jackson's roots, Grouseland was a deliberate attempt to remind Harrison of the world he left behind.

Historians generally rank the three one-term Northern presidents (Millard Fillmore, Franklin Pierce, and James Buchanan) who led the country in the decade before the Civil War as among the weakest. Strict constructionists, each was perceived by northerners as too sympathetic to the South. Their homes are among the least visited of presidential homes, in part because of the obscurity of their presidencies. Fillmore lived in a small house in East Aurora, New York, for four years, from 1826 to 1830, as a fledgling lawyer before moving to neighboring Buffalo. The house contains the original horse-sleigh that Fillmore used, which is a marked contrast to the elaborate carriages of wealthier presidents and a sign of Fillmore's humble origins. Pierce lived in a small house in Concord, New Hampshire, from 1842 to 1848, after his retirement from the senate. The house contains a letter that Pierce sent to Jefferson Davis on the eve of the Civil War that proved controversial, as it was seen as evidence of his pro-Confederate sympathies. Buchanan's elegant, Federal-style estate in Lancaster, Pennsylvania, was named Wheatland because it was once a wheat farm. Buchanan lived there from 1849 to 1888, except for when he was ambassador to England and when he was president. He is the only president who never married, though the house offers no secrets to his personal life.

The homes of the presidents from Ohio who were elected after the Civil War are generally more modest, more comfortable middle-class homes rather than estates. The one exception is the ancestral estate of Rutherford B. Hayes—Spiegel Grove, in Fremont, Ohio. It was originally a small summer home belonging to Hayes's uncle, but Hayes retired there after having served as president and turned it into a thirty-five-room estate with two hundred fifty acres of farmland. It's the most impressive of the Ohioan presidential homes. Hayes was the first president with a telephone; the telephone directory for Fremont from the late nineteenth century lists him under "General Hayes," however, not "President Hayes"—illustrating Hayes's sense of himself primarily as a Civil War general rather than a former president.

In contrast, the most significant aspect of the homes of James Garfield, Benjamin Harrison, and Warren Harding is the front porch, from which they conducted their "front porch" campaigns—arguably Ohio's major contribution to electoral politics. Garfield lived at Lawnfield in Mentor, Ohio, on the outskirts of Cleveland. He purchased the house in 1876 and transformed it into a large, twenty-room estate that became the site of the first of the front porch campaigns. After his assassination in 1881, Garfield's wife and mother expanded the house and turned it into a memorial to him. Its prized possessions include a memorial wreath sent by Queen Victoria to the funeral.

Benjamin Harrison was born in Ohio but settled in Indianapolis, Indiana; his house in Indianapolis is modest and unassuming on its exterior, though it boasts sixteen rooms. Harrison is most famous as the man who prevented Grover Cleveland from serving two consecutive terms by winning the electoral college vote (though not the popular vote) in 1888; four years later, Cleveland defeated Harrison and returned to the White House. One-term presidents deal with defeat in a variety of ways: some run again; others go on to serve in Congress or to serve on the Supreme Court, doing their most important work after being president. Benjamin Harrison virtually retired from politics, remarried (his wife died while he was in the White House), and began a new life as a lawyer, living in his comfortable Indianapolis townhouse until his death in 1901.

Warren Harding ran on a nostalgic vision of America "returning to normalcy" after World War I and revived the "front porch" house campaign to do so. His home in Mentor, Ohio, was built as a wedding gift in 1891, and Harding lived there for the next thirty years, until he went to the

White House. Harding was the first president elected when women were allowed to vote; among the house's possessions is a quilt from the GOP women's group of Leyton, Utah, stitched in 1920.

Presidential homes sometimes can seem interchangeable and generic: yet another Southern plantation, yet another front porch. This is not the case with Theodore Roosevelt's estate, Sagamore Hill, in Oyster Bay, New York. It remains among the most individualistic and unique of presidential homes, the one that most fully conveys the personality of its owner. Roosevelt's belief in "muscular Christianity," the belief in the moral virtues of the outdoors, is revealed in the decoration of the house, which includes elephant tusks, bear and tiger rugs, an inkwell made of a hippo foot, and numerous elk heads; at times, the house resembles a hunting lodge.

Only one president remained in Washington, D.C., after being in the White House: Woodrow Wilson. He and his wife, Edith Galt, moved to an elegant townhouse on what is now Embassy Row. Wilson's decision to remain in D.C. was partly based on health considerations, partly on the fact that Edith was a Washington widow when he met her, and partly because he desired proximity to the Library of Congress. Wilson only lived for three more years; though Edith continued to live in the house until her death in 1961, the restoration emphasizes the years that they lived there together. The house is decorated with the gifts they received while in the White House, including a movie projector from Mary Pickford and Douglas Fairbanks Jr. that Wilson used to screen silent movies.

Birthplaces and Childhood Homes

Unlike the homes in which presidents lived as adults, the birthplaces and childhood homes of presidents tend to offer a much more tenuous relationship between the site and the president's sensibility. This is especially true of more recent presidents. John Adams was born a farmer's son in Braintree, Massachusetts, six miles south of Boston. After receiving a Harvard education, he married and moved into a small house adjacent to the one where he was born and where his son and future president, John Quincy, was born. They lived in the house for the next twenty years. John Adams and John Quincy Adams were men of Massachusetts all their lives. Contrast this with some recent presidents: Gerald Ford was born in Omaha, Nebraska, but left when he was two years old for Grand Rapids, Michigan; George H. W. Bush was born in Milton, Massachusetts, and his son, George W. was born in New Haven, Connecticut, but they are identified with Texas, not New England. The importance of a presidential birthplace in shaping his ideology was truer in ages with less geographical mobility.

The most famous presidential birthplace is obviously that of Abraham Lincoln. Everyone knows that Lincoln was born in a log cabin in Kentucky in 1809 to parents who migrated to Kentucky from Virginia. So hallowed in myth are Lincoln's origins that they obscure a more complicated history. Lincoln lived in his birthplace for little more than two years. When Lincoln was seven years old, his parents left Kentucky altogether, migrating first to Indiana, where they lived for the next decade, and then to Illinois, which likes to boast of itself as the "land of Lincoln." By 1837, Lincoln moved to Springfield, Illinois, and lived there for the next twenty-four years of his life—longer than he lived in any other place. He set up law offices across from the State Capital Building, where he gave his famous "A House Divided" speech. He married Mary Todd, and they lived in a modest house in Springfield from 1844 until he left for the White House. It was not only the house he had lived in longer than any other but also the house to which he planned on returning after the presidency. But the deification of the Lincoln of the log cabin origins (the original log cabin is enshrined in a memorial building) has superseded our image of Lincoln as an intellectual. Both houses are restored and preserved, but the public's association of Lincoln with the log cabin and not the law office says much more about the American public than about Lincoln.

Birthplaces of presidents can also be of questionable authenticity. Lincoln's log cabin was enshrined in a mausoleum, but his is not the only presidential birthplace to have been altered. Andrew Johnson, Lincoln's vice president, a Southern Democrat from Tennessee, was born in Raleigh, North Carolina, in 1808 in a house that, like the Lincoln birthplace, was not much bigger than a log cabin. The house has since been moved to a more central part of Raleigh and is now part of a historical theme park. Theodore Roosevelt was born on East 20th Street in New York City and lived there until he was fourteen years old. The house was demolished and was then rebuilt after his death. Despite claims of historical veracity, if a house is relocated or razed and then reconstructed, how authentic is it?

Visiting the birthplaces and childhood homes of presidents often reveals more about the parents than the future president. Although Grover Cleveland is associated with New York, where he served as governor before becoming president, he was actually born in Caldwell, New Jersey, in 1837, where his father served as a pastor of the First Presbyterian Church from 1834 to 1841. Cleveland only lived there for four years before his father moved to another parish in Fayetteville, New York. The house reflects the living quarters of a minister in the mid-decades of the nineteenth century, rather than offering any insights into the future president—though it does contain Cleveland's baby cradle.

William Taft was born in Cincinnati in 1857 and lived in the pleasant Mt. Auburn family home until 1874, when he left for Yale. Just as the Cleveland home in Caldwell, New Jersey, reflects how a minister lived in the second half of the nineteenth century, the Taft house reflects how a successful lawyer lived in the second half of the nineteenth century. Taft's father, Alphonse, migrated from New England to Cincinnati in 1839 and purchased the house in 1851. Alphonse was a founding member of the Ohio Republican party, which would prove a great asset to his son's career. Most of the few original pieces in the house belong to Alphonse, not William—the only original furnishing associated with William is the chair he sat in while serving as Secretary of War in Theodore Roosevelt's cabinet.

The boyhood home of Calvin Coolidge in Plymouth Notch, Vermont, is unique because the simple farmhouse was where Coolidge was sworn in as president. Coolidge was visiting his father there in 1923 when he received news of Harding's death. His father, who was a farmer, a church deacon, a part owner of the general store, and most significantly, a notary public, administered the oath of office.

If most presidential birthplaces embody the world of their fathers, the birthplaces of Franklin Delano Roosevelt and John Fitzgerald Kennedy embody the spirit of their mothers. Roosevelt was born and lived most of his life at his family's estate at Hyde Park, New York; his father died in 1900, and his widowed mother, Sara Delano Roosevelt, continued living there until her death in 1941. The house belonged to Sara Delano Roosevelt longer than it did to Franklin, though it does possess, among its belongings, Roosevelt's actual wheelchair—a potent reminder of the great physical adversity and courage that marked his personal life.

John Fitzgerald Kennedy's birthplace also embodies the spirit of his mother, Rose—the daughter of a former mayor of Boston and the wife of an ambitious banker, who molded her children into future leaders. Kennedy was born in 1917 in a house in Brookline, Massachusetts, a wealthy residential neighborhood adjacent to Boston. His parents moved into the house as newlyweds and had their first four (of nine) children there. His parents moved from the house in 1921 when Kennedy was only four years old, but the house embodies the Boston family saga that his parents represented.

The benefit of preserving houses of more recent presidents is that the great majority of items are authentic and not recreations or replicas. Eisenhower's boyhood home in Abilene, Kansas, is virtually entirely as it was when Eisenhower lived there because his parents continued to live in the house until 1946, at which time it was opened to the public.

Only three presidents were actually born in hospitals (Carter, Clinton, and George W. Bush), though obviously that number will increase. As such, the preservation of houses in which presidents were born, although not revealing a great deal about the future presidents, is an important reminder of birthing practices in the eighteenth and nineteenth centuries for future generations.

Graves and Monuments

The earliest presidential estates were also where the presidents were buried; this is the case with Washington, Jefferson, Madison, and Jackson. Surprisingly, only three presidents were actually buried within churches: John and John Quincy Adams are buried in the United First Parish Church in Quincy, Massachusetts, and Woodrow Wilson is buried in the National Cathedral in Washington, D.C., the only president to be buried in the nation's capital. Whether the president is buried on an estate or within a church, the tomb is usually simple, unadorned, and deliberately eschewing anything ostentatious.

The mid-decades of the nineteenth century, however, witnessed a preference for presidents being buried in public cemeteries. Some of these cemeteries are little more than small country churchyard (such as the Princeton cemetery in which Grover Cleveland is buried), but others were part of the Rural Cemetery Movement of the nineteenth century, which sought in the creation of public cemeteries a pastoral retreat from urbanization and industrialization. Cemeteries became landscaped public parks, and presidential tombs became works of art.

Two presidents (James Monroe and John Tyler) are buried in Richmond's Hollywood Cemetery. Monroe was originally buried in 1831 in the Marble Cemetery in New York City, a small burial ground, but was reinterred in 1858 in the elaborate Hollywood Cemetery. His move was ostensibly to commemorate the anniversary of his birth, but it was also intended to be seen, as the inscription on his monument reads, "as evidence of the affection of Virginia for her good and honored son." It was a way of reclaiming him as a son of the South on the eve of the Civil War. Four years later, in 1862, John Tyler joined him in the cemetery—his bust atop his tomb looks outward to the James River below.

When Zachary Taylor died in office in 1850, his body was returned to his family estate, Springfield, in Louisville, Kentucky, for burial on the estate grounds in a family vault. In the 1920s, at the foot of what was the Springfield estate, a national veteran's cemetery was created, and the Taylor burial ground was incorporated into the new cemetery. Taylor's body was removed from the family vault and placed in a newly built mausoleum, and the new national cemetery was named after him. It is fitting that Taylor is buried in a national cemetery, surrounded by veterans of World War II and the Korean War, as Taylor's greatest accomplishments were as a military hero (particularly in the Mexican–American war), rather than as a president (where he spent a scarce sixteen months in office).

The most beautiful of presidential graves, however, belongs to Chester Arthur, who is buried in Albany's Rural Cemetery, founded in 1844. Victorian statuary of weeping angels makes it among the most beautiful

An angel guards Chester A. Arthur's gravesite in Albany's Rural Cemetery. (Courtesy of Tony Giffone)

cemeteries in the world; Arthur's grave is guarded by a large, winged angel, whose arms gracefully lay a palm across the tomb.

Along with the burial of presidents in public cemeteries came the creation of special memorial monuments. In many ways, these monuments are probably the most authentic indication of a president's status at the time of his death, as opposed to how history has rendered its verdict over time.

Lake View Cemetery in Cleveland, Ohio, was founded in 1869 and contains the James Garfield monument and tomb. Garfield, ironically, is most noted for being assassinated in office just months after his inauguration. Had he served his complete term, he would not be memorialized in such a fashion, but his monument is a reminder of just how shocking his assassination was in 1881, less than two decades after Lincoln's. Shaped as a tower, the interior is decorated with stained glass and mosaic windows that symbolize the thirteen colonies plus Ohio. In addition, the dome is designed as an ornate allegory that demonstrates the nation's grief at his death.

The tomb of Ulysses S. Grant in New York City is a reminder of his status at the time of his death. In the nineteenth century, it was Grant, not Lincoln, who was perceived as having saved the Union in the Civil War. Though now a much less mythic figure than Lincoln, Grant was the only president between Andrew Jackson (the seventh president) and Woodrow Wilson (the twenty-eighth president) to serve two consecutive terms, from 1868 to 1876, presiding over the nation's centennial. Though born in Mt. Pleasant, Ohio, Grant spent the last years of his life in New York; his monument and tomb, overlooking the Hudson River, is a reminder of his popularity at the time of his death in the 1880s. Other presidents interred in public monuments died in office; Grant is the only president who did not die in office to be afforded such a public tomb.

By the end of the nineteenth century, so widespread was the movement to erect monuments to presidents that James Polk, who had previously been inconspicuously buried, was reburied in a much more public space. Polk, a protégée of fellow Tennessean Andrew Jackson, died in 1846 in a cholera epidemic and was buried in the city cemetery in Nashville. He was later reburied on a family estate, but when that estate was demolished, he was reburied yet again, in 1893, on the grounds of the State Capital Building.

McKinley's assassination in 1901 also shocked the nation. A native of Ohio, he was assassinated by an anarchist only twenty-eight years after Garfield's assassination while attending the Pan American Exposition in Buffalo. Theodore Roosevelt, McKinley's vice president and successor, appointed a committee to construct a monument to McKinley, completed in 1907. Situated at the foot of a long esplanade adjacent to the small West Lawn Cemetery in Canton, Ohio, the tomb sits at the citadel of 108 steps.

Harding died of natural causes, but by the time of his death in 1923, the construction of public monuments for presidents who died in office was *de rigueur*. The Harding Memorial in Marian, Ohio, is a circular monument of white marble columns that recalls a Greek temple.

Whether the president was buried in a public cemetery, a family estate, or a church, the idea that permeates all presidential burials is that they are buried in their own home state: The United States does not have the equivalent of Britain's Westminster Abbey or a national pantheon. Only two presidents have broken with this tradition and have not been returned to their home state: Taft and Kennedy are both buried in Arlington National Cemetery in Arlington, Virginia, on the outskirts of Washington, D.C. Kennedy's grave is lit with a perpetual flame that embodies his principles and is among the most visited of presidential graves.

Conclusion

Part of the appeal of visiting presidential homes and graves is a confirmation that who is president does matter. Much historical scholarship has turned away from the idea that history is shaped by "great leaders" and instead studies history from "the bottom up." At the same time, many

Americans increasingly feel that who is president does not matter; steady declines in voting suggest that Americans perceive that their elected officials are, at best, figureheads, and that policy decisions are made by an unelected "permanent government" that acts behind the scenes.

Pilgrimages to these sites contradict these two trends: they reconfirm the importance of great leaders as stewards of the nation, and they suggest that the individual's domestic life reveals who he is—and that the individual and his vote do matter.

In the twentieth century, the creation of presidential libraries (for all presidents since Herbert Hoover) has partially usurped the role and function that the preservation of historical houses once played. Presidents Hoover, Franklin Roosevelt, Truman, Eisenhower, Nixon, and Reagan are even buried on their library's grounds, just as earlier presidents were buried on family estates. At most, presidential libraries should complement rather than replace the preservation of presidential homes, for while the libraries excel at documenting the political life of the president, nothing can replace the homes in offering glimpses into their private life.

The childhood homes of recently deceased presidents (Johnson, Nixon, and Reagan) and some living presidents (Clinton) have already been preserved as museums; both Midland and Odessa, Texas, are reportedly in the process of turning the childhood homes of George W. Bush into museums as a way of luring tourists and bolstering their sagging economies.

Visitors to presidential homes are inevitably asked which their favorite is. It's a difficult question to answer: Pilgrimages to presidential homes are best as a cumulative experience; one needs to visit as many of these sites as possible to get a sense of the breadth of American presidential history, despite our relatively short history. Your favorite house might not belong to your favorite president. Although historical scholarship, by its very nature, must judge some presidents as being more successful or significant, based on their accomplishments, the most magnificent houses sometimes belong to the least significant of presidents. Those who have been given minimal space in the history books are given equal weight in the preservation of their houses and graves.

CHAPTER 7

LIBRARIES

BENJAMIN HUFBAUER

The national dream is that any American child, no matter how humble his or her beginnings, may someday grow up to be president. This idea finds material expression in monuments such as the Lincoln Memorial, which is engraved on our currency and in our consciousness. During the twentieth and twenty-first centuries, however, presidential monuments have changed, making it unlikely that monuments of the kind built for George Washington and Abraham Lincoln in Washington, D.C., will ever be built again. The presidential monuments with which we are most familiar retain their relevance, but there has been a profound transformation of presidential commemoration since the Lincoln Memorial was dedicated in 1922. The presidential monument of the past—the obelisk, temple, or statue built by posterity—has largely been replaced by the presidential library. Presidential libraries are monuments built outside of Washington (usually) with the help of the commemorated president. Since Franklin Delano Roosevelt's library was completed in 1940, more than a dozen presidents have assisted in designing their own memorials. The twelve existing federal presidential libraries now draw a combined average of approximately 1.5 million tourists and scholars a year.[1] They house archives and museums that preserve and celebrate materials related to each president. In many ways, presidential libraries go beyond earlier presidential memorials, because a presidential library is not just a monument but also a popular history museum, an archive, and sometimes even a school of public affairs.

The presidential library is an unusual commemorative form that reflects the extraordinary power of modern presidents—militarily, constitutionally, and culturally. The presidential library reflects the dramatic increase in presidential authority that has occurred during an era when the United States itself has become the most powerful country in the world.[2] Architectural historian Carol Krinsky has written that the Lyndon Baines Johnson Library "manifests the power of the president . . . and country that collaborated to build it,"[3] and this statement is valid for other presidential libraries as well.

The Rutherford B. Hayes Library

In 1910, Webb Hayes, the son of nineteenth-century President Rutherford B. Hayes, created an institution that provided a model for the first federal presidential library. Hayes deeded his parents' twenty-five-acre estate, Spiegel Grove, to the State of Ohio under the condition that "a suitable fireproof building" be erected "for the purpose of preserving and forever keeping" the records and relics of his parents.[4] The Rutherford B. Hayes Library near Fremont, Ohio, opened in 1916. The Hayes family and the Ohio Legislature provided the money for the neo-classical library, privately administered by the Ohio Historical Society and the Hayes Foundation.[5]

Originally, the entrance to the library opened on a memorial hall honoring Hayes. On either side were small rooms displaying President Hayes's relics as well as Webb Hayes collection of Americana. An expansion to the Hayes Library in the 1960s expanded research, storage, and display space, and now visitors enter from the side of the building. The preserved Hayes presidential home is filled with antiques that evoke how it might have looked during the lifetimes of Rutherford and Lucy Hayes. Entrances to the estate are marked by outmoded White House gates that were transported from Washington when they were no longer needed there. On the grounds of Spiegel Grove are also the graves of Rutherford and Lucy Hayes. For Webb Hayes, the Hayes Library was a place where visitors could come to remember his father and mother and to see interesting relics from the recent past. Hayes's interest in having tourists visit a small museum displaying presidential and historical materials alongside a library reflects the transformation of presidential commemoration from places of reflection to educational experiences.

Franklin Delano Roosevelt Library

The first presidential library supported by the federal government was completed in 1940 for Franklin Delano Roosevelt in Hyde Park, New York.[6] One of Roosevelt's goals in creating a federally administered Roosevelt Library was to escape a pattern of destruction and disbursement that had adversely affected earlier presidential records since George Washington's. The private ownership of presidential papers was a tradition established when Washington, at the end of his second term, shipped all of his documents to Mount Vernon.[7] During retirement, Washington wanted to erect a stone building at Mount Vernon "for the accommodation and security of my Military, Civil and private Papers which are voluminous and may be interesting."[8] Washington had in mind a precursor to the presidential library, but he was unable to carry out his plan, and on his death his papers went to his nephew, Bushrod Washington.[9] Bushrod lent large portions of the papers to Chief Justice of the Supreme Court John Marshall, who confessed that after many years they were "extensively mutilated by rats and otherwise injured by damp."[10] The remains of Washington's papers, like the remains of most presidential papers, were eventually purchased by the Library of Congress, but only after many were lost forever. Even some presidential papers that found their way to the Library of Congress had unusual restrictions placed on them. For instance, many of Abraham Lincoln's papers were sealed and unavailable to historians until 1947.[11]

On viewing Egypt's pyramids during the Second World War, Franklin Roosevelt noted that "man's desire to be remembered is colossal,"[12] and what he observed about the pharaohs was true for himself and his successors. Roosevelt collected many things during his life, from books to stuffed birds, from model ships to millions of documents relating to his government service. As a student of history, he knew the danger of leaving the fate of these collections to chance: They needed an archive to remain intact after his death and remain a testament to his life. To appeal to the public, Roosevelt wanted a tourist-friendly history museum to be part of his library, which he hoped would draw "an appalling number of sightseers."[12]

As President Roosevelt began to make plans for preserving his own collections, he sent the Director of the National Archives to investigate the Hayes Library and learned that it was "a veritable gold mine for historical scholars."[13] Roosevelt was influenced by the Hayes Library, but it was Roosevelt's library, the first federal presidential library supported by annual appropriations from the national government, that would set the precedent for his predecessor, Herbert Hoover and his successors. In fact, Roosevelt largely invented the federal presidential library as we know it today by imagining that tourists would be drawn to a museum run by the national government that contained his personal collections, along with exhibits on his life and career. Roosevelt could make a compelling case for a presidential library because of the loss of some earlier presidential records. By donating his papers to his presidential library, a branch of the National Archives, they would escape the pattern of destruction and restriction.[12] Consequently, 80 percent of Roosevelt's papers were opened to scholars in 1950, just five years after his death.

Presidential libraries have the power to draw people because they promise to provide an authentic experience of a presidential life, and to a large degree they deliver. Tourists visiting the Roosevelt Library see his childhood clothes, his wheelchair (which he usually hid from the press while he was president to conceal his paralysis from polio), as well as his presidential desk, preserved as it was on the day of his death. These are the kinds of items in a presidential library that become the relics of a presidential life. They give visitors the sense that Roosevelt was not just someone in a history book or television documentary but a human being who conquered his own fears and physical disability to win the presidency and then take on the challenges of the Great Depression and fascism.

However, the Roosevelt library's administrators have also learned that although for older visitors, contact with relics of the past is effective, younger visitors require a multimedia approach. Verne Newton, Director of the Roosevelt Library for most of the 1990s, noted that to reach a younger audience, a presidential library today "must become a mini-Disneyland. It needs to entertain, educate, and even create a marketable product."[14] The Roosevelt Library has done this by creating multimedia displays of Roosevelt's life, including a simulated set of the White House's Second World War map room, with a recording of an actor simulating the president's voice for an animatronic "Roosevelt." The library has even created a video game of Roosevelt's presidency, which places you in Roosevelt's shoes in the first year of the Second World War. In the game, as Great Britain struggles for survival against the bombings of Adolf Hitler's Luftwaffe in 1940, Prime Minister Churchill begs Roosevelt for assistance while Roosevelt's Secretary of War warns that the homeland is almost completely defenseless. You as Roosevelt must decide whether to overrule your own advisors and strong isolationist public opinion to aid England. Those who take the seemingly easier path to only defend the United States soon find that America is isolated and trying to defeat the Nazis alone. The game is especially popular with students on field trips to the library, who often stand in lines five or six deep for their turn to "be the president" at one of the Library's video consoles.

The Harry S. Truman Library

The Harry S. Truman Library, which opened in 1957 in Independence, Missouri, displayed the first replica of the Oval Office in a presidential library. The replica, which allows visitors to stand in one corner of the room behind a wooden railing, presents this presidential room as it appeared during Truman's presidency. This exhibit has been so popular that the Hoover, Kennedy, Johnson, Ford, Carter, Reagan, and Clinton Libraries have all replicated the Oval Office the way the room appeared during their respective terms. First built in 1909, the Oval Office's rise to the status of premiere presidential symbol occurred during the presidencies of Roosevelt and Truman. President Truman was the only president to authorize the use of

The replica of Harry Truman's Oval Office in the Truman Presidential Museum and Library. (Harry S. Truman Library)

nuclear weapons in war, and especially during and subsequent to his presidency, the Oval Office became associated with the president's military authority.

The Oval Office replica at the Truman Library, as at other presidential libraries, is a symbol not only of the presidency but of America's enlarged place in the world since 1945.[15] At the Truman Library, this reference is given emotional punch through a work by a well-known American artist that frames the entrance to the replica—Thomas Hart Benton's "Independence and the Opening of the West." This colorful mural, which was commissioned especially by Truman to welcome visitors to the lobby of the building and lead them into the Oval Office, is a dramatic portrayal of the concept of "Manifest Destiny"—the idea that the United States, from its small beginnings, was destined to become a great power in North America, stretching from the Atlantic to the Pacific. The mural portrays mid-nineteenth-century Independence, the town of Truman's birth, when it was a jumping-off spot for Western expansion.

Benton's painting is meant to be a microcosm of American history that explains the victory of European Americans over Native Americans. The nomadic way of life of the Native Americans on the left of the mural is contrasted with the productive and settled life of Independence on the right. The key to the painting is the looming conflict between the white settlers and two Indians in the portion of the mural over the door that leads to the Oval Office replica. In this center area of the painting, four armed white men prepare to defend the women and the children at their camp from two approaching Pawnee men. Two white men raise their rifle muzzles into the air, but in spite of this harsh greeting, the first Native American offers his "peace pipe." This Indian chief represents the possibility of peaceful accommodation between whites and Native Americans, a possibility undermined by a warrior who stealthily readies an arrow to shoot at the family. In the moment after the painting takes place, it appears that one of the settlers will shoot him dead. This will lead to an escalation of violence, resulting in the victory of the whites and the displacement of Native Americans to reservations.

Visitors pass under this looming conflict through a door that leads to the Oval Office replica. Although Benton's painting is likely to remind viewers of Hollywood's Western stereotypes, the Oval Office recalls films about Cold War anxiety. As tourists look at the recreation of this famous room, a recording of Truman's voice is played: "I am glad you have come to this historical institution. You are very welcome. This is Harry S. Truman speaking. This room is an exact reproduction of the Presidential Office in the West Wing of the White House, as it was in the early 1950s." It is an uncanny experience to have the single most important room of the government described with the voice of a disembodied dead president, but this is one of the reasons that the room is by far the Truman Library's most popular display.[16] The Oval Office replica provides a calm, symbol-laden environment in which tourists can visualize presidential authority.

The Dwight D. Eisenhower Library

The Eisenhower Library in Abilene, Kansas (1962), grew out of a memorial museum honoring Abilene's most famous son. After Eisenhower's presidency, an impressive marble archive was completed near the museum. Replicated rooms similar to those found in the Truman and the remodeled Hoover Library museums were not included in the museum until after Eisenhower's death, when a display featuring Ike's study from his postpresidential home in Pennsylvania was added. His staff car is featured in the Military Hall, highlighting another common display in presidential libraries—presidential vehicles. A tank, a big gun, and other military equipment are also on display, highlighting the museum's role as a memorial to those who served in the Second World War. Clothing and military uniforms also make up part of the displays at the Eisenhower Library Museum, detailing the transformation of American life and the American military in the first half of the twentieth century into a more modern form. Female visitors tend to be drawn more to the displays of Mamie Eisenhower's clothing, whereas male visitors generally spend more time looking at the cars on display, reflecting a division of interest common to the displays in many presidential libraries.

The Herbert Hoover Library

Although the Hayes Library provided a model for the preservation and commemoration of a president, federally supported presidential libraries did not come into being until FDR initiated the more elaborate, federally supported form. As a result, Herbert Hoover, FDR's predecessor, opened his presidential library in 1962, in the same year that the Eisenhower library opened to the public. The Herbert Hoover Library, which is run by the National Archives and Records Administration of the federal government, was opened to the public. Hoover decided to establish his own presidential library along the lines laid out by Franklin Roosevelt. The Hoover Library includes a museum and archive of presidential papers, the common denominator of all presidential libraries, near his preserved early-childhood home in West Branch, Iowa, at the Herbert Hoover National Historic Site. Near the museum and home are several preserved buildings from the nineteenth century. The museum was completely updated in 1992, and it now includes an Oval Office replica, a replica of part of the Hoover vacation cabin, and a recreated room from Hoover's post-presidential home in the Waldorf Towers in New York City. The replicas and the preserved homes are places where visitors can imagine life in the past.

The John F. Kennedy Library

Although President Kennedy held office from 1961 to 1963, his library, on the University of Massachusetts, Boston, campus was delayed for years and was only opened to the public in 1979. President Kennedy, like other modern presidents, actively helped plan his library. He hoped to have it built on the campus of his alma mater, Harvard University, but after a long conflict over the size of the library and its site, it was instead built along Boston Harbor. After Kennedy's assassination, his family endeavored to produce a library that would serve as both a memorial and an expression of the goals of his presidency. Even the architecture of the library reflected these goals, for President and Mrs. Kennedy had strongly supported the arts during his time in office, and the family wanted the design of the building to reflect the their interest in the arts. The Kennedy Library was designed by architect I. M. Pei, whose modernist work became prominent in the latter part of the twentieth century. As at many other presidential libraries, an Oval Office replica is included. This replica is split apart, so that visitors can walk through the office on their way to other displays. It is designed to recreate preparations for Kennedy's speech on civil rights, and television cameras are prominently placed in front of his desk. A 110-foot-high glass-enclosed hall hung with a huge American flag frames Boston Harbor and provides a place for contemplation. Although most visitors are aware of President Kennedy's assassination and the intense feeling of loss felt throughout the nation, the museum displays emphasize his life and presidential goals and achievements rather than his death. There is only a small exhibition on his funeral near the end of the exhibition.

An auditorium that features a film on President Kennedy's life signals yet another way that modern presidents are remembered in presidential libraries. Increasingly, short movies like the one in the Kennedy Library have been developed that highlight experiences from a president's life that prepared him for the presidency and that feature key events that help form his presidential legacy. Film, photographs, and audio recordings are increasingly used throughout the galleries to evoke the presidency.

The Lyndon Baines Johnson Library

The Lyndon Baines Johnson Library in Austin, Texas (completed in 1971), is built on a scale as colossal as that of the Lincoln Memorial. The Johnson Library, designed by another prominent architect, Gordon Bunschaft, is covered in Italian travertine marble and rises eighty-five feet in the air (compared with eighty for the Lincoln Memorial). The building symbolizes that Lyndon Johnson was, in Bunshaft's words, "an aggressive . . . big man," who forcefully used the federal government to prosecute the Vietnam War as well as to broaden civil rights and promote social programs.[17] Johnson's belief in government power is built into this stark and yet elegant structure, visited on average by more than two hundred thousand tourists a year.[18]

The Johnson Library's museum has extensive exhibits, that are periodically redesigned and updated, which cover not only Johnson's life but also connect his life to American history. The library's massive archive has more than forty million documents relating to Johnson's career, as well as hundreds of thousands of photographs, miles of film, and thousands of hours of audio and video tape.[19] Next to the Johnson Library is the Johnson School of Public Affairs, part of the University of Texas at Austin, which turns out scores of graduates each year—many of whom go on to serve in the public sector.

In the Johnson Library, architect Gordon Bunshaft designed a majestic Great Hall of Achievement for the museum displays. One of President Johnson's black Lincoln limousines is parked beneath the monumental

President and Lady Bird Johnson in front of the Lyndon Baines Johnson Library and Museum. (Lyndon Baines Johnson Library and Museum)

marble stair to the Great Hall. Cases filled with elaborate gifts of state given to the Johnsons from nations around the world, from gold-encrusted swords to African masks, are featured prominently in elegant display cases at the rear of the hall. A photomural etched into huge magnesium sheets first pictures a young Johnson with one of his first political mentors, President Roosevelt, when they met in 1937. Succeeding photographs picture Johnson with Presidents Truman, Eisenhower, and Kennedy. The final panel depicts Lyndon Johnson alone as president. Rising high above the marble stairs and the photomural is a wall of glass four stories high that displays forty-four thousand red archive boxes filled with the papers of President Johnson's administration.

Bunshaft resisted designing an Oval Office replica for the museum until President Johnson himself called to ask for it, but Johnson knew how popular the Oval Office replicas were. As a consequence, a seven-eighths scale replica was squeezed into the library's eighth floor so that visitors can see the Johnson Oval Office, with its three television screens and push button phone. (Everything on display inside is also a replica—its seven-eighths scale meant that real objects once used by Johnson seemed out of proportion and had to be reproduced in a smaller size.)

The Richard Nixon Presidential Library

The Nixon Presidential Library and Birthplace in Yorba Linda, California, replicates the Lincoln sitting room during Nixon's term, with labels that emphasize the room as a gathering place for the Nixon family. The Oval Office is absent. Replicating the Oval Office for display in the museum might have been awkward, because many of Nixon's self-recorded misdeeds that were part of the Watergate scandal that led to his resignation occurred there. As it is, the Nixon museum tries to explain Watergate through television screens that use short segments of the Watergate tapes with interpretations that attempt to make them less incriminating. Because of lengthy legal battles between Nixon and the National Archives over his papers, Nixon's library is the only later presidential library that is not, as of this writing, run by the National Archives and Records Administration. The Nixon Library is instead a privately run institution that does not contain Nixon's presidential papers, which were impounded by the government during Watergate and are stored near Washington, D.C. After Watergate, Congress passed a law making all subsequent presidential papers federal property rather than the personal property of each president. However, as this book went to press, the National Archives was in the process of absorbing the Nixon Library into its presidential library system to ensure its long-term survival and was preparing to transport Nixon's presidential papers to California. A presidential library is an expensive proposition, and running a large one without federal funding is difficult.

The Gerald R. Ford Archive and Museum

The Gerald R. Ford archive and museum are separate. The archive is located at the University of Michigan in Ann Arbor, President Ford's alma mater. Both the Ford Library and the Ford Museum feature short films that emphasize President Ford's time in office as a period of healing after President Nixon's resignation during the Watergate Crisis. Since the establishment of the Johnson Library at the University of Texas at Austin, presidential libraries have almost all been associated with the prestige, facilities, and faculty of research universities. The Ford Library has been active in helping to develop a presidential studies program at the University of Michigan.

The Gerald R. Ford Museum is located 130 miles away in Grand Rapids. The museum hosts swearing-in ceremonies for new American citizens. The Ford Museum also has an Oval Office replica. A gallery focusing on the popular culture of the 1970s features an interactive display on the period as well as examples of fashion from bellbottom jeans to platform shoes. A "Constitution in Crisis" gallery features the tools used in the 1972 Watergate break-in and directly addresses President Nixon's involvement. A Vietnam-era Huey helicopter is featured at the museum, as is a gallery that allows visitors to see White House rooms and learn about their history across the centuries.

The Jimmy Carter Library

The Jimmy Carter Library in Atlanta, Georgia (1986), is designed as a series of interconnected circles that look out on a Japanese garden with a small lake. An Oval Office replica is part of the displays, as is an interactive town meeting display. A display featuring Rosalynn Carter's activities as first lady is prominently placed in the museum and reflects the increasingly large public role of modern first ladies. The Carter Library display features photos of Rosalyn's visits to foreign countries, her support of the arts while in the White House, as well as a White House table setting and one of her gowns. Like all presidential libraries, the Carter Library also has an archive and museum.

The Ronald Reagan Library

The Reagan Library (1991) is located on an isolated summit in Simi Valley, California, and is not associated with a home—as were earlier presidential libraries—or a university—as are more recent libraries. The Reagan Library looks like a huge Mission-style hacienda with red-tiled roofs, a spacious courtyard, and low profile (made possible because a substantial part of the building is underground), which almost gives it the appearance of an imposing family home rather than a government institution.

Displays prominently feature First Lady Nancy Reagan, the President's early life, an Oval Office replica, and a piece of the Berlin Wall. "Meet President Reagan," an interactive display similar to the one at the Carter Museum, allows visitors to hear short video-taped answers from President Reagan to preprogrammed questions. The Library has featured a film series of Ronald Reagan's Hollywood films.

The George H. W. Bush Library

As architects and presidential staff increasingly became aware of the needs of museums for flexible display and storage spaces, the shapes of the libraries have become more monumental. This is evident in the George H. W. Bush Library (1997) on the campus of Texas A & M University in College Station, Texas, which features a vast hangar-like space with a façade that makes a postmodern reference to the ancient Roman Pantheon. After passing through the entrance rotunda that divides the museum and the library, visitors pass a temporary gallery with changing displays and then walk along a gallery path that leads from one exhibit to another. Hanging above the display cases is a bomber like the one President Bush flew during the Second World War. Stairs up to the plane allow visitors a closer view. It features two replicas: a room at Camp David, which emphasizes Bush's work in foreign affairs, and a mock-up of part of Air Force One. It also features a children's reading room with a comfortable couch and shelves of books for younger children, which refers to First Lady Barbara Bush's literacy campaign.

The William Jefferson Clinton Library

Federal presidential libraries have become larger over time—so large that they have the potential to have a significant economic effect on the cities in which they are located. Franklin Roosevelt wanted a building that would look almost like a home, albeit a mansion, and one that would blend in with other mansions in the area, whereas Bill Clinton had the larger ambition to "have a building that was beautiful and architecturally significant that people would want to walk in 100 years from now."[20] Reaching out into space toward the Arkansas River to architecturally visualize Clinton's 1996 campaign slogan to "build a bridge to the twenty-first century," this gleaming steel and glass building, designed by the acclaimed architectural firm of James Polshek and Associates, conveys, as do many other presidential libraries, the awesomeness of the office it commemorates. The Library, which opened in 2004 features two replicated presidential rooms, an Oval Office and a Cabinet Room, and ranks of interactive displays that take the media forms in use at earlier presidential libraries and multiplies them.

Museum visitors to presidential libraries far exceed the number of students, scholars, and journalists who make use of the preserved materials in the archives. Presidential library museums provide an opportunity for visitors to gain access to American political history far from Washington, D.C., where, before the advent of presidential libraries, much presidential commemoration was located. For most visitors, the displays that chronicle the life and decisions of the president they commemorate are the primary attraction, with the recreated rooms, preserved cars, airplanes, and inaugural ball gowns shaping the museum experience. Objects like this have become part of popular culture in part through exhibitions displaying the relics of first ladies and presidents in the Smithsonian. Presidential libraries might be thought of as "mini-Smithsonians," spread across the country, which focus on the presidents and their eras. Unlike the Smithsonian, however, which generally provides a fairly balanced approach in its historical displays, the library staffs at newer presidential libraries have been successfully pressured by presidents and their supporters into creating purely celebratory displays. As the decades pass, however, more balanced and historically accurate displays have been created at older libraries, such as at the Truman and Hoover libraries.

In addition to these museum displays, education programs are an increasingly important part of the public practices of the presidential libraries. Presidential library education programs oversee field trips and provide study guides for teachers and activities for students that are meant to help them to connect with history and American politics. At the Truman Library, students can participate in the White House Decision Center that has been constructed to look like a portion of the West Wing of the White House. Students take on the roles of President Truman, the Secretary of State, and the Press Secretary and attempt to deal with crises such as the Soviet blockade of Berlin in 1948. For many high school students using the program at the Truman Library, it seems a natural fit to step into White House roles because of how frequently they have seen them dramatized in films and television programs. As one participant at the White House Decision Center said, "It's very fun to play a role. It's kind of like 'West Wing' in a way."[21] Just as elements of the television program *The West Wing* began to infiltrate the Truman Library, the program *The West Wing* was infiltrated by a fictional "Lassiter Presidential Library." In an episode titled, "The Stormy Present," broadcast in January 2004: an ex-president spends much of his last years in the Oval Office replica in his presidential library. As his fictional wife says, "He'd come here to think. He took to eating here, and sleeping here," and eventually he dies in a bed in his Oval Office replica. This *West Wing* episode helps reveal the degree to which presidential libraries have become central to the popular cultural understanding of the presidency.

Although the libraries present a public memory of the presidents, they also have a crucial role to play in the public commemoration of a president's passing. Funerals at presidential libraries have become transfixing national events. Since Franklin Delano Roosevelt was buried near his library at Hyde Park, most subsequent presidents have been interred at their libraries as well. These funerals are media events that help transform presidential libraries into sacred national sites.

Presidential libraries go through a life cycle.[22] Because presidential libraries are constructed with privately raised money, even though they are federally run, a presidential library is born as the culmination of a huge fund-raising drive. The president to be commemorated is usually heavily involved in this fundraising and also has a hand in selecting his library's architects—and even its first director. After years of construction, a presidential library's museum is opened to tourists, and after several more years its archive is opened to scholars. While the president is in living memory there is nostalgic interest from many people who reminisce in presidential museums to gain an experience linked to memories in their own lives. During this period there is immense work behind the scenes as archivists painstakingly catalog and organize presidential materials, which are slowly released for use by scholars, who then write works that often become bestsellers.

The federal presidential library as a commemorative form has become so popular that a few presidents who lived before the federal system was created have recently had presidential libraries created for them by private historical societies. These libraries are not eligible for federal funding and are, with one exception, much smaller and less impressive than federal presidential libraries, and as a result they draw only a small fraction of the number of tourists that a federal presidential library draws. The one exception is the Lincoln Presidential Library, which as of this writing is under construction in Springfield, Illinois. The Lincoln Library received substantial funding from the state of Illinois and is likely to be a large and impressive institution.

Presidential libraries, with their museum collections, archival holdings, houses, and graves, mark a shift in commemoration reflective of changing technologies of memory. Each generation of presidential library directors, curators, and archivists reconstruct the stories of their president and first lady for every new generation. The technology of display changes as well, from glass cases filled with relics to computer-controlled exhibits that simulate a presidential meeting. As the living memory of a president and first lady passes away, those who commemorate them help them make the transformation into the realms of history and popular culture.

Notes

1. *Office of Presidential Libraries Briefing Book*, National Archives and Records Administration, Washington, D.C., Office of Presidential Libraries, 2002.

2. Arthur M. Schlesinger Jr., *The Imperial Presidency* (Boston: Houghton Mifflin, 1989).

3. Carol Herselle Krinsky, *Gordon Bunshaft of Skidmore. Owings, & Merrill* (Cambridge, Mass.: MIT Press, 1988), 247.

4. "Dedication of the Hayes Memorial Library." *Ohio Archaeological and Historical Quarterly* 25 (1916):401–484.

5. Ibid.

6. http://www.archives.gov/presidential_libraries/index.html, the National Archives and Records Administration's site for presidential libraries.

7. Frank L. Schick, with Renee Schick and Mark Carroll. *Records of the Presidency* (Phoenix, Ariz.: Oryx Press, 1989).

8. George Washington, Letter to James McHenry, 3 April 1797. *George Washington: Writings* (New York: Library of America, 1996), 993.

9. John D. Knowlton, "Properly Arranged and So Correctly Recorded." *American Archivist*, 27 (July 1969):371–374.

10. Ibid., 372.

11. Donald David Herbert *Lincoln*. New York: Simon and Schuster, 1995.

12. Benjamin Hufbauer, "The Roosevelt Presidential Library: A Shift in Commemoration," *American Studies*, 42 (Fall 2001):173–193.

13. Donald W. Wilson, "Presidential Libraries: Developing to Maturity," *Presidential Studies Quarterly* 21 (Fall 1991):187–194.

14. Ibid., 188.

15. Benjamin Hufbauer, *Presidential Temples: The Transformation of Presidential Commemoration Since 1900* (Lawrence: University Press of Kansas, forthcoming).

16. http://www.trumanlibrary.org/trivia/oval2.htm (accessed March 24, 2005).

17. Krinsky, *Bunshaft*.

18. *Office of Presidential Libraries Briefing Book*.

19. http://www.lbjlib.utexas.edu/johnson/archives.hom/holdings/intro .asp (accessed March 24, 2005).

20. Bill Clinton, "Speech by President at WJC Presidential Center," http://www.clintonpresidentialcenter.org/legacy/120900 (accessed December 9, 2004).

21. The White House Decision Center: Students experiencing history and making decisions, VHS, 7 minutes, Harry S. Truman Library, n.d.

22. Wilson, "Presidential Libraries."

CHAPTER 8

NEWSPAPERS

ELLIOT KING

In 1844, John Tyler, the tenth president of the United States, married Julia Gardiner, the daughter of a prominent Long Island family. It was the first time that a president would marry in office, and the union could have been grist for the gossip mills. After all, Tyler was more than twice the age of his new bride, who was only twenty-four years old and a fixture on the Washington society circuit.

Was the romance between the President and the socialite young enough to be his daughter covered widely in the newspapers at the time? No. In fact, at first, the president's wedding was kept secret, and when it did become public knowledge, it did not receive widespread press attention. For example, The *Baltimore Sun* carried only a short notice that the president and his new bride would be passing through Baltimore on their way to a reception in their honor in Washington, D.C. The *New York Herald*, a newspaper known as a supporter of Tyler's policies, also carried a short, relatively lighthearted article on the wedding.[1]

In 1886, Grover Cleveland, the twenty-second president of the United States, married a much younger woman while in the White House. Like Tyler, Cleveland was eager to keep his wedding a private affair, but he did not succeed. On the day of the ceremony, a huge press entourage followed the couple through the ceremony and then on their honeymoon. The *New York World* had five columns of coverage on page one and another column and a half on page two. It had another feature story about White House weddings and presidential mistresses. Finally, it ran a story about Deer Park, Maryland, the couple's honeymoon destination. The public was fascinated by the events. As a result of this in-depth reporting, many women began to imitate the new first lady's hair and fashion styles.[2]

Many felt that the coverage had gone too far and that the newspapers had published material that should not have been made public. The *Nation*, for example, argued that people did not have the right to know everything, and the intense press scrutiny about the president's engagement, wedding, and honeymoon was inappropriate.[3] Another magazine, the *Forum*, carried an article that described the coverage of the Cleveland wedding as "press espionage" and argued that the press should not pry into the private lives of public figures.[4]

Newspapers responded vigorously to the criticism. For example, the *New York World* argued that that president "is public property," and newspapers had the duty to report what its reporters deemed newsworthy and appropriate.[5]

The difference in coverage reflects changes in the role of the president in American popular culture as well as a change in the part that newspapers play in the public's understanding of that role. In his seminal work *Public Opinion*,[6] Walter Lippmann, the most prominent newspaper columnist of his era, argued that the media create the pictures of the world that people carried in their heads. Writing in the 1920s, Lippmann suggested that most of what people "know" about the world around them came not from personal experience but through mass media. The same thought was echoed by the humorist Will Rogers in the 1930s, with his signature line that all he knew is what he read in the newspapers.[7]

The observations of Lippmann and Rogers reflect on the central role of media in general and newspapers in particular in the development of the shared social knowledge that serves as the basis of popular culture. As Robert Darnton has pointed out, what a society writes, publishes, and reads is a guide to its culture.[8] Through the distribution of printed material, folk culture, which can be seen as being generated primarily through interpersonal interaction, begins to give way to a culture in which the bonds among people are mediated through broadly distributed cultural objects.

Newspapers are the most regularly read printed material in the United States. First weekly and now daily, newspapers publish information that the reporters and editors that produce them believe is important for people to know. As Benedict Anderson observed, the creation of shared knowledge is a primary agent in the creation of a community of identity that can reach beyond interpersonal and tribal bonds. The content shared through newspapers is part of the glue that binds people together and creates a common identity.[9,10]

The founders of the United States understood that the perception of the president would be shaped, in part, by newspapers, and that in a democracy, citizens must be informed about the government and its leaders. Newspapers usually see the president of the United States as a political figure—the role of the press is to report on the president's political policies, successes, and failures—but the president has an effect on American culture beyond politics. He influences style, manners, and Americans' self image. For example, President John F. Kennedy selected two silk top hats for his inauguration, as reported by the *New York Times*.[11] However, when pictures of a bare-headed Kennedy in the reviewing standing of the Inaugural Parade were published in newspapers around the county, the era of the well-dressed man routinely wearing a hat came to an end.[12] In addition, as the opening wedding examples suggest, the American public has increasingly become interested in the personal life of its presidents. The president not only influences popular culture but his personal and, sometimes, private life has become part of the culture.

Beginnings

When George Washington became president of the United States, nobody knew exactly what role the president should play in the political life of the country. There was no understanding about the role of the presidency rooted in folk culture, leavened over time and steeped in tradition. People were well aware of the role of a king in the cultural life of a country; the presidency, however, was a new idea.

As a consequence, the decisions that editors made in their reporting about George Washington set the foundation for the way that president would be mediated through the print media. Since mediated content is inextricably intertwined with the development of popular culture, newspaper reporting played a role in establishing the image of the presidency in the popular mind, in addition to establishing the role of the presidency in the political culture of the country.

In many ways, Washington's assumption of the presidency under the new Constitution in 1789 marked the beginning of a national popular culture. Washington was the first iconic figure shared by all citizens of the country. As president of the United States, Washington was the first political figure who could claim to represent every citizen. In turn, every citizen had, in some fashion, a relationship to Washington. The image of Washington was a shared cultural resource.

Newspapers, or what could be better described as the periodical press, were important in agitating for the American Revolution and for the U.S. Constitution, but the consensus that had led to Washington's selection as first president quickly broke down. As competing factions emerged, newspapers were launched to promote their ideals.

Thomas Jefferson, who served as secretary of state in the Washington administration, led one faction. He sponsored the *National Gazette*, putting its editor, Philip Frenau, on the State Department payroll. Secretary of Treasury Alexander Hamilton led the other faction, with *The Gazette of the United States*, edited by John Fenno, serving as its partisan press. As Washington refused to favor either faction, he came under political attack by both papers, as well as the *Aurora*, edited by Benjamin Bache, the grandson of

Benjamin Franklin. Far from being presented respectfully and with dignity, Washington was regularly accused of allowing corruption in his government, of wishing to be king, and of defying the will of the people.[5]

But if the newspapers in the capital treated Washington simply as one more political actor, deserving of no more respect than any other political actor, other images of Washington emerged as well. These images presented Washington not as a political figure but as a national symbol. Almost from the beginning of his presidency, Washington was seen as the "Father of his Country." This reporting came outside the bounds of reporting on politics, and it can be seen in poems written about him, the reporting on monuments built in his honor, and reflections on his birth and death, as well as attempts to put his life in perspective.[13]

In short, reporting on George Washington was conducted on two tracks. In one sense, as president of the United States, Washington was a political figure and was treated in the same fashion as other political figures. In another sense, however, he was a cultural figure, the "father" of the country. He was portrayed as a teacher to the entire civilized world. In this sense, Washington's political stands mattered little. His character, and what he represented, was what counted.

Presidential Character

The notion that the president's character in some way reflected the American character became a fixed feature in the way that newspapers portrayed the president. For example, in the election of 1828, which many historians see as a turning point in the development of popular politics in the United States, supporters of John Quincy Adams began long before the election to conduct a campaign in newspapers, attacking the eventual winner Andrew Jackson as an adulterer who had lived with his wife without the sanction of marriage. In an early salvo, the *Cincinnati Gazette* reported that Jackson's relationship with his future wife, Rachel Donalson Robards, was the cause of the break-up of her marriage with her first husband. The implication of the newspaper campaign was that a vote of Jackson was a vote for sin, and that Jackson was unfit to be president.[14]

This attention to character and image continued in the campaign of 1840. William Henry Harrison, who had a long and distinguished military career and was a descendent of one of the most prominent families of Virginia, was presented in the newspapers as a man who was content to live in a log cabin and drink hard cider. Harrison was a man of simple tastes compared to his aristocratic opponent Martin Van Buren.[15] A simple man, it was argued, was more suited to lead the common people of the United States. The campaign of 1840 was the first in which inexpensive mass-circulated newspapers affordable for working people played a significant role, and political parties campaigned extensively among the general population, many of whom were newly enfranchised. Massive rallies were held in cities around the country, and for the first time, campaign paraphernalia such as trinkets were mass produced.[16]

Henry Clay, another candidate for the Whig nomination for the presidency, was the first to make what was intended to be the disparaging comment that Harrison would be happy to spend his days in a log cabin sipping cider. His remark was picked up by a Baltimore newspaper, which argued that it was a slur against the common man in the West by aristocrats in the East. Other newspapers and speakers who campaigned for Harrison carried the theme into the election.[17] In fact, scores of campaign newspapers with names like *Log Cabin Herald* and *Log Cabin Rifle* were launched to promote the Harrison candidacy. Horace Greeley's *Log Cabin*, published simultaneously in New York City and Albany, reached a circulation of eighty thousand and became the launching pad for the *New York Tribune*, one of the most important newspapers of the nineteenth century.[5]

The message that Harrison was in touch with the common man was driven home by a widely republished campaign print that showed Harrison greeting a wounded soldier at a cabin at the North Bend of the Ohio River, with a barrel of hard cider outside on the porch.[18] Through the newspaper press, Harrison was transformed from a Virginian aristocrat into a person of the people.

Abraham Lincoln's popular image was also remade by the press during his campaign for the presidency and while he was in office. After engineering Lincoln's nomination as the Republican candidate for president in 1860, Horace Greeley, editor of the *New York Tribune*, published an exuberant editorial titled "Honest Old Abe"—the nickname stuck.[19]

The twin notions that a president's character is perhaps as significant as his policies and that his private life reflects on his character have continued to influence the way in which presidents have been popularly portrayed. For example, Theodore Roosevelt, a member of a patrician New York family, was a prolific writer who chronicled, among other topics, his adventures as a cowboy and rancher, as well as his experiences leading a regiment in the First U.S. Volunteer Calvary—dubbed the Rough Riders—in the Spanish-American War.[20] Roosevelt also actively courted reporters. In fact, Richard Harding Davis of the *New York Herald*, Edward Marshall of the *New York Journal*, and Stephen Crane of the *New York World*, which represented the newspapers with the largest circulations in New York City at the time, accompanied the Rough Riders in Cuba.[21] Roosevelt used his relations with reporters to burnish his image as a robust adventurer and man of action even after he assumed the presidency.

From the time of Theodore Roosevelt on, the assessment of a president's character increasingly became a common element in the newspaper coverage of the president. Newspaper assessment of Roosevelt's successor,

William Howard Taft, was very favorable when he took office in 1909. The Toledo Blade asserted that "[h]e enters the White House today greatly admired," and the *New York Times* described him as "a strong and healthy man . . . in keen and active sympathy with the best spirit of his times and his nation."[22] Taft's discomfort, however, with the rough and tumble of everyday politics hurt his popularity. Newspaper pictures of the overweight (he weighed over three hundred pounds) president only made matters worse—especially when contrasted with his physically fit predecessor. Press coverage of Taft's attempts at exercise—playing golf—only reinforced the public's poor perception of him. As Conlin notes: "batting a little white ball around an oversized lawn was considered a sissy's game in the early twentieth century."[23] Taft would finish third behind Wilson and Roosevelt in the 1912 presidential election, garnering only eight electoral votes.

Woodrow Wilson's victory in the 1912 election would signal a change in style of leadership. Wilson, a strong orator, wanted to communicate directly with the American people: He saw the press as a nuisance, at best. Not surprisingly, though his popularity remained high, his relationship with the press quickly deteriorated. By early 1913, he was writing to a friend that he should not "believe anything you read in the newspapers. . . . Their lying is shameless and colossal."[24]

During Wilson's reelection campaign in 1916, rumors about a possible sex scandal involving the president surfaced. The press convention in place at this point, however, was to ignore the private life of the president, which would work to Wilson's benefit and would prevent the erosion in the public's perception of his character that President Bill Clinton would later face. The first of Wilson's problems dealt with possible infidelities with a friend of the family, Mrs. Peck. The rumors were that Mrs. Peck had a longstanding affair with the president and that there were incriminating letters between the two.[25] Given the unwillingness of the press to closely examine the private life of the president, neither the *New York Times* nor the *Washington Post* covered the story at the time. The first mention of "Mrs. Peck" in either paper did not occur until January 4, 1925, when both papers covered the possibility of a congressional investigation into charges by Mrs. Peck that she had been offered $300,000 by the Republican National Committee "to enlist in a precious enterprise which had as its objective the impeachment of the President of the United States."[26]

Complicating the Peck rumors was Wilson's marriage to Edith Bolling Galt in 1915—just one year after the death of his first wife. For an America not many years removed from the Victorian era, Wilson's action was insensitive, if not downright scandalous. The newspapers closely covered the engagement and marriage ceremony. Although they seldom explicitly commented on the propriety of his engagement and marriage so soon after his first wife's death, the papers' attention to the details of their courtship certainly allowed for popular moralizing about the president. The *Washington*

Post, however, was partly responsible for contributing to the sometimes lewd jokes that were told about the couple throughout the nation. The president and Mrs. Galt had attended a play, and a *Post* reporter noted that instead of watching the play, "the President spent most of his time entertaining Mrs. Galt."[27] In the *Post*'s first edition, however, "entertaining" became "entering."

Republican Warren G. Harding won the presidential election of 1920. When he was nominated, the *New York Times* called him "the firm and perfect flower of the cowardice and imbecility of the senatorial cabal."[28] His likeability would soon change the presses' view, however—within four months, the *Times* would be extolling him for "gradually assuming undisputed leadership."[28] Like Wilson, rumors of sexual affairs surrounded Harding; most histories of Harding suggest he had affairs with at least two women, including one (Nan Britton) who may have borne an illegitimate son. As with their treatment of Wilson, however, newspapers chose not to investigate and report them. As Summers concludes: "during his entire term in office, voters did not read anything about Harding's adultery. The charges and more general suggestions of turpitude waited for his demise and the disgrace of his administration."[29] The disgrace would come in the form of political scandals—most notably the events surrounding the leasing of oil reserves in Teapot Dome, Wyoming. Harding would die in August 1923.

Newspaper reaction to new president Calvin Coolidge was quite positive. The *New York Times* wrote that "[t]he sorrow of all Americans at Mr. Harding's death is not sharpened by any doubt or fear such as has sometimes been felt when a Vice President became President, regarding the caliber and the qualifications, moral and intellectual, of his successor."[30] The *Philadelphia Enquirer* agreed and added that "[h]e is calm, thoughtful and sober-minded; he thinks twice before he speaks once."[30] Coolidge got along well with newspaper reporters, starting with his first news conference, when he cracked jokes and the reporters applauded.[31] Coolidge also connected well to the popular culture of the 1920s. Newspapers photographed him in all sorts of outrageous outfits and places—fishing in a formal suit, wearing skis on the White House lawn, and posing in ten-gallon hats and Indian war bonnets. When Coolidge was asked about his costumes, he replied that "the American public wants a solemn ass as president and I think I'll go along with them."[32] Conlin concludes by noting the connection with popular culture: "[p]erhaps the photos were Coolidge's quiet way of saying that he was at one with the American people of the 1920s in enjoying novelties and pranks."[33]

Herbert Hoover became president in early 1929; the stock market crashed in October of that year, and the economy followed soon afterward. Hoover's relationship with the press started well, but as the stock market and the economy deteriorated, the relationship worsened to the point that he would often criticize reporters openly. Sometimes at press conferences, he simply read prepared statements. By the end of his term, press conferences became nearly nonexistent.[24]

The *New York Times* opined on the day before Franklin Delano Roosevelt's inauguration that "No President . . . ever came to greater opportunities amid so great an outpouring of popular trust and hope."[34] Roosevelt worked hard to win over reporters and editors, especially as some were quite critical of his administration and the New Deal. To that end, Roosevelt held frequent press conferences that proved to be both lively and informative.[35] As with Wilson and Harding before him, the press would not make the rumored sexual affairs of the president public until long after Roosevelt's death. Nor would the press call attention to Roosevelt's physical limitations—only once in his twelve years in office did a photograph of the president in his wheelchair appear in print.[36] "The photographs that appeared in the newspapers and newsmagazines of the day generally showed a smiling president, head thrown back in delight, as he waged war against the ills associated with the depression. . . . Then, as now, the image of Roosevelt that radiated through the media was that of a man who had conquered the physical afflictions of polio by dint of his strong will."[37]

Postwar America would see many changes. One that would have a major effect on popular culture and its relationship to the president was television. *New York Times* columnist Russell Baker places the first Kennedy–Nixon debate in 1960 as the moment when television became more important than newspapers: "That night, television replaced newspapers as the most important communications medium in American politics. After that, the Bill Lawrences of the press would gradually yield the stage to technicians of the electronic arts until we came to a time when it no longer mattered how newspapers treated you as long as you could handle yourself well on camera."[36] John F. Kennedy would be the first president to effectively use the new medium, but he also successfully used newspapers— he had worked as a journalist, and he knew many reporters from his congressional days. Pierre Salinger, his press secretary, claimed that if Kennedy had the time, he could have been his own press secretary.[38] After eight boring years of Eisenhower, the press was excited by the vigor of the new president, and whether owing to his friendships with reporters or the unwritten code that frowned on such coverage, Kennedy's sexual escapades received no attention from the press while he was alive.[29]

Richard Nixon was dogged through much of his national political career with questions about his moral character. His opponents frequently referred to him as "Tricky Dick" and described him as shifty and untrustworthy. Nixon's character problems began in September 1952, shortly after he was nominated to run for the vice presidency, when syndicated newspaper columnists Drew Pearson and Jack Anderson broke the story that Nixon had a "slush" fund for his personal use, created by wealthy friends for whom he had performed political favors. Although most large newspapers did not vigorously pursue the story, it soured Nixon's relationship with the press and, in turn, tainted his public image.[39] When Nixon was president, events surrounding the break-in at the Watergate would reopen questions about his character. The scandal was not just political—popular culture could also be found on his "enemies list." In addition to the expected enemies from politics and journalism, his list contained celebrities including Carol Channing, Steve McQueen, Barbara Streisand, Gregory Peck, Bill Cosby, Tony Randall, and Joe Namath. Nixon would blame the press for Watergate: He said he had "never heard or seen such outrageous, vicious, distorted reporting in my twenty-seven years of public life."[40] For many Americans who lived through the period, however, Watergate and what it symbolized are called to mind whenever Richard Nixon's name is mentioned.

In the last decades of the twentieth century, the sex lives of presidents and presidential candidates reemerged as a major issue in the assessment of a potential president's character. The rules began to change in 1987, when reporters from the *Miami Herald* and the *Washington Post* revealed information indicating that presidential candidate Gary Hart was engaged in an extramarital sexual relationship. *Washington Post* editor Ben Bradlee defended the reporting, arguing that there was a legitimate public interest in Hart's private life and that, consequently, the press was free to investigate his possible sexual escapades. Bradlee did concede that the ground rules on coverage of a candidate's private life had changed.[41]

The full effect of the changes to acceptable levels of coverage came to bear in the candidacy and then the presidency of Bill Clinton, when reporters felt free to grill the candidate about rumors concerning his marital infidelity. In mid-January 1992, while campaigning for the New Hampshire primary elections, candidate Clinton was asked by reporters whether he had ever had an extramarital love affair. Although he declined to answer, both he and his wife responded in ways that did not rule out that Bill Clinton may have been unfaithful.[42]

Then, on January 23, the *Star*, a tabloid, faxed copies of a story it planned to publish on Monday, January 27, detailing allegations by a woman named Gennifer Flowers that she had engaged in an affair with Clinton.[41] On January 24, the *New York Daily News*, the *New York Post*, *New York Newsday*, and the *Boston Herald American* carried the Flowers allegations as their front-page headline stories. Some newspapers even used the same headline: "Sex, Lies and Audiotape," playing off a popular movie at the time, titled *Sex, Lies and Videotape*.[43] Gennifer Flowers's allegations ultimately did not prevent Clinton's victory, but the presidential candidates' and presidents' sex lives were now clearly on the public agenda.

The issue resurfaced with a vengeance in President Clinton's second term. Even before his taking office, President Clinton had been dogged by accusations of corruption and wrongdoing. Ultimately, a special prosecutor was appointed to investigate those charges. In January 1998, the special prosecutor's office learned that the president had conducted an affair with a young White House intern named Monica Lewinsky and may have cajoled Lewinsky to perjure herself in yet another lawsuit being brought against the president. When the special prosecutor asked Clinton about the alleged affair while the president was under oath in front of a grand jury, the president tried to evade the question. After Matt Drudge, an Internet columnist, leaked a report prepared by *Newsweek* in which the *Newsweek* reporter described hearing tapes of Lewinsky detailing the affair, the story was then picked up by every major newspaper and news organization in the country.[44]

From that point, the Clinton–Lewinsky affair became a national scandal, leading to the impeachment of the president. According to a study by Journalism.org, the coverage of the scandal had six story lines: the existence of a blue dress with DNA evidence of the affair; the existence of witnesses of an affair; the existence of other staffers who had also had affairs; the existence of talking points for Tripp and Lewinsky to lie about what they knew; the role of Vernon Jordan; and the role of Betty Currie. And though these story lines were often initiated by other types of media such as tabloids and cable talk shows, newspapers added to the reporting.[45] The coverage peaked when the special prosecutor's report recounting the affair in prurient detail was posted first on the World Wide Web and then published verbatim in many newspapers, including a number of important ones—newspaper coverage had just legitimized the scandal. When the coverage was limited to the tabloids and cable talk shows, it was just gossip; when the newspapers covered it, it became news.

Washington Society

Perhaps ironically, the role the president and first lady play in fashionable society can be understood as being analogous to the role kings and queens played in Europe. Because the entire country looks to them, they can set a certain tone—a tone that is transmitted through the press. The presidency of John Kennedy is perhaps the most striking example. When Jacqueline Kennedy's designer was dispatched to Paris to identify the latest fashions, it was dutifully reported in the *New York Times*.[46] In November of that year, the *Times* published a pictorial spread showing Mrs. Kennedy greeting different heads of state, noting that her presence often makes the meetings more pleasant.[47] In 1962, the *Times* summarized the Kennedys' influence domestically and abroad "on matters domestic, social and familiar,"[48] adding that Jackie Kennedy hoped that the lasting nonpolitical achievement of the Kennedy administration would be that the people of America truly felt that the White House is a home that belonged to them. The Kennedy family has been widely seen as American royalty.

When Ronald Reagan, a former Hollywood matinee idol, replaced Jimmy Carter, a Southern Baptist who drank no alcohol, newspapers noted the return of elegance and sophistication to Washington's social life. For example, the *New York Times* reported that in the second year of the Reagan administration, Washington society was entertaining more lavishly and more frequently than in years. The reason was simple: Members of the Reagan administration liked to go out. Although an assassination attempt on his life cut down on his social schedule in his first year, Reagan and his wife, Nancy, could be found at dinner parties hosted by Katherine Graham, publisher of the *Washington Post* and other venues.[49] Despite the economic recession that plagued the United States in the early 1980s, the newspaper reporting on the parties attended by Ronald and Nancy Reagan in some ways made it fashionable to lavishly entertain again.

Inauguration Day

Although reporting on the president's role in Washington society has echoes of the attention paid to royal courts, reporting on the inauguration of a new president represents an important junction in the rhythms of American democracy. The inauguration of a new president is a central ritual of American political life—the peaceful transfer of power from one administration to another based on the will of the people. Inauguration Day is a national day of hope; the hopes of the nation and sometimes the world are pinned to the fortunes of the new president.

In addition to reporting on the speeches, the parades, and the festivities that followed the presidential inauguration, newspapers often used the occasion to try to take the measure of the new president as a person, a leader, and a symbol. The first full-fledged inaugural parade took place in 1829, with the ascension of Andrew Jackson to the presidency. It ended with a drunken bacchanalia at the White House, which was seen as evidence of the growing frontier presence in the Capitol.[50] To James Gordon Bennett, then the Washington correspondent for the *New York Courier and Enquirer*, which supported Jackson, however, the scene was a "lesson for the monarchies of Europe. The mummery of a coronation, with all its pomp and pageantry, sinks into merited insignificance, before the simple and sublime spectacle of twelve million freeman, imparting this Executive Trust to the man of their choice."[51] The Jackson presidency and the reporting about it signaled the growing democratization of American politics and culture at the expense of the patricians from Virginia and New England.

Writing in the *New York Times* when Franklin Roosevelt was elected, the editor of the British newspaper *The Daily Express* observed that "Mr. Roosevelt brings to his work more of personal magnetism than any President since his famous namesake, and an unblemished record of integrity. It may yet be that he shows he possesses the strength of character and insight which enabled Lincoln seventy years ago to lead his country from extraordinary dangers to one of the greatest triumphs in history."[52] In the same edition of the *Times*, another writer opined that no other new president had ever come to office amid such a great outpouring of hope and popular trust.

The *Wall Street Journal* also assessed Roosevelt and the tasks he faced on Inaugural Day. The *Journal* wrote, "It is a young and ardent spirit which today assumes the Presidency of the United States. . . . Mr. Roosevelt appears to have been born with, and so far to have retained, an exceeding useful resilience of temperament and those reserves of courage and enterprise which naturally accompany it."[53]

These images of the president taking office reassure readers that the country is in strong hands, particularly in time of peril. Indeed, in times of peril the president often rises above politics, and so, too, is the president lifted above politics on the day he assumes office.

Death of a Sitting President

In the same way the president is lifted above politics on the day he enters office, he transcends politics when he dies. The death of a sitting president calls forth a period of national mourning, regardless of his specific record. At death, once again, the president becomes invested with a shared, common understanding.

Assessments, however, change over time, and competing assessments can often emerge. For example, although *Frank Leslie's Illustrated Newspaper* had maintained a distinctly mixed stance towards Lincoln during most of his administration, when he was assassinated, its praise was unstinting. In its eulogy following his death, "All that was mortal of Abraham Lincoln, the man of the people; the tried but always faithful President, will soon be consigned to the grave; but that grave will be the Mecca of a great nation, and will divide the reverential tribute of mankind with that which has made Mount Vernon holy, and a shrine before which all good men bow, as before the symbol of our faith and the emblem of our salvation."[54] At the moment of his death, Lincoln had been elevated from controversial politician and the target of hostile criticism, to something resembling a deity.

A competing view, based on his earlier frontier days, also emerged. In this view, Lincoln was an earthy son of the West. Neither view excludes the other, of course, and popular cultural memory is shaped by many factors, but in commentary as new presidential biographies emerge and birthdays and anniversaries of deaths are published, newspapers play a role in the production of those popular images.[55]

James A. Garfield would be another example. Garfield had been elected in 1880 in a very close election. In fact, he had won only about 10,000 more votes than his Democratic opponent Winfield S. Hancock. On July 2, 1881, he was shot by Charles Guiteau, a frustrated office-seeker. For 10 weeks, Garfield lingered between life and death. When he died, however, the closeness of the election and his short time in office were forgotten. The *New York Times* wrote, "As time passes, his character will be idealized as that of no other Presidents save Lincoln and Washington have been . . . the potency of his death may prove, in the providence of God, greater than aught which could have attended the unflagging and best directed energies of his life."[56]

On September 14, 1901, William McKinley died, also felled by an assassin's bullet. Like Garfield, McKinley had emerged victorious in a hotly fought campaign the year before, defeating William Jennings Bryan, who pioneered many modern campaigning techniques, for the second time. Upon his death, however, *The Baltimore Sun* looked not at his politics. It wrote that McKinley was "one of the most important and significant figures in contemporary history . . . a representation of a new regime of aspiration . . . an architect of national greatness and a molder of national destiny."[57]

When Franklin D. Roosevelt died on April 12, 1945, the entire world joined in America's sorrow. Roosevelt had emerged as the leader of the victorious Allied countries during World War II, defeating Germany and Japan. As the expressions of sympathy poured in, the *New York Times* noted that in his first inaugural speech, Roosevelt had revived the country itself with his stirring remarks that "the only thing we have to fear is fear itself."[58] Noting that Roosevelt had served as president longer than anybody else in history and had faced the gravest problems, the *Times* wrote that he had emerged as the leader of much of the world. Beloved and hated by millions, the *Times* wrote, Roosevelt did more to mold the future of the world he lived in than anybody else, and "his character and policies dominated."[59] It was not just his policies that made a difference—it was his character.

When John F. Kennedy was assassinated in Dallas on November 22, 1963, as with the death of Roosevelt, the world joined in mourning. The next day, the *New York Times* was filled with messages from leaders and countries from Australia to Canada to India, expressing their grief and disbelief about the death of this young and vibrant leader. The *Times* also published an editorial reflecting on the slain President. It wrote that every action that Kennedy had taken represented youth and strength. It described the loss as personal, deep, and crushing. The *Times* wrote that Kennedy "represented the vitality and the energy, the intelligence and the enthusiasm, the courage and the hope of these United States in the middle of this 20th Century."[60] At the moment of his passing, John F. Kennedy had become not just a political figure but also the embodiment of the country itself.

At the death of a president, newspapers become the vehicle in which mourning can be expressed, and the process of transforming the president from his role as an active politician to a historical figure begins. Over time, the president becomes part of the country's and the world's historical memory and culture. In Kennedy's case, within two years of his death, aides Arthur Schlesinger Jr. and Theodore Sorenson published memoirs of the Kennedy years in office, which was portrayed as Camelot—a storied period in American politics. Through reviews of these books and in subsequent reflections in the newspapers, the myth of Camelot was perpetuated. A president is remembered not only for his particular political achievements but also for way the country itself could be understood during his term in office.

Conclusion

The president of the United States is primarily a political figure, and thus the coverage of the activities of the president is overwhelmingly devoted to politics. Day in and day out, newspapers chronicle the political fortunes of the president.

However, this is not the only role the president plays. The president is a symbol to which every American can lay claim, and from time to time, newspaper reporting focuses more on the symbolic aspect of the presidency than on the political dimension. In those times, the president can be seen as a stand-in for what is popularly held to be the American character. When the press lauds or criticizes the personal character of the president, it reveals what it believes are the personal characteristics admired or scorned by the people, and as the president has a symbolic relationship with all the people, the president has the potential to have an effect in social life beyond politics. The president can establish a social tone for a particular era.

Moreover, newspaper reporting on the presidency creates a public space in which the country can celebrate or mourn together. The celebrations occur every four years, with the inauguration of a new administration. The mourning occurs less frequently, but most intensely, with the passing of a sitting presidency.

Newspapers have been called the first draft of history. The reporting in newspapers represents the first ideas and first efforts in a process that ultimately lodges each president within our historical memory.

Notes

1. Steve Wick, "A Long Island Social Climber," Newsday.com, http://www.newsday.com/community/guide/lihistory/ny-history-hs525a,0,6961090.story?coll=ny-lihistory-navigation March 16, 2005.

2. "Frances Folsom Cleveland," *World Book Encyclopedia*, http://www2.worldbook.com/features/features.asp?feature=presidents&page=html/clevel and_frances.htm&direct=yes.

3. John Tebbel and Sarah Watts, *The Press and The Presidency* (New York: Oxford University Press, 1985).

4. Joseph Bucklin Bishop, "Newspaper Espionage," *Forum* 1 (Summer 1886):528–537.

5. James Pollard, *The Presidents and the Press* (New York: MacMillan, 1948).

6. Walter Lippmann, *Public Opinion* (New York: Harcourt Brace, 1922).

7. Jennifer Tebbe, "Print and American Culture," *American Quarterly* 32 (1980):259–279.

8. Robert Darnton, "Reading, Writing and Publishing in Eighteenth Century France: A Case Study in the Sociology of Literature," in *Historical Studies Today*, ed. Felix Gilbert and Stephen R. Graubard (New York: Norton, 1972), 238.

9. Steve Fox, "The New Imagined Community," *Journal of Communication Inquiry* 28 (January 2004):47–62.

10. Benedict Anderson, *Imagined Communities* (London: Verso Books, 1991).

11. *New York Times*, "Kennedy Selects 2 Top Hats" January 19, 1961, 20.

12. *New York Times*, "Capital Paraders Don Overcoats to Pass in White House Review," Russell Baker, January 21, 1961, 1.

13. Barry Schwartz, "Social Change and Collective Memory: The Democratization of George Washington," *American Sociological Review* 56 (April 1991):221–236.

14. Norma Basch, "Marriage, Morals and Politics in the Election of 1828," *The Journal of American History* 80 (December 1993): 890–918.

15. R. D. Monroe, "The Campaign of 1840," http://dig.lib.niu.edu/message/campaignhistory-1840.html.

16. Roger A. Fisher, *Tippecanoe and Trinkets Too* (Urbana: University of Illinois Press, 1988).

17. Freeman Cleaves, *Old Tippecanoe* (New York: Charles Scribner's Sons, 1939).

18. "American Political Prints," Harpweek.com, http://loc.harpweek.com/LCPoliticalCartoons/IndexPeopleList.asp.

19. Harry J. Maihafer, *War of Words: Abraham Lincoln and the Civil War Press* (Washington, D.C.: Brassey's, 2001), 21.

20. Theodore Roosevelt, *The Rough Riders* (New York: C. Scribner's, 1899).

21. Edmund Morris, *The Rise of Theodore Roosevelt* (New York: Coward, McCann and Geoghegan, 1979).

22. Emil Dansker, "William Howard Taft," in *Popular Images of American Presidents*, ed. William C. Spragens (New York: Greenwood, 1988), 211.

23. Joseph R. Conlin, *The American Past*, 5th edition, vol. 2 (Ft. Worth, Tex.: Harcourt Press, 1997), 648.

24. James David Barber, *The Presidential Character* (Englewood Cliffs, N.J.: Prentice Hall, 1992), 50.

25. Hope Ridings Miller, *Scandals in the Highest Office* (New York: Random House, 1973).

26. "Inquiry Into Bribe Story of 'Mrs. Peck' Proposed in White House," *Washington Post*, Janury 4, 1925, 1.

27. Miller, *Scandals*, 182.

28. Barber, *Presidential*, 217.

29. John H. Summers, "What Happened to Sex Scandals? Politics and Peccadilloes, Jefferson to Kennedy," *The Journal of American History*, 87 (December 2000). Paragraph 18. http://www.historycooperative.org/cgi-bin/justtop.cgi?act=justtop&url=http://www.historycooperative.org/journals/jah/87.3/summers.html (accessed January 7, 2005).

30. "Editors Write of New President," *Washington Post*, August 6, 1923, 3.

31. Barber, *Presidential*.

32. Conlin, *The American Past*, 716.

33. Ibid.

34. Barber, *Presidential*, 287.

35. Robert E. Gilbert, "Franklin Delano Roosevelt," in *Popular Images of American Presidents*, ed. William C. Spragens (New York: Greenwood, 1988), 347–385.

36. Doris Kearns Goodwin, *Every 4 Years*, The Newseum, http://www.newseum.org/everyfouryears/essay.htm (accessed January 9, 2005).

37. Gilbert, "Roosevelt," 366.

38. Benjamin Bradlee, *A Good Life* (New York: Simon and Schuster, 1995).

39. Joseph C. Spear, Presidents and the Press: The Nixon Legacy (Cambridge, MA and London: The MIT Press, 1984), 51.

40. Barber, *Presidential*, 164.

41. Thomas B. Rosentiel, "Clinton Allegations Raises Questions on Media's Role," *Los Angeles Times*, January 29, 1992, A1.

42. Samuel P. Winch, *Mapping the Cultural Space of Journalism* (Westport, Conn.: Praeger, 1997).

43. Jonathan Alter, "The Cycle of Sensationalism," *Newsweek*, January 27, 1992, 25.

44. "A Chronology: Key Moments in the Clinton-Lewinsky Saga," http://www.cnn.com/ALLPOLITICS/1998/resources/lewinsky/timeline/.

45. "The Clinton/Lewinsky Story: How Fair? How Accurate?" http://www.journalism.org/resources/research/reports/clinton/story/default.asp.

46. "Cassini Sees Styles of Paris Courtiers," *New York Times*, August 4, 1961, 24.

47. "V.I. Lady and V.I.P's," *New York Times*, November 26, 1961, SM 65.

48. Marilyn Bender, "The Kennedys, in White House a Year, Bring New Look to Domestic Scene," *New York Times*, January 20, 1962, 14.

49. Lynn Rosellini, "The Pleasure of their Company," *New York Times*, February 9, 1982, B12.

50. Warren Weaver Jr., "From George Washington to George Bush, Speeches and Parades, Dances and Tradition," *New York Times*, January 21, 1989.

51. Tebbel and Watts, *The Press*, 81.

52. "British Papers Bid Roosevelt Lead," *New York Times*, March 4, 1933, 5.

53. "Mr. Roosevelt Begins," *Wall Street Journal*, March 4, 1933, 8.

54. Edmund C. Steadman, "Abraham Lincoln," *Frank Leslie's Illustrated Newspaper*, April 29, 1965, 81–82.

55. Don E. Fehrenbacher, *Lincoln in Text and Context* (Stanford Calif.: Stanford University Press, 1987).

56. "James A. Garfield," *New York Times*, September 20, 1881, 4.

57. "The Death of a President," *Baltimore Sun*, September 14, 1901, 4.

58. "Country Revived by First Anaugural," *New York Times*, April 13, 1945.

59. "Roosevelt Regime, From '33, Longest in History," *New York Times*, April 13, 1945, 6.

60. Weaver, "From George Washington," 27.

CHAPTER 9

MAGAZINES AND TABLOIDS

KATINA R. STAPLETON

The office of the presidency confers instant fame and scrutiny on those who hold the office; presidents are the star attraction in news media coverage of American politics. "This is true not just when the president is the subject of scandal and impeachment. It is true for all presidents."[1] Some presidents, however, become media celebrities in their own right—this is not new. "Since the turn of the twenty-first century, the signs have been clear that the American political system has changed into a celebrity regime in which politicians are subjected to Hollywood-style tabloid coverage."[2]

Despite an environment crowded with radio, television, and the Internet, America's magazines and tabloids are major sources of presidential news. Since the first periodicals were founded in the mid-eighteenth century, the magazine industry has grown by leaps and bounds; at this time, there are over forty-seven thousand general magazines, circulating around four hundred million copies each year.[3] Modern magazines are a vital part of American culture; they chronicle societal changes and political life. Although newsmagazines provide the bulk of periodical coverage of the president, coverage is not limited to them. General interest magazines and special interest magazines also regularly cover the president as a politician and as a man.

The tabloid press has been a significant cultural force since 1919, when the *New York Daily News* became America's first successful tabloid picture paper. Since the beginning, tabloids represented the voice of the common people.[4] Modern "supermarket" tabloids, such as the *National Enquirer*, the *Star*, the *Globe*, the *National Examiner*, and the *World Weekly News* occupy the coveted check-out counter positions in supermarkets, drugstores, and convenience stores across the nation. Supermarket tabloids are important culturally because they preserve and shape American folklore. The term "folklore" traditionally refers to the body of orally preserved, beliefs, tales, and stories of a people. Tabloids provide an important means of transmitting established oral legends and tales as well as creating new ones.[4] American tabloids have been crucial in shaping presidential mythologies and helping transform specific presidents from being commanders-in-chief to celebrities-in-chief.

This essay begins at the nation's founding and explores how magazines and tabloids help shape the images of American presidents. Creation and maintenance of public images is crucial for American politicians, especially presidents. Some images, like that of the president as a common man, are broader, recurring images that usually reflect the prevailing value system of particular historical eras. Other images are personal, adopted by presidents to "look tough on crime, strong on defense, caring and compassionate, and so on."[5]

Presidential image-making often involves humanizing the president, so we often see him presented as close to the people or as a family man.[1] To this end, many presidents cultivate images as sportsmen or true-blue sports fans. Sometimes presidential images are mythic in nature—they can be presented as legendary lovers, heroes, or even nefarious villains and crooks. According to Orman,[6] periodical coverage can add to or take away from presidential images. Stories that portray the president as decisive or as a winner positively affect his image, as do portrayals of the president as a tough, strong, or aggressive leader. However, stories that portray the president as weak, indecisive, or passive detract from his image. It is no surprise that negative portrayals of the president as a loser, a corrupt politician, or unable to govern also negatively affect his image.[6]

The Early Presidents

When George Washington, the "father of the nation," became president, he already had a strong positive image. Washington was famous before he entered office because of his military leadership during the Revolutionary War. Magazines predated the Washington presidency by over forty years; in 1741, colonial publishers Andrew Bradford and Benjamin Franklin fought to publish the first American magazine. Eighteenth- and nineteenth-century magazines were a curious mix of the arts, history, politics, sciences, religion, and moral criticism. Most important, these magazines "reflected the political and cultural birth of the U.S."[7] Today, they provide a valuable record of the renowned status of the nation's first leader.

According to Darrel West and John Orman, authors of *Celebrity Politics*,[2] George Washington was the precursor to the modern celebrity politician. During his presidency, Washington made for glamorous copy. Washington's lasting historical image as an American icon began to be developed in the periodical press of his time. Consider this 1789 passage from the *Gentlemen and Ladies Town and Country Magazine*,[8] describing the "Illustrious George Washington, president of the American empire." "He has shown forth the political favour of his country and the admiration of mankind," writes the author, "his performance exhibits everything great and noble. He is upwards of six feet high, and exceedingly well proportionate; he has a [majestic] carriage, serene countenance, and dark coloured hair."[9]

Washington realized the significance of being the nation's first president. In April 1789, he wrote James Madison, "as the first of everything, in our situation will serve to establish a Precedent."[10] This held true for presidential image-making. Later presidents were held up standards of greatness set by Washington during his tenure. Moreover, as the first president, Washington also established lasting trends in magazine/president relationships. He was covered by, contributed to, and supported the periodical press. Magazines like *New York Magazine* published his speeches and analyzed his policy decisions. The *Universal Magazine* showcased his talents as a poet, publishing his work "The Genius of America," and popular magazines published biographical accounts of his life. The president even subscribed to three magazines to gauge public opinion.[5]

John Adams, Washington's successor, was known as a political philosopher, but not as an effective speaker. Adams gave only six public speeches during his presidency, and when he did give public addresses, periodicals such as the *New York Magazine*, the *Time Piece*, and *Philadelphia Repository and Weekly Register* published them.

Thomas Jefferson was a staunch proponent of freedom of the press. The irony of Jefferson's presidency is that his belief in the necessity of a free press continued even as his public and private lives were assailed.[11] "Like many presidents who would follow him, Jefferson made a favorable beginning, but again, the honeymoon was brief. He became the target for all sorts of accusations, personal as well as partisan."[12] For example, publicity given to Jefferson's "free thinking" during a presidential campaign led to concern in the nation's religious periodicals.[13] In addition, reports of Jefferson's supposed infidelity could be found in a number of publications. For example, the Federalist *Port Folio* magazine pilloried Jefferson, making fun of his literary skill, his friends, and the "scandalous reports of Jefferson's intimacies with a slave of his household."[14]

Political, general, literary, religious, and even ladies magazines of his time contributed to Jefferson's presidential image. They covered his messages to Congress, presidential addresses, views, character, and personal life. Perhaps one of the most important functions of popular periodicals was to familiarize the public with what Jefferson looked like. Unlike today, there was no ready reference to his appearance for the average person. Engraved prints, which were reprinted in magazines such as *Literary Magazine* and *American Register* thus became important sources for his likeness.[15]

Nineteenth-Century Presidents

After Andrew Jackson, it was common for presidents to associate themselves with the image of the common man. Jackson was the first American president to consciously link himself to the common man, even going so far as to invite ordinary Americans to celebrate his electoral victory at the White House. This coincided with changes in American politics, which had become more democratic during the 1820s. "Mass rallies, bonfires, processions, and the formation of political clubs all characterized a political system stirring public enthusiasm for electoral participation."[16]

During the nineteenth century, "domestic women's status and leverage increased."[17] Women's magazines have always been integral to American journalism; however, the growth of women's magazines was nurtured during the Jacksonian period. Many gained a national following, and others were niche publications.[18] Magazines such as *Godey's Lady's Book* (1830–1880) were intended to educate as well as entertain the women of America. Whereas some of these magazines concentrated on domestic topics such as health and fashion, other ladies magazines covered political figures and issues of the day (and some did both). Mary Barney, editor and publisher of the *National Magazine: Or, Lady's Emporium*, was determined to treat women as "thinking, sentient beings in 1830 and not as housewifely appendages or fashion plates."[19] Barney published several critical articles about Andrew Jackson, writing that the president was "depraved, obstinate, and frivolous."[20]

America's sixteenth president, Abraham Lincoln, carefully constructed images of himself as a regular guy and as a self-made man within the nation's periodical press. "Although Lincoln had become a prosperous lawyer, his background—born in a log cabin and raised in poverty with little formal education—was a perfect fit for the self-made man myth."[21] His nicknames "Honest Abe" and the "Rail Splitter" followed him throughout his presidency. Although Lincoln was proud of his reputation of "impeccable honesty," the president apparently was embarrassed by mentions of his frontier past.[5]

The extraordinary political circumstances of his term, which included the Civil War, further developed Lincoln's image in the magazines of the day. However, it was the actions of John Wilkes Booth that immortalized Lincoln's image as that of a tragic hero. In the wake of the Union victory in the Civil War and a successful reelection, Lincoln's life was cut short. The April 14, 1865, assassination of Lincoln by Booth plunged the nation into mourning. Consider this eulogy from *Our Young Folks: An Illustrated Magazine for Boys and Girls*: "There is no reader of this magazine too small or too young to have heard and to understand that Abraham Lincoln has been removed from this life by an act as awful and as wicked as any that history records."[22] Even those who differed with Lincoln politics embraced his hero image. According to the editors of the *Godey's Lady's Book and Magazine*, "never, perhaps, has there been a ruler so endeared personally to the people as Abraham Lincoln...those who opposed him on such grounds, now remembered only his grand, noble nature, his pure attributes, his devotion to his country, and above all his kindness and never failing goodness."[23]

Lincoln's successor, President Andrew Johnson, and America's eighteenth president, Ulysses S. Grant, faced a periodical press concerned just as much with presidential character as presidential policy making. Johnson, who was known at the beginning of his presidency as an honest, honorable man, suffered a reversal of fortune when he became the first president to be impeached. His trial was closely covered by the nation's periodicals. During the scandal, he was characterized in the *Atlantic Monthly* as being "insecure as well as stubborn, vain as well as ill tempered."[24] Early in President Grant's term, his intellectual character was called into question by several of the nation's magazines. The *Old Guard* presented him in its editorials as a "nincompoop," and the *Nation* ascribed to Grant, "the entire ignorance of the intellectual and political life of the nation."[25] Not all images of Grant that appeared in magazines were bad; he was drawn in *Harper's Weekly* "as a strong silent hero."[26]

Twentieth- and Twenty-First-Century Presidents

Theodore Roosevelt

As were their predecessors, modern presidents are frequently scrutinized by the nation's periodical press. Magazines are well known for stereotyping American presidents.[27,28] For example, researchers studying *Time* magazine found that the magazine stereotyped presidents by emphasizing their personalities rather than their news activities. For example, *Time* stereotyped Truman as "blunt, sarcastic, belligerent," as well as "harried, lazy, vain, angry, sly, curt, and cold." Eisenhower was described by the magazine as "cautious, warm, charitable, modest, happy, amiable, firm, cordial, effective, serene, frank, calm, skillful, and earnest."[29]

In addition to facing coverage by news and opinion magazines, modern presidents face a wide range of magazines that consider the personal lives of presidents to be fair game. Picture magazines and news magazines have existed since the nineteenth century. As discussed earlier, illustrated magazines like *Collier's Weekly*, *Godey's Lady's Book*, and the *Ladies' Home Journal* covered the early presidents. So did the predecessors of modern news and opinion magazines such as the *Literary Digest*, *North American*

Review, Independent, New Republic, Crisis, Harper's Monthly, Harper's Weekly, and others.[30]

Modern presidents find themselves the topic of modern mass magazines from *Life* to *People*. Because many of these magazines regularly practice "personality journalism," it is common for them to cover the personal lives of president. It is not unusual to see presidents gracing the pages of *Life, Jet, Rolling Stone, Sports Illustrated*, and even *Playboy*. Since the early 1920s, modern newsweeklies—in particular *Time, Newsweek*, and *U.S. News and World Report*—have become critical in shaping both personal and political images of American presidents.

Since Theodore Roosevelt, how have presidents shaped their images in magazines and tabloids? When the nation's twenty-sixth president came to the White House in 1901, he was already a war hero. However, Roosevelt's lasting political image is that of an activist, master politician.[5] He had a tough-talking public image—the president was well known for quoting an African proverb, "Walk softly and carry a big stick." In 1903, *Collier's* documented how Roosevelt's use of the proverb became a "permanent part of the American language."[31]

Part of Roosevelt's tough-guy image came from his crusade against some members of the magazine industry. When Theodore Roosevelt assumed the presidency in 1901 after the assassination of William McKinley, he faced a magazine industry increasingly critical of government. During the early 1900s, America's muckraking magazines began a fight to expose corruption in society, government, and business. *McClure's*, the *Ladies' Home Journal, Collier's Weekly*, and *Good Housekeeping* all took on social and political causes. Roosevelt thought that magazine investigations like these only concentrated on the bad while ignoring the good. In response, he began a personal crusade against what he nicknamed the "muckraking press."[32]

The lasting effect of the muckraking era is that magazines usurped newspapers' role as the sole influencer of public opinion by directly discussing pubic affairs. According to James Wood's history of the social and economic influence of American magazines, "all important general newsweeklies and monthlies began to give more coverage and more thorough discussion to public matters and thus to exert a greater influence on the minds of their readers."[33]

Roosevelt often used magazines as a platform. Similar to their early predecessors, modern magazines often made it a practice for statesmen to contribute articles. Roosevelt, a prolific writer, wrote for a wide variety of magazines, including *Harper's Monthly Magazine* and the *Ladies' Home Journal*. In the latter, Roosevelt urged men to engage in civic activity and be good family men. "Roosevelt himself was regularly pictured in the magazine as an actively engaged father."[34] Roosevelt also popularized the practice of writing letters to women's magazines such as the *Ladies' Home Journal* and the *Woman's Home Companion*.[35]

Wilson and Coolidge

After Teddy Roosevelt, several different images of the president emerged or re-emerged in the nation's magazines. Woodrow Wilson was an activist president and embraced using presidential rhetoric to influence policy and to shape his political and personal images. "Silent Cal" Coolidge had a reputation for being a man of few words. However, even as the nations' magazines acknowledged the common perception, they argued it was a myth. For example, in the *New Republic*, Charles Mertz argued "Mr. Coolidge is not a silent man, but a very noisy man."[36] The *Literary Digest* concurred: "Only because Mr. Coolidge has this amazing reputation as a man of silence from whom it is difficult to prod a single extra word, is it worth noting."[37] So where did Silent Cal speak? The article goes on to explain that Coolidge was always willing to talk at a range of public gatherings and to send felicitations noting all sorts of significant life events.[38]

Roosevelt and Coolidge were both widely regarded as sportsmen. During his presidency, Roosevelt became "the most photographed president up to that time, being photographed performing all sorts of activities from hiking [to] equestrian sports. However because tennis was considered to be an 'effete sport,' the president would not allow himself to be photographed playing the game."[39]

Like Roosevelt, Coolidge was able to cultivate a connection with sports-loving Americans. Coverage of Coolidge in the *Literary Digest* illustrates this point. Throughout his term, the magazine covered the importance the president placed on personal fitness.[40] Coolidge's "well trained and athletic body and mind" supposedly made him fit for the job.[41] In particular, the magazine focused on the president's love of walking and fishing. According to the *Digest*, Coolidge's use of worms supported his image as a common man: "When the choice is between fish for breakfast with worms, and a fishless breakfast with gaudy flies all sensible men take the worms. And nobody denies that President Coolidge is a sensible man."[42]

Franklin Delano Roosevelt

American's thirty-second president, Franklin Delano Roosevelt, transformed expectations of American presidents. After Roosevelt, the "presidency was now an office that no mere mortal—or common man—could expect to inhabit."[43] Roosevelt was portrayed in the nation's magazines as an activist president. When *Time* named him man of the year in 1941, they described him as an "extraordinary man, who, like some astonishing Shakespearean character, full of great speeches and thundering images, appears only when the going gets hard."[44] Roosevelt was elected to four terms, overseeing the nation through the Great Depression and World War II.

Roosevelt's personal struggles, however, were largely kept from the American public during his presidency. Although Americans knew that the president had contracted polio in the 1920s, most were unaware the president was wheelchair bound—vitality was the president's preferred public image. Roosevelt, who did not wish to be viewed as disabled, purposefully misled the public, and the periodical press helped. At the time, there was a gentleman's agreement between the press and Roosevelt that they would not show photographs of his disability. Very few photographs of Roosevelt exist showing him in a wheelchair. Magazine readers instead saw the President photographed from the waist up or standing. In this way, Roosevelt's image as a vital man of action was not undermined by visual portrayals of infirmity.[45]

John F. Kennedy

After Roosevelt, John F. Kennedy was the next president to dramatically change the way presidential images were portrayed in magazines. With the help of his father, Joseph, John F. Kennedy was able to successfully cultivate a war hero image for himself in the nation's periodical press. In 1943, Kennedy survived a World War II military accident. In 1944, John Hersey's *New Yorker* article chronicled Kennedy's war experience. "Survival," writes the author of *The Kennedy Obsession*, "is the true beginning of the production of John F. Kennedy as a popular hero."[46] The story told in "Survival" is that of Kennedy emerging from the sawing in half of his PT boat by a Japanese destroyer to save both himself and his crew.

Once president, Kennedy recognized the importance of the nation's magazines in shaping his image, even discussing image-making in an article in *TV Guide*. America's picture magazines frequently cooperated, idealizing Kennedy and his young wife. *Life*, in particular, presented numerous photo essays of the "perfect" first family to the American public.[47]

Kennedy carefully controlled his family image: "No photographs were allowed showing him eating, smoking cigars, playing golf, or kissing his wife."[48] Curiously absent from magazine coverage of Kennedy was evidence of suspected extramarital affairs. Though Kennedy was suspected of womanizing, during his lifetime this was suppressed. Even the tabloid press hesitated to discuss it for many years after his death.[49]

Two explanations exist for this. First, just as the media agreed not to picture Roosevelt's infirmity, they also had a gentleman's agreement not to discuss Kennedy's infidelities. Second, Jacqueline Kennedy did a very successful job of shaping Kennedy's image after his 1963 assassination. The first lady was concerned about how history would remember her husband and their relationship, so she called on family friend and journalist Theodore White to tell her story. Through White's article in *Life* magazine, the nation was introduced to the mythic imagery of Camelot, in which the Kennedy administration was likened to King Author's court.[50]

According to S. Elizabeth Bird, author of *For Enquiring Minds*, John F. Kennedy is unique (even among presidents) for the type and amount of tabloid attention he still garners. It seems that in life, Kennedy garnered no more tabloid attention than other politicians, but in the years after his death, tabloid coverage increased as Kennedy's life and death rose in mythic consequence.[51] In particular, the Kennedy-is-alive myth has captured America's imagination for decades. Although history records the president's death as fact, both oral and written rumors persist that the president was not successfully assassinated. The Kennedy-is-alive story has been an on-going favorite of the tabloids, continuing into the 1990s. As Bird points out, "the notions of a dead mythic hero (or villain) being alive and ready to return, or returning in the form of another person, are widespread heroic motifs."[52]

American popular culture is replete with rumors and speculation about the how and why Kennedy was killed. Tabloids have contributed their own theories behind the president's untimely death: The CIA did it, or alternately, it was either a Buddhist curse or a Kennedy family curse. The *National Enquirer* even went so far as to offer a $100,000 reward in 1975 for proof of a conspiracy surrounding the president's death.[51] This type of speculating was not unusual. Tabloid stories represent only a small portion of pop culture conspiracy theories surrounding Kennedy's untimely death. The public's fascination with Kennedy seems destined to be long-lived in part because his life was so short-lived. The hero image cultivated in his youth did not get a chance to grow old and be sullied. Moreover, the circumstances surrounding his death only added to the Kennedy mystique. Together, his life and tragic death have made the legend of John F. Kennedy a permanent part of America's collective consciousness.

Lyndon B. Johnson

President Lyndon B. Johnson had tough shoes to fill after Kennedy's assassination. Despite this, Johnson cultivated a master politician image. He put together an impressive list of legislative accomplishments as part of his "Great Society" program. However, controversies over civil rights and American involvement in Vietnam weakened his popularity. His coverage in *Time* illustrates the conflict faced by the nation's magazines when reporting on Johnson. On one hand, the magazine portrayed Johnson as perhaps the best twentieth-century president since Franklin Roosevelt. On the other hand, *Time* presented him as a president who couldn't take criticism well and who was often uneasy with persistent issues facing the nation.[53]

On a much lighter note, magazines often covered Johnson's First Dogs. His canines proved to be both an image-making help and a hindrance to Johnson. Johnson's love for his dogs was featured in a wide range of the nation's magazines—from women's magazines to newsweeklies. The president's beagles, Him and Her, were Johnson's most well-known dogs. The president frequently played with the dogs and was often photographed with them. However, when President Johnson picked up Him by the ears in front of an audience that included photographers, it caused a national uproar. *Newsweek*'s coverage "Him, Her, and LBJ"[54] discussed the political fallout. Dog owners (which constitute a fair proportion of the voting public) and a host of animal rights organizations expressed outrage by lighting up the White House switchboard.

Richard M. Nixon

President Richard Nixon's coverage in the periodical press is a two-part tale. From the beginning Nixon considered his image just as important as policy. According to the thirty-seventh president, "in the modern presidency, concern for image must rank with concern for substance."[55] Nixon created the Office of Communications within the White House to help control his image, but it had varying success influencing the nation's periodical press. For example, *Time* magazine's pre-Watergate coverage of Nixon characterized him as a skilled politician with a dogged, hardworking personal style, but it also hinted at his tendency toward secrecy.[53]

In particular, the details of one little-known incident were kept largely out of the public eye for over fifteen years. Only a few days before Christmas 1970, Elvis Presley met Nixon at the White House after sending the president a six-page letter asking to meet him. At the time, there was no coverage of the Elvis–Nixon meeting in the nation's magazines because Elvis requested that his visit be kept private. White House officials also didn't think the visit was important enough to leak to the American press. Columnist Jack Anderson uncovered the visit in 1972, but his revelations barely caused a stir.[56] It wasn't until December 1986 that public interest revived, after approximately 1.5 million pages of Nixon White House documents were released, including documentation of Elvis's visit. Subsequently, his White House meeting was briefly covered by magazines like *The Economist* and *U.S. News and World Report*. However, it was a report in an Elvis fan magazine that really piqued Americans' interest. The article made people aware that photos of Elvis and Nixon were publicly available through the National Archives.[56] Requests rushed in, and the photo of Nixon shaking hands with Elvis remains the archives' most requested photo.

Ultimately, political subterfuge would rule periodical coverage of Nixon. After Nixon was linked to the 1972 break-in at the Democratic National

President Lyndon Johnson picks up his dog, "Him," by the ears and gets widely criticized by animal lovers. (Lyndon Baines Johnson Library and Museum)

Committee offices at the Watergate hotel, his coverage took a turn for the worse. Prose describing the president was almost always negative in tone. For example, Nixon was characterized by *Time* as an ineffectual and erratic president besieged by scandal—even photos of Nixon in *Time* after Watergate created negative impressions.[53] Negative coverage wasn't limited to *Time*, however. Nixon received the poorest periodical coverage of any president in the twentieth century during the 1973 portion of the Watergate scandal.[57] Debate over whether or not Nixon was telling the truth when he declared "I'm not a crook!" played out in the nation's magazines.

Coverage of his struggles continued through Nixon's 1974 resignation and subsequent pardon by Gerald Ford.[58]

Jimmy Carter

Thirty-ninth President Jimmy Carter illustrates how presidential image making can backfire. During his 1976 campaign, Carter cultivated the common-man imagery successfully used by presidents in the past. Carter hoped that the press would cover him as both an outsider to Washington politics and as just a regular guy from Plains, Georgia. He used his nickname, "Jimmy," rather than his given name, James.[59] In his infamous 1976 campaign interview with *Playboy* magazine, Carter admitted that he was no better than other men because he, too, had "lusted in his heart," even though he had never cheated on his wife. Once in office, Carter's common-man imagery was not enough for him to gain consistent, positive coverage in the nation's magazines. Unfortunately for Carter, presidents who sought to use common-man imagery after Roosevelt largely failed. Ordinary men weren't seen as good enough to be president; rather, extraordinary men were expected to lead the nation.[58]

Ronald Reagan

President Ronald Reagan presented almost the opposite image of Carter's to the American public. He was no common man; rather, Reagan was already a full-blown celebrity when he took office. As a former 1940s Hollywood film star, Reagan brought glamour back to the White House. Together, Reagan and his wife Nancy made a storybook couple and great celebrity copy. Reagan was a recurring feature in the nation's magazines, receiving more magazine coverage than any twentieth-century president before him.[57] Reagan was on the cover of *Time* forty-four times, including as "Man of the Year" both in 1981 and 1983. What might explain the case of Reagan's near-mythical celebrity appeal? Perhaps his reported grace after being shot by a would-be assassin only 69 days after entering office contributed to his popularity. In 1986, *Time* reporter Lance Morrow attempted to explain why people seemed drawn to the president: "Ronald Reagan has a genius for American occasions. His is a Prospero of American memories, a magician who carries a bright, ideal America like a holograph in his mind and projects its image in the air.... Reagan, master illusionist, is himself a kind of American dream." "How does he pull it off?"[60] asked Morrow of *Time* readers. The answer lies in Reagan's background as an actor. He brought to the White House the amiability of his on-screen image, a ceremonial presence gained through years on Hollywood, and an appeal to the young. Simply put, he was likable and came off as authentic. This, combined with the image-making prowess of his press office, led to the prevalence of positive images of the president rather than negative ones.

For the most part, the Teflon president's shield even protected him from public inquiries into whether Reagan was too old to be an effective president. Reagan's battle with Alzheimer's disease, a progressive form of dementia that usually starts in the forties or fifties, only became public many years after he left office. During his presidency, "some journalists feared Reagan was 'sinking into senility,' but did not report it publicly."[61] Once Reagan left office, his health became a matter of speculation for the nation's magazines and tabloids. In "Brave Reagan is Still 'Swingin'"[62] and "Brave Reagan's Still Smiling,"[63] Reagan is presented as a gusty, optimistic former president bravely facing life with a debilitating illness. As Reagan's condition deteriorated, America's tabloids and magazines began presenting the former president's condition as tragic; sympathy turned to his family, who had to care for him and watch his painful decline. The December 15, 2003, edition of *People* magazine, for example, gave readers an "intimate look" at the private world of the Reagan family.

George H. W. Bush

When George H. W. Bush became president, he faced the task of cultivating a dynamic presidential image. This was difficult for two reasons. First he rejected the stage-managed presidential style favored by Reagan. Second, he was handicapped by his unflattering vice presidential coverage.[58] For example, in a 1987 *Newsweek* cover story, Bush was characterized as a wimp. As president, his negative image was compounded because his political strategy and message seemed incoherent.[64] In addition to the "wimp factor," two more deleterious images emerged: "George Bush as the silly politician, and a new image, George Bush as the uncaring, out-of-touch-with-the-needs-of-ordinary-Americans president (the antithesis of the common man image)."[65]

However, the president's interest in sports did provide a connection with two overlapping segments of the population: sportsmen and sports fans. Following in the footsteps of Teddy Roosevelt and Coolidge, George H. W. Bush established himself as a physically active president. He was an avid tennis player, golfer, and fisherman. *Sports Illustrated* began chronicling Bush's sports activities while he was vice president and continued during his presidency.[66] Because the president loved watching sports, he was often characterized as the nation's "number-one sports fan." The president would often even call winning sports teams after their televised victories and invite them to the White House.[67]

William Clinton

Like George H. W. Bush, William Jefferson Clinton's presidency was characterized by multiple (and often bad) public images. By the time Clinton first ran for president, he was already somewhat notorious for his sexual exploits as the governor of Arkansas. Clinton would find that neither American magazines nor tabloids afforded him the same "blind-eye" given to former presidents Kennedy and Reagan.

William Jefferson Clinton faced a hostile media environment in part because reporters had been previously exposed to the manipulation techniques of the Reagan era.[64] Clinton, long rumored to be a womanizer, faced intense scrutiny during his 1992 campaign when The *Star*, a tabloid, printed an account of Gennifer Flowers's alleged twelve-year affair with Clinton. Although he denied the allegations, the scandal became a major campaign issue: "the mainstream press had no recourse but to report how he was dealing with it."[68] Unfortunately for Clinton, sexual scandals haunted him throughout his presidency. When Paula Jones alleged that then-governor Clinton had sexually harassed her, the subsequent investigation led to the biggest political scandal of his career: President Clinton allegedly had an affair with White House intern Monica Lewinsky, lied about it, and got caught. He was impeached for lying under oath, tried, and found innocent.

Although this was a story made in tabloid heaven, the supermarket tabloids were initially scooped by *Newsweek* magazine and an Internet journalist. For over a year, *Newsweek* journalist Michael Isikoff had been pursuing allegations that the president had harassed Paula Jones while he was governor. As part of the Jones case, former White House intern Monica Lewinsky gave a deposition in which she denied having sex with the president. However, a tape existed on which Lewinsky reportedly admitted to having a romantic relationship with the president. According to reports by the magazine, *Newsweek* was given access to the tape the day before *Newsweek* was to go to press. *Newsweek* editors decided to double-check their facts before going to print.[68]

However, this caution—usually applauded as part of good journalism—caused *Newsweek* to fall victim to the journalistic equivalent of "you snooze, you loose." Matt Drudge, editor of the Internet Web site the *Drudge Report*, learned that the magazine had decided to hold the story for confirmation. Drudge didn't see any need to wait and broke the story on Monday, January 19, 1998. As Witcover observed, "the story spread like an arsonists handwork."[69] Richard Fox and Robert Van Sickel, authors of *Tabloid Justice*,[70] calculated that collectively, *Time*, *Newsweek*, and *U.S. News and World Report* (the nation's three most prominent newsmagazines) published 497 articles (including twenty-five cover stories) on the Clinton/Lewinsky scandal in 1998.[71]

The tabloids soon found themselves competing head-to-head with the mainstream press over this traditional "tabloid" story. The oversaturated media environment resulted in a free-for-all; in an effort to outdo each other, many mainstream news organizations began moving closer to tabloid style. "This means sensationalism, scandal, prurience, triviality, even rumor and gossip, and speculation instead of facts" became increasingly prevalent.[72]

Even Clinton's weight was a concern of the nation's magazines. Magazines like *Men's Health* concentrated on the president's poor diet, while others like *Sports Illustrated* focused on his physical fitness efforts—especially his jogging routine. *People* even chronicled the caps Americans gave the president to wear while jogging.[73,74] Clinton, a passionate basketball fan, replaced George H. W. Bush in *Sports Illustrated* as the nation's "First Fan."[75]

George W. Bush

Like his father, George W. Bush has faced challenges in shaping his image for the periodical press. At the beginning of his presidency, two characterizations of Bush existed that magazines could draw from. At one extreme was an image of him as being not very bright and riding on his father's coattails, but at the other extreme was a representation of Bush as an effective and skilled leader.[64]

Bush's image in the tabloids seems to teeter-totter from one image to the next. As early as the 2000 election, Bush's struggle with alcoholism became a much talked-about tabloid topic. Tabloid headlines proclaimed: "How Laura Bush Saved George W from the Bottle"[76] and "The Night I Got Drunk with George Bush."[77] His malapropisms and problems with language can also be found in the nation's tabloids. For example, in "Is Our Children Learning," the *Globe* proclaimed "George W. Bush is a butcher—when it comes to the English language."[78] The tabloid attributed a list of verbal blunders to the president including "Will the highways on the internet become more few?"

Not all tabloid coverage of Bush has been critical. Immediately after the terrorist 2001 attacks on America, tabloids began covering Bush as a strong leader in the face of a national tragedy. For example, the *Globe* published "Bush Shows His Hand of Strength"[79] and "In Safe Hands."[80]

Like many presidents before him, Bush has been able to harness his image as a family man. For example, the first couple was featured in the *Ladies' Home Journal*, which has a history of interviewing presidents and their wives. In the October 2003 *Ladies' Home Journal* interview with the President and Laura Bush, the couple discussed their marriage, their children, and their religious faith.[81] This interview was not unusual; the first couple's relationship has been profiled in periodicals from *People* magazine to *U.S. News and World Report*. Like his immediate predecessors, Bush is portrayed in American magazines as a sportsman. For example, in a 2003 Q&A with *Sports Illustrated*, the president discussed his participation in Little League and his former role as managing partner of the Texas Rangers.[82]

Conclusion

Hero, lover, liar, the common man, the family man, the strong man, the weak man, the first sportsman, and Sports Fan–in-Chief—these are all images of the president that have been developed over time in the nation's periodical and tabloid press. From George Washington to George W. Bush, magazines and tabs have shaped public perceptions of American presidents. However, over the years the standards for covering the president in the nation's periodicals have changed. The legacy of the nation's last twentieth-century president and first twenty-first-century president is that personal problems can find themselves in print in the blink of an eye. Magazine (and even tabloid reporters) hesitated to show the public Franklin Roosevelt's physical disability, report on Kennedy's affairs, or speculate on Reagan's memory lapses, but Clinton's sexual relations and Bush's diction became public spectacle. Future presidents have the difficult job of maintaining positive presidential images in the periodical and tabloid press in an age in which presidential image-making is perhaps just as important as presidential policy-making. They must also govern in a world in which tabloids matter.

Notes

1. Richard Davis, *The Press and American Politics*, 3rd edition (Upper Saddle River, N.J.: Prentice Hall, 2001), 229.

2. Darrell West and John Orman, *Celebrity Politics* (Upper Saddle River, NJ: Prentice Hall, 2002), x.

3. David L. Paletz, *Media in American Politics*, 2nd edition (New York: Longman, 2003).

4. S. Elizabeth Bird, *For Enquiring Minds*, (Knoxville: University of Tennessee Press, 1992).

5. Richard Waterman, Robert Wright, and Gilbert St. Clair, *The Image-Is-Everything Presidency: Dilemmas in American Leadership* (Boulder, Colo.: Westview Press, 1999), 12, 23, 172.

6. John Orman, "Images of the Presidency in the Periodical Press," *Presidential Studies Quarterly* 25 (1995):683–695.

7. *Description of Collections: American Periodical Series, 1741–1935.* Computer Indexed Systems, http://www.comp-index.com/describe-collections .asp (accessed July 1, 2003).

8. "Brief Account of the Illustrious George Washington, President of the American Empire," *The Gentleman and Ladies Town and Country Magazine: Consisting of Literature, History, Politics, Arts, Manners, and Amusements, With Various Other Matters*, April 1, 1789: 153. APS Online database, Proquest (College Park, Md.: University of Maryland at College Park) http:proquest.com/ (accessed December 24, 2003).

9. Ibid., 3.

10. George Washington, "Letter to James Madison," May 5, 1789. *Teaching American History Document Library: Founding Era*, http:// teachingamericanhistory.org/library/index.asp?document=390 (accessed May 20, 2004).

11. James E. Pollard, *The Presidents and the Press* (New York: The Macmillan Company, 1947).

12. Ibid., 73.

13. Luther Mott, *A History of American Magazines: 1865–1885* (Cambridge, Mass.: The Belknap Press of Harvard University Press, 1957).

14. Ibid., 227–228.

15. Noble E. Cunningham Jr., *The Image of Thomas Jefferson in the Public Eye* (Charlottesville: University Press of Virginia, 1981).

16. Davis, *The Press*, 35.

17. Mark E. Kann, *The Gendering of American Politics: Founding Mothers, Founding Fathers, and Political Patriarchy* (Westport, Conn.: Praeger, 1999), 142.

18. Kathleen L. Endres, "Introduction," in *Women's Periodicals in the United States: Consumer Magazines*, ed. Kathleen L. Endres and Therese L. Lueck (Westport, Conn.: Greenwood Press, 1995).

19. Sammye Johnson, "The National Magazine: Or, Lady's Emporium," in *Women's Periodicals in the United States: Consumer Magazines*, ed. Kathleen L. Endres and Therese L. Lueck (Westport, Conn.: Greenwood Press, 1995), 251.

20. Ibid., 248.

21. Henry Louis Stephens, "Three to One You Don't Get It," *Vanity Fair*, September 1, 1860, 117. Reprinted in "Cartoons: Lincoln's and the Republicans," *Explore History: Cartoons from Harper's Weekly and Other Leading Journals*, HarpWeek, http://elections.harpweek.com/1860/cartoon-1860-Medium.asp?UniqueID=13&Year=1860 (accessed May 21, 2004).

22. "Abraham Lincoln," *Our Young Folks: An Illustrated Magazine for Boys and Girls* (1865–1873) (Boston, MA: June 1865) 1:6. APS Online database, ProQuest (College Park, Md.: University of Maryland at College Park) http://proquest.umi.com/pqdweb?did=410048891&Fmt=2&clientId=41143&RQT=309&VName=HNP (accessed December 24, 2003).

23. *Godey's Lady's Book and Magazine* (1854–1882) (New York: July 1865) 71:88. APS Online database, ProQuest (College Park, Md.: University of Maryland at College Park) http://proquest.umi.com/pqdweb?did=336771391&Fmt=2&clientId=41143&RQT=309&VName=HNP (accessed December 24, 2003).

24. Pollard, *The Presidents*, 285.

25. Ibid., 286.

26. Ibid.

27. John C. Merrill, "How Time Stereotyped Three U.S. Presidents," *Journalism Quarterly* 42 (1965):563–570.

28. Fred Fedler, Mike Meeske, and Joe Hall, "Time Magazine Revisited: Presidential Stereotypes Persist," *Journalism Quarterly* 56 (1979): 353–359.

29. Merrill, "How Time Stereotyped," 567–568.

30. William H. Taft, *American Magazines for the 1980s* (New York: Hastings House, 1982).

31. F. A. Emery, "A Presidential Epigram," in *A Cavalcade of Colliers*, ed. Kenneth McArdle (New York: A. S. Barnes and Company, 1959), 73.

32. Mark Neuzil, "Hearst, Roosevelt, and the Muckrake Speech of 1906," *Journalism and Mass Communication Quarterly* 73 (1996):33–34.

33. James P. Wood, *Magazines in the United States; Their Social and Economic Influence* (New York: Ronald Press Company, 1949), 141.

34. James L. C. Ford, *Magazines for Millions* (Carbondale: Southern Illinois University Press, 1969), 173.

35. Kathleen L. Endres, "Women's Home Companion," *Women's Periodicals in the United States: Consumer Magazines*, ed. Kathleen L. Endres and Therese L. Lueck (Westport, Conn.: Greenwood Press, 1995), 444–455.

36. Charles Mertz, "Silent Mr. Coolidge," *The New Republic* June 2, 1926:51–54.

37. "Just How Silent is Mr. Coolidge?" *Literary Digest* June 19, 1926:40.

38. Ibid., 40–42.

39. Waterman, Wright, and St. Clair, *Image-Is-Everything*, 33.

40. "Extry! Mr. Coolidge is Learning to Play," *Literary Digest* August 21, 1926:42–48.

41. "How President Coolidge Keeps Fit," *Literary Digest* November 10, 1923:61.

42. "Exposing the President as a Worm Fisherman," *Literary Digest* June 9, 1927:38.

43. Waterman, Wright, and St. Clair, *Image-Is-Everything*, 28.

44. "Man of the Year," *Time Magazine*, January 5, 1942, 13.

45. Waterman, Wright, and St. Clair, *Image-Is-Everything*, 38.

46. John Hellman, *The Kennedy Obsession: The American Myth of JFK* (New York: Columbia University Press, 1997), 38.

47. Hellman, *The Kennedy Obsession.*

48. Ibid., 132–133.

49. See notes 4 and 5 above.

50. Linda Czuba Brigance, "For One Brief Shining Moment: Choosing to Remember Camelot," *Studies in Popular Culture* 25 (2003), http://pcasacas.org/SPC/spcissues/25.3/Brigance.htm (accessed December 20, 2003).

51. See note 4 above.

52. Ibid., 179.

53. See note 31 above.

54. Kenneth Crawford, "Him, Her, and LBJ," *Newsweek*, May 11, 1964, 34.

55. AmericanPresident.Org, "Office of Communications (EOP, The White House Office)," http://www.americanpresident.org/action/orgchart/administration_units/officeofcommunications/ (accessed March 24, 2005).

56. Peter Carlson, "Elvis Meets Nixon," *The Washington Post*, October 2, 1988, final ed., W81.

57. John Orman, "Covering the American Presidency: Valenced Reporting in the Periodical Press, 1980–1982," *Presidential Studies Quarterly* 14 (1984):381–390.

58. See note 5 above.

59. "Man of the Year: I'm Jimmy Carter, and . . ." *Time*, January 3, 1977, 11–21.

60. Lance Morrow, "Yankee Doodle Magic: What Makes Reagan So Remarkably Popular a President?" *Time*, July 7, 1986, 12–16.

61. West and Orman, 48.

62. "Brave Ron is Still 'Swingin,'" *Globe*, December 3, 1996, p. 43.

63. "Brave Reagan's Still Smiling," *Star*, November 11, 1995.

64. See note 3 above.

65. Waterman, Wright, and St. Clair, *Image-Is-Everything*, 61.

66. Curry Kirkpatrick, "Playing in the Bush League," *Sports Illustrated*, August 19, 1991, 32.

67. See note 2 above.

68. Jules Witcover, "Where We Went Wrong," in *The Media and Morality*, ed. Robert M. Baird, William E. Loges, and Stuart E. Rosenbaum (Amherst, Mass.: Prometheus Books, 1999), 121–132.

69. Ibid., 128.

70. Richard Fox and Robert W. Van Sickel, *Tabloid Justice: Criminal Justice in an Age of Media Frenzy* (Boulder, Colo.: Lynne Rienner Publishers, 2000).

71. Ibid., 64.

72. Paletz, *Media in American Politics*, 76.

73. Stephen Perrine, "All the President's Menus: Lessons from B. Clinton's Eating Habits," *Men's Health* January/February 1994.

74. Rick Reilly, "Get a New Game, Bubba; B. Clinton's Jogging," *Sports Illustrated*, November 16, 1992, 78.

75. Alexander Wolff, "The First Fan: B. Clinton and Arkansas Razorbacks Basketball Team," *Sports Illustrated*, March 21, 1994, 24–26.

76. "How Laura Bush Saved George W from the Bottle," *Globe*, April 22, 2000, p. 4.

77. "The Night I Got Drunk with George Bush," *Star*, March 27, 2001, p. 6.

78. "Is Our Children Learning?" *Globe*, October 30, 2002, 9.

79. "Bush Shows His Hand of Strength," *Globe*, October 9, 2001, 14.

80. "In Safe Hands," *Globe*, October 9, 2001.

81. Peggy Noonan, "Be Proud of What We Stand For," *Ladies' Home Journal*, October 2003, 118.

82. Don Yaeger, "Q&A: George W. Bush: Interview with George W. Bush," *Sports Illustrated*, September 29, 2003, 45–46.

CHAPTER 10

POLITICAL CARTOONS AND COMIC STRIPS

SANDRA CZERNEK

If one picture can be worth a thousand words, then cartoons and comic strips have tremendous storytelling potential. The artist may amuse, mock, or provoke in telling a tale through visual imagery. In political cartoons, artists attempt to comment on an immediate—and often temporary—issue. Many of their works, however, have left lasting impressions on posterity.

The United States is often personified in its president. Along with the character of "Uncle Sam," the president is a universally recognized symbol of America—for good and for bad. This chapter will examine the presidents as portrayed in cartoons and comic strips throughout the nation's history.

The Early Republic

There are few cartoons available from the Early Republic period because of the expense of engravings and the shortage of newsprint. The third president, Thomas Jefferson, was often accused of democratic extremism—conservative contemporaries were especially concerned with his support of the French Revolution. Small wonder, then, that a cartoon entitled "The Providential Detection" appeared after the presidential election of 1796. The anonymous (undoubtedly Federalist) artist shows an eagle stopping Jefferson from destroying the U.S. Constitution by throwing it into the flames at the "Altar of Gallic Despotism." This is an early example of the power of a cartoon—even an illiterate could understand the artist's message.[1]

Before the War of 1812, the young nation was beset by many external threats, and political cartoons reflected these preoccupations. After the war, however, and especially after the Era of Good Feelings, the national outlook changed. Americans were more confident, more relaxed, and much more willing to laugh at their elected officials. Commercial lithography became feasible during the 1820s and made reproduction of pictures faster and cheaper than ever. The advances in lithography coincided with the administration of a political giant—Andrew Jackson.[2]

From Jackson to Lincoln

Andrew Jackson was a cartoonist's dream. In particular, his face lent itself to caricature. Jackson was a military hero and a rough-hewn product of the frontier. He acted on strong, sometimes violent, passions throughout his life and never mellowed with age. Because of his well-known stubbornness, opponents labeled him a "jackass," but Jackson turned the insult to his advantage by using a donkey as his campaign symbol. By the end of his first term, artists often drew donkeys with Jackson's face to represent presidential obstinacy on issues. One famous cartoon even has a pack of dogs howling tribute to Jackson as "the greatest and best ass we ever knew!" It would be difficult to imagine such crass statements in print about any of Jackson's six predecessors—popular culture was already reflecting the leveling effect of Jacksonian democracy.

Jackson's personality and effect on the role of the presidency naturally led to opposition. As fitting for the enemies of kings, the other side were called "Whigs." Whig sympathizers delighted in portraying Jackson in a variety of unflattering roles, most commonly as "King Andrew I." In oddly anachronistic outfits of both Carolingian and Tudor adornments, Jackson is often portrayed with a royal scepter in one hand and a veto in the other. The Constitution is typically under his foot. Slightly less sarcastic cartoons depict Jackson as an old woman cleaning his "Kitchen Cabinet" of rats after the Peggy Eaton affair and as a mother feeding her infant son— successor Martin Van Buren. Martin Van Buren was also drawn as a fox in numerous cartoons of the era, in reference to his nickname, the "Sly Fox of Kinderhook," and to his shrewd political acumen.

Over the next two decades, presidents would struggle with the issues of slavery and sectionalism. The chief executives appeared to be either unwilling or unable to deal with the problems that confronted the nation. The leadership void thus provided artists with plenty of situations to mock. The most humorous cartoons were produced by Henry Louis Stephens for the magazine *Vanity Fair*. Stephens did a series of caricatures of the fifteenth president, James Buchanan. Buchanan was the only confirmed bachelor to reside in the White House and was mockingly called "Miss Nancy" for his effeminate mannerisms. In a classic illustration of the popular view of Buchanan, *Vanity Fair* ran a cartoon in its issue of January 7, 1860, entitled "The Bewildered Old Woman."[3] Buchanan appears as an elderly matron, complete with dress, apron, and bonnet, running from an impending storm. The caption begins

President James Buchanan as the Bewildered Old Woman. (University of Michigan Making of America collection)

"Sakes Alive! I know no North, no South, no East, no West—no Nothing!" The quote is a reference to the famous Henry Clay statement of nationalism—with a new, sad twist.

Abraham Lincoln

No figure would bear the brunt of caricature more than 1860 president-elect Abraham Lincoln. From a modern perspective, it is difficult to imagine anyone criticizing or mocking a figure so universally admired, yet Lincoln would be the focus of more cartoon humor than any other president before him. By 1860, most newspapers were running illustrations with their texts.[4] Lincoln's physical appearance was easily mocked. He was very tall and lanky, with strikingly gaunt facial features. Not surprisingly, artists with Confederate sympathies portrayed Lincoln in the most venomous fashion.

Hundreds of caricatures of Lincoln were published between 1860 and 1865, especially in popular venues such as *Harper's Weekly*, *Vanity Fair*, and *Frank Leslie's Illustrated Newspaper*. Artist Frank Bellew's elongated caricature of Lincoln in *Harper's Weekly* of November 26, 1864, is a testament to the man's dominating presence. In "Long Abraham Lincoln, A Little Longer" the president literally and figuratively towers over his era.[5]

One of the few artists who genuinely appreciated Lincoln before he was assassinated was Thomas Nast. Nast had met the new president in early 1861 and would remain an unabashed supporter of Lincoln, the Union, and the Republican Party throughout his life. His pointed sarcasm would have numerous targets, but he never caricatured Lincoln. His cartoons in *Harper's Weekly* deriding Lincoln's 1864 election opponents are believed to have garnered thousands of votes for the incumbent.[6]

In a Christmas cartoon of 1864, Nast draws Lincoln as a magnanimous host of a national dinner, extending his arm to invite Southern leaders to take their rightful place at the table. The picture is beautifully done, with intricate detail, and has a religious quality to it. Lincoln's sweet, forgiving nature is evident and seems to portend his status as a martyr within four months.

The living Lincoln had been the perfect subject for artists until his assassination. After April 15, 1865, portrayal of Lincoln as anything less than the Great Emancipator or the Savior of the Union seemed sacrilegious. What an irony—Lincoln was certainly one of the wittiest and most self-deprecating of all American presidents; that there are no posthumous cartoons that mocked him would have surely amused him.[7]

Lincoln's transformation from man to monument was rapid. Cartoonists perceived the sadness now associated with Lincoln and needed subjects worthy of their satire. How fortunate that the Gilded Age was at hand! The period between 1865 and 1896 was marked by a series of uninspiring presidents that was the sorry equal to the era between Jackson and Lincoln. Cartooning was about to enter its heyday.

Andrew Johnson

Lincoln's unfortunate successor, Andrew Johnson, is remembered as the first president to have impeachment charges brought against him. Johnson had the unenviable task of dealing with the complex issues of the Reconstruction. Initial support for Johnson waned as he appeared to appease the South and move away from ensuring civil rights for former slaves. The progression of popular opinion turning against Johnson is reflected in the cartoons of the era, especially in those of Thomas Nast.

Nast reflected popular sentiments toward Johnson. Many former Johnson supporters saw him as a traitor, and his offensive public statements were bitterly resented. Cartoons associating Johnson with the Ku Klux Klan in the defeated Confederate states tapped popular beliefs about Johnson's own Southern background. As with the Whigs of the Jackson era, many people feared that Johnson was setting himself up as a king or dictator.[6] Nast rarely used contemporary popular culture references and instead relied on classical allusions. In March 1867, in one of his first cartoons of Johnson, entitled "Amphitheatrum Johnsonianum,"[8] Nast portrayed him as an indifferent Roman emperor watching a race riot in New Orleans. Later that year, he cast the president as Medusa in "Southern Justice."[9] Nast's fondness for Shakespeare is revealed in "Reconstruction and How It Works," with a parody of Johnson as Iago beguiling a black Union veteran as Othello.[7] The constant image of Johnson is one of contempt—just look at the furrowed brow and scowling mouth. Such negative depictions of a president would not be seen again until Richard Nixon assumed the office.

Ulysses S. Grant

As early as February 1864, Nast had demonstrated his admiration for Ulysses S. Grant. In "Columbia Decorating Grant,"[10] Nast celebrates the general who has just been acknowledged by Congress for his string of Union victories.[11] Nast would remain a supporter of Grant even after corruption was revealed about members of his administration. However, other cartoonists were not as blind to Grant's faults. Grant was caricatured as a drunkard, a thief, and a loafer by many artists. Grant was also rumored to be fond of fast horses, expensive cigars, and whiskey—charges that had followed him since his service in the Mexican War.[12]

The public would be bombarded with competing images in the 1872 election, referred to by Paine as "a campaign of caricature—the first great battle of pictures ever known in America."[13] Initially good-natured humor targeted both Horace Greeley, the Democratic candidate, and the Republican incumbent Grant. As Morgan's portrayals of Grant became more pointed, however, Nast's depictions of Greeley became equally scurrilous. Grant was shown as a leering Belshazzar on a throne, a drunken dancer before "Boss" Tweed, and an embezzler. Greeley was portrayed as the candidate of ex-Confederates, Tammany grafters, eccentrics, and any group unworthy of citizenship.[14] As the campaign wore on, the viciousness of the cartoons dismayed many responsible journalists. According to the respectable press, the pictures went too far—and partisan audiences loved them for it.

The Gilded Age

The Gilded Age presidents could never be called inspiring or charismatic. They were competent, but common. In an era known for widespread business and political corruption, these men squandered numerous opportunities to demonstrate the strength to stem the tide. Amazingly, considering the quality of the presidents, Americans expressed an interest in their leaders that defies logic. Perhaps the shift in cartoon content can explain this phenomenon.

As Thomas Nast's influence declined, other cartoonists caught the nation's attention. Both *Puck* (pro-Democratic party) and *Judge* (pro-Republican party) were magazines that used artists who were beginning to exploit popular culture to lampoon their political foils.[7] Artists such as Joseph Keppler and Frank Beard had a wealth of incipient fare from which to choose. The price of publication was also now a factor: A reader would have to have paid thirty-five cents to see a couple of black and white Nast prints, but for a mere dime one could get three full color lithographs of Keppler's in *Puck*. The cover price and increasing popular culture references quite naturally expanded readership to a large middle class. A golden age of presidential cartoons was at hand.

Gilded Age cartoonists apparently never tired of gender bending their targets. One of the first, and funniest, cartoons was Keppler's "Forbidding the Banns" which appeared in *Puck* on August 25, 1880.[15] James A. Garfield is portrayed as a demure, blushing bride in the process of marrying groom Uncle Sam. An objector rushes in to stop the wedding ceremony with the baby "Credit Mobilier" in his arms. (Garfield was rumored to have profited from the scandal.) The obvious question of illegitimacy was seen as shocking and, of course, wickedly funny. The age was also obsessed with spectator and participatory sports. Political contests were often depicted as boxing or tennis matches, baseball or football games, or bicycle races. Other types of competition—such as dog shows or country fair exhibitions—allowed the reader to see a president as a poodle or a pumpkin.[16] In one of the silliest cartoons of the era, Keppler drew several presidential hopefuls in a garish 1884 cartoon entitled "The Contest of Beauty."[17] Among the candidates, the lovely Miss Chester A. Arthur appears to receive the most votes in her ballot box.

President Grover Cleveland looked like a cartoon creation. With his corpulent frame and oversized head, he was easily depicted in any number of absurd situations. Cleveland was visually linked with numerous popular culture references. In this era of amusement parks, shows and spectacles, and all sorts of silliness, Cleveland and his contemporaries were perfectly suited as players in the game of politics. Frank Beard mocked Cleveland's 1884 election chances by depicting him on a merry-go-round along with six Democratic predecessors who lost.[18] *Uncle Tom's Cabin* was the most popular melodrama of the nineteenth century; artist Bernhard Gillam tapped the public's familiarity with it by drawing the demise of the Cleveland administration in "The Last Scene in Uncle Grover's Cabin" for *Judge* in 1889.[19] In another cartoon, emulating the typical daredevil stunts of the era, Cleveland is a tightrope walker attempting to cross Niagara Falls while balancing issues and colleagues in "Cleveland Will Have a Walk-Over."[20]

P. T. Barnum also had a strong influence in American popular culture during the Gilded Age; not surprisingly, cartoonists found obvious ideas for caricature with numerous circus and freak show references. Gillam mocked Cleveland's girth by consistently drawing him as Jumbo, "Sacred Civil Service Reform White Elephant." Cleveland's entire reelection effort was easily portrayed as a traveling circus.[20] The cartoons of the Gilded Age reflect the levity of this period in American history. Amazingly, in the last three decades of the nineteenth century, voter participation reached an all-time high. Eighty percent of eligible voters went to the polls; politics had clearly become our favorite sport.[21]

Theodore Roosevelt

If politics became a sport at the beginning of the twentieth century, one man would attempt to make it his own amusement park in September 1901. On William McKinley's assassination, Vice President Theodore Roosevelt remarked, "It is a dreadful thing to come into the presidency in this way. But it would be a far worse thing to be morbid about it." No one could ever accuse Teddy Roosevelt of being morbid about anything, and he intended to enjoy his time in the White House. The nation and its artists were welcome to come along for the ride.

Roosevelt would shatter outdated notions of dignity that had been cultivated by every president since Rutherford B. Hayes. He embodied the new middle-class lifestyle—enjoyment of leisure, self-improvement, and creature comforts—and reflected their values like a mirror. Teddy would change expectations of the presidency and would deliberately enlist the media to help him market this new image.[22]

Roosevelt would sustain cartoonists for years. His features were relatively easy to draw—the close-cropped moustache, round eyeglasses, and the trademark grin were instantly recognizable to all Americans. In his typically good-natured fashion, Teddy rarely took offense at cartoons that mocked him. He was known to have been annoyed at only one cartoon, which it showed him mounting a horse with the wrong foot.[1]

Few, if any, presidents possessed Roosevelt's ability to coin a phrase. Catchy lines such as "rough riders," "muckrakers," "bull moose," and "speak softly and carry a big stick" naturally translated to visual interpretations.[23] From saving bears to busting trusts, Teddy's manic persona jumped from every page. A fitting tribute is found in Jay "Ding" Darling's "The Long, Long Trail."[24] Drawn at the time of his death in 1919, we see the old cowboy riding a spectral horse into the clouds. He is shouting and waving his hat goodbye, and he appears to have more energy in death than most people could ever hope to have while alive.

© 1999 J.N. "Ding" Darling Foundation

Jay "Ding" Darling's tribute to Theodore Roosevelt (J. N. "Ding" Darling)

Franklin Delano Roosevelt

During World War I, President Woodrow Wilson established the Committee on Public Information (CPI) to manage news about the war. As part of the CPI, a Bureau of Cartoons was created to encourage artists to use their craft to support the war effort (and sell more war bonds). When cartoonists become cheerleaders, it is unlikely that their work will lampoon presidents, or much of anything else. After Wilson, the presidents of the 1920s were a group of dutiful dullards worthy of the Gilded Age. Not until another Roosevelt came along would cartoonists return to the White House with enthusiasm.

Franklin Delano Roosevelt began his presidency in 1933 as the nation was mired in the Great Depression. The daunting economic circumstances would have challenged even the most competent leader, and Roosevelt gave no indication that he was qualified to handle the task before him. Most early observers commented on his charming, but "light" personality and openly wondered if he could be taken seriously. He could indeed.

Roosevelt's "New Deal" resulted in a number of new governmental agencies created to address the problems of the day. Some Americans resented the direction of Roosevelt's program and believed it smacked of socialism. The "alphabet soup" of the various agencies was an easy target for cartoonists. The majority of cartoonists were conservative, or at least their editors were;[25] thus, "New Deal Tyranny" was portrayed as an ominous Trojan horse at the gate of the Constitution, or on a less sinister note, Roosevelt was a benign kindergarten teacher leading his young students in a game of ring-around-the-rosy. The comic strip creator of Little Orphan Annie, Harold Gray, was anti-Roosevelt and anti–New Deal and he expressed these views through his character, Daddy Warbucks. Daddy even suffered a heart attack when Roosevelt was nominated for a fourth term but was miraculously revived after Roosevelt died. Roosevelt's jaunty air and toothy grin were accompanied by the ever-present cigarette holder—a symbol of his social status. Roosevelt was also mocked for the activism of his wife Eleanor, who challenged traditional notions of the proper role of a first lady.[26]

John F. Kennedy

After World War II, syndication would become a factor in the cartoon business. The syndicates would choose which cartoons would be published largely based on a broad, mostly inoffensive appeal.[27] The unique, often provocative opinions of freelance artists were no longer welcomed. As a result, political cartoons became predictable and gag-oriented during the 1950s.[28] Harry Truman playing a piano and Ike swinging a golf club would be standard fare in this vanilla era—even the dynamic John F. Kennedy couldn't shake the artistic doldrums.

Kennedy had a radiant, cultured wife; two beautiful children; and an active extended family. His personal charisma and wit easily won over members of the media, and cartoonists were no exception. Their depictions of Kennedy were very flattering and "utterly boring as cartoons and caricatures.[29] Even the humor magazine *Mad* reserved its acerbic wit when dealing with the Kennedys. *Mad* often used popular tunes for its parodies; in a feature on Kennedy, Gilbert and Sullivan's lighthearted operetta *HMS Pinafore* is the backdrop on the first family. Perhaps it was just easier to mock Cold War antagonists such as Fidel Castro or Nikita Khrushchev than the beloved Kennedy clan.

Whether the kid-glove treatment by cartoonists would have continued for Kennedy can never be known. Kennedy's tragic assassination stunned the nation on November 22, 1963. Famed cartoonist Bill Mauldin captured the nation's grief in one of the most powerful cartoons in United States history. The muted simplicity of Abraham Lincoln with head in hands is beautifully eloquent.[30] The two presidents are often equated in the national consciousness: both dealt with national crises, civil rights for African-Americans, and becoming martyrs in their primes.[7]

Lyndon B. Johnson

With Lyndon B. Johnson's presidency, the fond, courteous attitude towards the president came to an abrupt end. Johnson enjoyed a brief honeymoon period, but his escalation of the conflict in Vietnam would prove his undoing. Despite his significant accomplishments in domestic affairs, Johnson became a visible symbol of the wrenching effect of the war on the American psyche. David Levine parodied a famous Johnson moment—lifting his shirt to show a scar from recent surgery. Levine drew the scar in the shape of Vietnam. An undignified presidential gaffe was now immortalized in popular culture.

Richard M. Nixon

Although Vietnam would prove to be political quicksand for Johnson, it also marked a turning point for cartooning. For the first time, mainstream cartoonists openly opposed governmental policy on a war.[1] Then came Richard Nixon. To cartoonists, Nixon was "a gift from the gods."[31] His resume included blatant red-baiting, questionable political deals, and a general seediness of character; the nickname "Tricky Dick" said it all. In addition, the five o'clock shadow, beady eyes, and heavy jowls delighted caricaturists. Nixon was as easy to draw as a Lincoln or a Roosevelt, and without any of the redeeming qualities that might temper an artist's poison pen. Nixon would come to symbolize all that Americans don't want in a leader—the "anti-Lincoln" in popular culture.

The presidency of Richard Nixon in general, and the Watergate scandal in particular, would usher in another golden age of cartooning. Not since the Gilded Age had so many absurd situations come under public scrutiny. Artists such as Herbert Block (Herblock), Patrick Oliphant, Doug Marlette, and Mike Peters had plenty of White House transgressions from which to choose. Cartoonist Paul Conrad alone drew more than one hundred Watergate-related cartoons between 1972 and 1974. The Pulitzer Prize winner earned a spot on Nixon's infamous "enemies list" for his body of work—the only cartoonist to be so honored.[1]

A young comic strip artist would be forever grateful to Nixon and his foibles. Garry Trudeau's groundbreaking "Doonesbury" owed a debt to Walt Kelly's "Pogo" comic strip, which had dared to stand up to Senator Joseph McCarthy in the early 1950s. "Doonesbury" would reflect the growing mistrust of elected officials that was now common among Baby Boomers. Since its debut in October 1970, more than sixty million readers have watched characters such as Joanie Caucus and Zonker Harris react to contemporary events. Trudeau would win the Pulitzer Prize in 1975—the first one for editorial cartooning ever given to a comic strip. As President Gerald Ford said in 1976, "[t]here are only three major vehicles to keep us informed as to what is going on in Washington, the electronic media, the print media and Doonesbury and not necessarily in that order."[32]

Ronald Reagan

If artists made careers off of Richard Nixon, "they grew fat and sassy during the administration of Ronald Reagan."[33] As they had with Teddy Roosevelt, cartoonists found a likable and easy subject for their creations. Unlike Teddy, however, Reagan was a product of Tinseltown. His career as an actor predictably inspired a number of cartoons based on Hollywood themes. The most common motif found him as a cowboy to tap familiarity with Reagan's numerous B westerns and television's *Death Valley Days*. Other metaphors were inspired by his association with "The Gipper" of Notre Dame lore and, on a lighter note, former costar Bonzo, the chimpanzee.[34]

Although popular culture references in cartoons had begun during the Gilded Age, their use would accelerate during the Reagan years. In particular, movies would be a common denominator for late-twentieth-century artists. The popular *Star Wars* films were easily translated into caricature by Reagan's own rhetoric: the antimissile defense as "Star Wars" and the Soviet Union as the "evil empire." Was anyone really surprised to see Andrei Gromyko as Darth Vader? Reagan was also portrayed as baseball player Roy Hobbs in *The Natural*—with a twist: the "Wonder Boy" bat became "Commie Basher." Sylvester Stallone's *Rambo* character naturally became "Ronbo" Reagan, who could single-handedly destroy all Cold War enemies.[7]

The movie references would continue throughout Reagan's second term, but with more caustic tones. The degree of Reagan's involvement in the Iran-Contra affair provided plenty of fodder for cartoonists. Reagan often seemed oblivious to the details of his support for rebel fighters in Nicaragua. The movie *The Untouchables* became "The Uncontrollables," with Reagan in the role of "the amnesiac." Oliver Stone's *Platoon* became *Buffoon*, with Reagan shooting himself in the foot. The tag line was telling and a play on the Hiram Johnson's famous quotation about truth being the first casualty of war: "the first casualty of a secret war is intelligence."[35]

Reagan's intellectual abilities had been in question long before the Iran-Contra scandal. As early as 1981, Garry Trudeau had sent television reporter Roland Hedly on a mission in search of Reagan's brain. As Reagan appeared more bemused with the passing years, artists noted his decline in their caricatures. Wrinkles and wattles became more pronounced, the neck and head grew smaller, and the suits got bigger. Only the trademark pompadour seemed immune to the ravages of time.[33]

George H. W. Bush

In November 1988, Reagan's vice president, George H. W. Bush, would win the presidential election. By this time, *Doonesbury's* favorite scenario was a four-panel strip with the White House in each panel. With these, Trudeau had been mocking every president since Nixon with his dialogues. In 1988, Bush did not wait for his turn and said of Trudeau, "He speaks for a bunch of Brie-tasting, Chardonnay-sipping elitists." Trudeau responded by drawing Bush as an invisible man with an evil twin and Vice President Dan Quayle as a floating feather. Fellow liberal cartoonist Pat Oliphant depicted Bush as an unsuccessful Pied Piper trying to charm rats of recession, deficit, and poverty. Perhaps illustrating the general coarsening of American culture, Oliphant also drew a "barf purse" on Bush's arm—a reference to an unfortunate incident in which the president vomited at a Japanese state dinner. So much for the dignity of the office.[36]

Coming to the aid of conservatives was the comic strip *Mallard Fillmore*, which debuted in 1991. Mallard is a duck hired as a reporter for WFDR to fill the station's "Amphibious-American" quota. The name is a play on words of the nation's thirteenth president, the hopelessly forgettable Millard Fillmore. Creator Bruce Tinsley uses Mallard to point out absurdities of political correctness, liberal media, and specifically the Democratic Party. Mallard Fillmore's growth in popularity coincides with a frequent target of conservative barbs in the 1990s—President Bill Clinton.

William Clinton

Bill Clinton was the first Baby Boomer president and was as fond of popular culture as any member of that generation. Before the 1992 presidential election, Clinton, an admirer of Elvis Presley, appeared on *The Arsenio Hall Show* during the campaign and enthusiastically performed Presley's "Heartbreak Hotel" on saxophone for a delighted national audience. Small wonder he was often depicted as a musician, complete with sunglasses and saxophone, in many caricatures. Gentle ribbing would give way to nastier humor later in Clinton's tenure. His bulbous nose and square jaw had always been easy to mock; now the ever-present bags under his eyes became symbols of the baggage he brought from Arkansas. Issues ranging from questionable real estate deals to numerous extramarital affairs hounded Clinton and provided fodder for artists. First Lady Hillary Rodham Clinton was also targeted because of her active, prominent role in her husband's administration. Not since the New Deal era had a first lady been featured in so many cartoons. Hillary was portrayed in a variety of unflattering roles: malicious figure skater Tonya Harding, husband-mutilator Lorena Bobbitt, Cat Woman, and even Richard Nixon.[33]

George W. Bush

As the nation wearied of the endless speculation on the president's affair with a White House intern, *Mallard Fillmore* summed up the end of the Clinton years for many Americans. Mallard speculated that it would take at least two months to fumigate the Oval Office before a Clinton successor could be inaugurated. That man, George W. Bush, would also have to deal with another wise-cracking bird. The comic strip *This Modern World* features a sarcastic penguin named Sparky who never misses an opportunity to point out absurdities of the Bush administration. President Bush is often depicted as a befuddled front man for Vice President Dick Cheney, who tells him what to say to the public. *This Modern World* uses a breezy fifties clip-art format that contrasts with its sharp political satire. By the end of the decade, *This Modern World's* creator, Dan Perkins (aka Tom Tomorrow), had a new rival for presidential criticism—Aaron McGruder of *Boondocks*.

Boondocks debuted in 1997 and has been controversial from the beginning. The comic strip features two black adolescents who keep readers amused with their insights on racial issues, consumerism, and politics. After the terrorist attacks of September 11, 2001, few cartoonists were bold enough to poke fun at the Bush administration; McGruder was. He pulled no punches in questioning the "War on Terrorism." As early as the first week of October 2001, McGruder had his main character, Huey, calling the Federal Bureau of Investigation terrorism tip line to report former presidents Reagan and Bush for their support of Osama Bin Laden and the Taliban.

Although many readers recoil at the indelicacy of such suggestions, McGruder is actually in keeping with the long tradition of cartoonists and the presidency. Throughout our nation's history, cartoonists have been keeping leaders honest by forcing them off their thrones and pedestals. The cartoonists' visual mixtures of poignancy, humor, and ridicule are all elements for healthy popular culture and democracy. With the continuing consolidation of newspapers, the job market for cartoonists is shrinking. This is unfortunate for the republic; who will be left to point out our emperors are not wearing any clothes?

Notes

1. Stephen Hess and Sandy Northrop, *Drawn and Quartered: The History of American Political Cartoons* (Montgomery, Ala.: Elliott and Clark Publishing, 1996).

2. Stephen Becker, *Comic Art in America* (New York: Simon and Schuster, 1959).

3. "The Bewildered Old Woman," *Vanity Fair*, January 7, 1960.

4. Becker, *Comic Art*, 291.

5. Frank Bellew, "Long Abraham Lincoln, A Little Longer," *Harper's Weekly*, November 26, 1964.

6. Albert Bigelow Paine, *Thomas Nast: His Period and His Pictures* (Gloucester, Mass.: Harper and Row, 1967).

7. Fischer, Roger A. *Them Damned Pictures: Explorations in American Political Cartoon Art* (North Haven, Conn.: Shoe String Press, 1996).

8. Thomas Nast, "Amphitheatrum Johnsonianum," March 1867.

9. Thomas Nast, "Southern Justice," 1867.

10. Thomas Nast, "Columbia Decorating Grant," February 1864.

11. Fischer, *Them Damned Pictures*, 97.

12. Ibid., 229.

13. Paine, *Thomas Nast*, 247.

14. Ibid., 248.

15. Joseph Keppler, "Forbidding the Banns," *Puck*, August 25, 1880.

16. Fischer, *Them Damned Pictures*, 136.

17. Joseph Keppler, "The Contest of Beauty," 1884.

18. Fischer, *Them Damned Pictures*, 136.

19. Bernhard Gillam, "The Last Scene in Uncle Grover's Cabin," *Judge*, 1889.

20. Fischer, *Them Damned Pictures*, 137.

21. Joseph R. Conlin, *The American Past* (Belmont, Calif.: Thomson Learning, 2004).

22. Ibid., 497.

23. Hess and Northrup, *Drawn and Quartered*, 80.

24. Jay Darling, "The Long, Long Trail," 1919.

25. Hess and Northrup, *Drawn and Quartered*, 94.

26. Ibid., 96.

27. Ibid., 103.

28. Ibid., 113.

29. Ibid., 110.

30. Bill Mauldin, 1963.

31. Fischer, *Them Damned Pictures*, 208.

32. Hess and Northrup, *Drawn and Quartered*, 130.

33. Paul P. Somers Jr., *Editorial Cartooning and Caricature: A Reference Guide* (Westport, Conn.: Greenwood, 1998), 30.

34. Ibid., 31.

35. Fischer, *Them Damned Pictures*, 130.

36. Somers, *Editorial Cartooning*, 33.

CHAPTER 11

FILM

SCOTT F. STODDART

> He who screens the history makes the history. When it is attempted, the aim of the exercise is to teach simple patriotism to a people become so heterogeneous that many of them have little or nothing in common with one another, including, often, the English language.
> —Gore Vidal, *Screening History*, 1992

Speaking of the screening of American history in Hollywood cinema, Gore Vidal acknowledges its power to control audience thought. This process of screening is what Martin Scorsese believes is the seamless manipulation of images to create an American vision that coincides with the predominant order—culturally, politically, and cinematically. The effects of Hollywood's prescriptive agenda control the average spectator's understanding of democracy—particularly in respect to the screening of the president of the United States.

Although the president has been the subject of newsreels and documentary films since the election of Theodore Roosevelt in 1904, this chapter will examine fictional film representations of the president.[1] Until the late 1960s, the use of the president in Hollywood cinema fell into a series of patterns that resulted in a similar message: Regardless of the man, the president faces unthinkable obstacles and manages to succeed through careful determination and sheer conviction, leading to a filmic resolution that illustrates the proper workings of the democratic system. Since then, as the culture has become more distrustful of authority, Hollywood films have used the president to tell stories of flawed men who attempt to overcome their personal limitations to achieve the power of the office. Richard Shenkman believes that the "most frequent complaint about presidential movies is that they get the facts wrong," while "the producers, directors, and actors seldom get the presidential character right" (Shenkman 2002, xi). Through its deliberate use of formula, Hollywood film uses the president to represent an ideal American: Whether flawed or genuinely heroic, he is one who sacrifices all to benefit the majority.

The effect of this use depends on the specific story form that the film takes. There are three distinct types of presidential film: the biographical, the historical, and the fictional. Each of these portrays the president as the embodiment of American male virtues of grace under pressure: The "right" course of action, taken with a quiet faith in the principles of right, results in a firm commitment to the ideals of the United States. Finally, Hollywood films that focus on the men who have held the office of president typically reflect a patriotic zeal, even if they openly question the president's intentions while he's in office.

The Biographical Film

The biographical film (also known as the bio-pic) is the most typical genre used to depict the president of the United States. George F. Custen defines the genre in the following manner:

> The biographical film routinely integrates disparate historical episodes of selected individual lives into a nearly monochromatic Hollywood view of history. One way this integration occurs is through the construction of a highly conventionalized view of fame. These films build a pattern of narrative that is selective in its attention to profession, differential in the role it assigns to gender, and limited in historical settings. Another way the Hollywood view of history is integrated is through the studio's use of star images in the creation of the stories of famous people. (1992, 3)

Custen's definition is important here because it solidifies the ideological foundation of the presidential bio-pic. In constructing the bio-pic's narrative, the director consciously selects events to highlight the strengths of the presidential figure, implying that only those of strong character rise up to become president.

Playing off the mythology of the common man who represents America is John Ford's *Young Mr. Lincoln* (1939). The plot focuses on the young Abraham Lincoln (Henry Fonda) in the years before his presidency (roughly 1850–1858), when he practiced law in frontier Illinois. Filled with homespun humor, the film consciously uses the image of the younger Lincoln to foreshadow his future greatness. Ford's careful direction shows that this common fellow is the Lincoln who, when put to the test, would emerge as arguably the nation's greatest president.

Henry Fonda in *Young Mr. Lincoln* (1939) (AP/Wide World Photos)

The film opens with a title card displaying Rosemary Benet's "Nancy Hanks," a dramatic monologue supposedly by Lincoln's mother, who died when he was a boy. Yet Ford's Lincoln is in his early twenties, wooing the prettiest girl in the area, hoping to settle down as a lawyer. The girl's early death affects the young man deeply, and a visit to her graveside sets the stage for a series of dissolves against the frozen river; the ice flows from right-to-left—the opposite of the camera's tracking—signifying the young lawyer's struggles ahead. Lincoln sets out for Springfield to practice law.

A lengthy montage of a July Fourth festival shows Lincoln as a man of the people, participating fully in the affairs of the day: he judges a pie contest, wins a rail-splitting contest, and devises the scheme to prevent the champions from winning a tug-of-war. The encapsulated American history lesson, from the Revolutionary War vets at the lead of the parade to the image of Lady Liberty at the end, foreshadow Lincoln's own role in preserving the nation. The film frames Lincoln as an iconic American figure as well as a human being.

Fonda's performance is remarkable because of his slow, awkward manner; for instance, the shy quality he affects in meeting Mary Todd (Marjorie Weaver), and his clumsy efforts to dance with her make an underdog of Lincoln. Ford's camera assists in making the 5'10" Fonda appear taller than he was, using low angles for some sequences and employing high angles from Lincoln's 6'4" perspective, particularly in the courtroom, to make others appear smaller. Fonda appears uncomfortable in his dark suits, noticeably shorter in the cuffs, and he seems appropriately easygoing only when he reclines in his shirtsleeves—all to create the illusion of the gangly future president. Each of these qualities assists in resurrecting a Lincoln right out of American lore—so much so that when Ford dissolves from the retreating young Lincoln to the iconic statue of the president at the Lincoln Memorial in the film's closing (scored to "The Battle Hymn of the Republic") the spectator almost believes that the one image grew into the other.

Another example of a bio-pic is Henry King's *Wilson* (1944). Nominated for ten Oscars, this film begins in 1909 with Wilson as president of Princeton University. Rather than focusing on his domestic life, the film follows his rise as a politician as he uses his linguistic acumen to stun the crowds. In one sequence, Wilson speaks to a huge crowd of dubious supporters, whom he gradually wins over through wit and deliberate politicking. Most likely copying a technique used in Welles's *Citizen Kane* (1941), King shoots Wilson from a low camera angle, making Wilson appear more stately and presidential than academic (Staples 2002, 120).

The film's use of actual newsreel footage (showing the real Woodrow Wilson) and montage are its real innovations, enlivening the political background to show the events of Wilson's two boisterous elections (in 1912 and 1916) and his subsequent campaign to create and align American sympathies with the League of Nations. These sequences add vibrancy to the bio-pic process, blending the stature of Knox's performance with images of the real Wilson driving through the throngs in Paris and of the crowds greeting him on his whistle-stop campaign.

The film carefully examines the national sensation that erupted when widower Wilson married Edith Galt (Geraldine Fitzgerald), a Washington widow whose vivacious charm lifted the grieving Wilson out of his despair (Caroli 1995, 144). However, the film egregiously exorcises Edith's contribution to the presidency when she acted in Wilson's stead after he suffered a debilitating stroke in 1919. For the remaining 45 minutes of the film, Wilson is shown only once in a wheelchair, and thereafter with a cane, offering the image of a man who quickly conquered his physical limitations to lead his country,

Ralph Bellamy stars as Franklin Delano Roosevelt in *Sunrise at Campobello* (1960) (AP/Wide World Photos)

---

rather than that of the sickly man who actually was carted from the White House without the use of his left side. The film's patriotic conclusion, as the now-retired Wilson and Edith stroll out of the White House after taking leave of supporters and enemies alike, to the strains of "Hail to the Chief," makes an impressive backdrop to Zanuck's ideology—showing an able, misunderstood leader who wanted peace, rather than war—which was an odd political message to be making at the height of Franklin Roosevelt's pro-war defense against the Axis powers.

Sunrise at Campobello (1960) is actually a screening of Dore Schary's Broadway play—a conjectured account of Franklin Roosevelt's (Ralph Bellamy) bout with polio. The story focuses on the struggles Roosevelt experienced with his children, his political allies, and his mother. Franklin's children want the father who engaged them in adventurous sailing and swimming expeditions, and they each find themselves pushed aside by his illness and ambition to continue as a politician. His allies continue to inspire Franklin's political ambitions, and his secretary Missy Le Hand (Jean Hagen) and advisor Louis Howe (Hume Cronyn) each have bittersweet moments where they reveal their fears for his mental and physical well-being. Sara Delano Roosevelt (Ann Shoemaker) antagonizes the situation as she urges her son to retire from public life and to live as a squire at their Hyde Park estate. One particular confrontation between the two obstinate Roosevelts reflects the bitter frustration in each as they wrestle with their personal attitudes toward this illness.

In an age in which the marital discord of the Roosevelts is so well-known, revealed in books by Doris Kearns Goodwin (*No Ordinary Time*, 1995) and Blanche Wiesen Cook (in her 1993 multivolume biography of Eleanor), the film appears a little comical now as it sanitizes Eleanor and Franklin's marital situation: It does not depict any dissension between the spouses. Instead, the film goes a long way toward making Franklin's polio a test for their marriage, with the marriage becoming stronger and more secure as Franklin's struggle to walk continues. As the wheelchair-bound Roosevelt struggles to recapture his manhood and assert his political clout, the naturally shy Eleanor endeavors to become Franklin's "eyes and legs," as he sends her to make speeches on his behalf.

Ideologically, the film domesticates the Roosevelts so they appear to be a typical American family, representing all the virtues of the American spirit, even though they are obscenely privileged. Schary's screenplay uses every excuse to permit Franklin to speak the rhetoric of the politician, articulating his rage against the Republicans' Teapot Dome Scandal and wrestling to uphold the principles of Woodrow Wilson's League of Nations. However, the film is overwhelmingly about the Roosevelts's home life—how this disease interrupted Roosevelt's great career, and how it ultimately brought the whole family together. The story reflects the American spirit of the individual who learns that he cannot stand alone without the full support of his loving wife and his devoted children, embodying the solidarity of yet another American myth.

In contrast to these earlier films, Oliver Stone's *Nixon* (1995) works to dissect the psyche of the man in office. Using his signature style, Stone blends actual footage (newsreels, television news bites) with staged action in color and in black and white, framing the film with Nixon reflecting on his downfall from power the night before his resignation. Cutting back and forth between actual footage and restaged scenarios immerses Stone's audience violently in the story. The film employs two narrative plains. The first details Nixon's struggle to the presidency, spanning his loss to John F. Kennedy in 1960 through his resignation after Watergate. The second, told in a variety of fragmented flashbacks, details Nixon as a young man, including the deaths of his two brothers, his relationship with his mother, his courtship of Pat, and his rise as a politician through the Alger Hiss scandal.

In an ideological sense, Stone makes Nixon into a tragic figure—a fallen leader whose desire to be loved by Americans in a Kennedy-esque fashion caused his downfall; this runs counter to the more "presidential" hero of the previously mentioned bio-pics. The constant reflections on Nixon's childhood and his marital strife serve as Freudian explanations to the larger problem: Nixon was a man who let his desire for popularity dictate his conscience. Stone's simple reasoning is part of the reason the film struggled at the box office, as this vision makes his Nixon pathetic, sympathetic, and unlikable—unpresidential, to say the least. As *Nixon* draws to its conclusion, replicating the fallen president's farewell speech to his staff, Stone uses actual news footage of Nixon and his family crossing the White House lawn to his helicopter, combining the historical moment with the reenactment. Here, the real Nixon takes his final bow as he retreats from the office he disgraced to enter the history books as the one president who resigned the office.

Historical Drama

Historical dramas place the president in the background of a narrative designed to depict a historical moment. These films present the facts of the moment as accurate. In earlier films, the president often enters the action to lend an air of verisimilitude.

Much good scholarship discusses the use of Abraham Lincoln as a background figure during the silent era, particularly in Griffith's *Birth of a Nation* (1915). Bryan Rommel-Ruiz argues that "the images of union and family" guide the early use of Lincoln, attempting to link the president's struggle to maintain the nation in the tradition of a "family tragedy/ melodrama" (2002, 78). Griffith's use of Lincoln throughout his epic was not to show him as "the rabid abolitionist Southerners feared and reviled on the eve of the Civil War but a distraught father of a divided family and a noble leader who kept radicals at bay" (Rommel-Ruiz 2002, 82). The image of Lincoln helps to codify Griffith's idea of how America should be seen in this new century—a philosophy that viewed the country as a family of distinct personalities that came together under one flag because of a selfless leader.

More recently, however, the president's presence, although lending credence to the film's narrative, is often peripheral to the story taking center stage. In some cases, the president is the object of satire. Philip Kaufman's *The Right Stuff* (1983), adapted from Tom Wolfe's journalistic account of the birth of the American space program, attempts to relate the social history of the 1950s and 1960s as the space program separated from the armed services. With a satiric tone, it uses then-president Dwight D. Eisenhower (Robert Beer) and future president Lyndon Johnson (Donald Moffat) to comic advantage. Eisenhower sits in the background of many of the comically staged meetings of inept advisors, making off-color remarks about the Russians. Senator Lyndon B. Johnson takes charge in scenes that capture his cantankerous attitude, most notably in the sequence that records John Glenn's

(Ed Harris) orbit of the earth. When mechanical failure postpones Glenn's initial take-off, the film's Johnson insists on seeing Glenn's wife Annie (Mary Jo Deschanel) to offer support—on television. Annie, who suffered from severe stuttering, refuses, and the fellow astronauts support Glenn in his refusing Johnson access to his home. A cut to Johnson, seated in his limousine outside the Glenn house, shows him hollering obscenities; a cut outside the vehicle shows it rocking back and forth as Johnson thrashes about inside. Neither image shows the presidency in a favorable light, which makes the first astronauts appear more heroic. Maligning the office in this way, Kaufman's film questions the authority of the president to highlight the individualist ideologies embodied in the astronaut—a perfect film for the Reaganomic America of the 1980s.

Steven Spielberg's epic *Amistad* (1997) uses former president John Quincy Adams (Anthony Hopkins) to question President Martin Van Buren (Nigel Hawthorne) about what democracy means. Detailing the slave revolt that took place aboard a trader in 1839, the film vividly recreates the anger and inarticulate frustration that led the slave leader, Cinque (Djimon Hounsou), to massacre *Amistad*'s American crew. The central story, screened in the first hour and told mainly in African dialect, puts the spectator in the precarious situation of the slaves. When Adams is solicited to represent the slaves before the Supreme Court, in an effort to show that the brutal circumstances of slavery led them to murder, Hopkins's approach is both lively and mannered, bringing the courtroom portion of the drama to life, as he embodies a former president convinced that America can be just.

The image of politically ambitious Martin Van Buren (Nigel Hawthorne) openly questions the ethics of the office. Van Buren quietly sits in the background, knowing that a public stand on the issue could ruin his chances for reelection. However, Adams's victory in court does not assist "Old Kinderhook," and the difference in the men's styles speaks volumes about the image of the presidency: When the president does not take a stand for freedom and justice, he looks ridiculous; when the president gives his all to champion those who cannot speak for themselves, he represents all that is good about America.

Oliver Stone's *JFK* (1991), part crime drama, part courtroom drama, blends historical fact and hypothetical reality. When it was released, the film set off a controversy over the factual veracity of the narrative in regard to the Kennedy assassination and the subsequent Warren Commission investigation.[2] Critics particularly questioned the objectivity of the portrayal of Jim Garrison, the New Orleans district attorney who put Clay Shaw, a prominent Louisiana businessman, on trial for murdering John F. Kennedy. Almost all of the reviews by prominent law professors, historians, and news journalists claim that Stone should have paid less attention to Jim Garrison's original theory and more attention to the facts of the case.

Presidential Fiction

Presidential fictions involve the adaptation of a fictional narrative that places the president in a central role in the story, often creating one steeped in the ideology of the times. For example, *The Gorgeous Hussy* (Clarence Brown, 1936), based on Samuel Hopkins Adams's novel, recounts the actual effects of the 1828 election on the marriage of Andrew and Rachel Jackson (Lionel Barrymore and Beulah Bondi). However, the main story focuses on the many loves of Margaret O'Neal (Joan Crawford), a fictional niece, who promises the dying Rachel that she will assist in the duties of first lady (in real life, Rachel's niece Emily Donelson served as first lady). Margaret, called "Peg of the Pot-house" by the crones of Washington society, marries the young "Bow" Timberlake (Robert Taylor) when her love for John Randolph (Melvyn Douglas) goes unrequited. Widowed when Bow dies at sea, Peggy devotes her immediate life to running her father's inn, where she cares for the Jacksons once they arrive in Washington, D.C., to serve Andrew's term as a senator.

Just as in actual life, Washington society greets Rachel Jackson with sneers and jibes—her dress is inappropriate, and her manners are unquestionably common (Bondi's performance is touchingly comic, right down to Rachel's pipe-smoking). She serves as a mother figure for Peg, giving her advice to ignore the two-faced Washington society women—advice she cannot follow herself. As she grows weaker after Jackson's election to the presidency, she makes Peg promise to serve as first lady, to remind the new president to "not say 'ain't' and 'git.'"

Barrymore's performance as Jackson is both comic and bittersweet. He creates a genuine character of Jackson, who appears uncomfortable in stylish clothes, and who throws the manners of upper-crust society aside for common sense. In one sequence, he and Rachel are in bed, awakened by the newly married Bow and Peggy, who giggle from her room. In their nightshirts, Rachel and Jackson confront the young newlyweds, Jackson armed with his infamous dueling pistols. "Uncle Andy" eventually approves of the marriage, but warns the rascally Timberlake that he will have to answer to him if he makes Peggy unhappy. In another sequence, following the death of Rachel, Jackson and Peggy arrive at a church to see the newly installed window Andrew donated to the local church in her memory. As he begins to think of all that she meant to him, Jackson begins to sob, opening his heart to Peggy by claiming he cannot go on to rule the country without his Rachel. Peggy, echoing the remarks Rachel made on her deathbed, reminds Andrew that Rachel is with him, and that she is guiding his every move. The scene is touching, as it brings the outrageous Jackson into focus with the softer elements of the woman's picture, making Jackson into a real father figure, and one who can capably rule the affairs of state. Given the fact that the picture was made at the height of the Depression, Brown wants to show how the gossip of the Washington socialites cripples the true American spirit, which takes risks to preserve the American way.

Made during the early years of World War II, *The Howards of Virginia* (1940), based on Elizabeth Page's novel *Tree of Liberty* (1990), uses future president Thomas Jefferson to embody the nobility of the American spirit—one that overlooks the limitations of class to embrace the common man to represent a film of the second era. The film tells the story of Matt Howard (Cary Grant), a frontiersman, who grows up with Thomas Jefferson (Richard Carlson) as his dearest friend. The film follows the Howards as they marry and retreat to the wilds of Abershame County to build a plantation of their own and also follows Jefferson's rise to prominence as a statesman and politician.

Jefferson's depiction in the film is as an ideal American—one born of privilege who sees that democracy will not flourish in the new nation without equal opportunity. The film uses montage effectively to capture the historical upheavals of the early nation, particularly the Boston Massacre and the Boston Tea Party. Through it all, Jefferson is depicted as a noble gentleman, learned enough to compose the Declaration of Independence but common enough to enjoy the easy comfort of the Howard family.

In recent times, the genre has made the president more human. Peter Hunt's filmed version of Peter Stone and Sherman Edwards's Tony-winning musical *1776* (1972) deserves mention for its unconventional portrayal of two future presidents, openly questioning their characters. Every one of the congressional members dislikes John Adams (William Daniels), primarily because he is frustrated with the Continental Congress's lack of action. The chorus of statesmen sings "Sit down, John!" during the opening number, as Adams urges them to vote for independence. Thomas Jefferson (Ken Howard), happily married and polished in manner and style, plays the Congress like his violin as he takes control of the writing of the Declaration of Independence.

Openly satirizing the Oval Office, *Dick* (Fleming 1999) sets itself up as a teen comedy focusing on the exploits of Betsy Jobs (Kirsten Dunst) and Arlene Lorenzo (Michelle Williams) as they encounter Richard Nixon (Dan Hedaya) during a high school field trip in 1972. *Dick* is a satire of Nixon's image: It is more concerned with filmed treatments of the Nixon presidency and of the rekindled interest in 1970s pop culture than in actually examining Nixon himself. The self-reflexive nature of the film actually dissects the image of Nixon in Oliver Stone's *Nixon* (1995) and the depiction of the Watergate scandal set forth in *All The President's Men* (Pakula 1976). The film replaces both Stone's tortured iconoclast and Pakula's self-styled heroes of the free press who brought down the Nixon regime—Nixon is no more than a bumbling, failed father figure, the paternal elder who is misunderstood, and Woodward (Will Ferrell) and Bernstein (Bruce McCulloch) are the hapless dupes who care more for glory than for truth and justice.

Hedaya's depiction of Nixon is central to the film, and his tweaking of Hopkins's characterization of Nixon in Stone's film is clearly intentional. This Nixon is also helplessly paranoid—a bungler who goes about whining that nobody likes him. Of course, Fleming explains part of Nixon's paranoia by depicting him devouring the cookies that Betsy and Arlene make (these "Hello Dollies" are laced with Betsy's brother's stash of marijuana, hidden with the walnuts in the family kitchen). The cookies even assist in détente, as Nixon feeds them to a belligerent Brezhnev (Len Doncheff), who becomes loveable when he begins to sing the Jerry Herman standard. Nixon's frustration in not being adored by the youth of America (emphasized by Stone in the Lincoln Memorial sequence) leads him to become a confidante to the girls, and they begin to talk on the phone at night about the new world order—the girls even assist in making Nixon understand that the bombing of Cambodia is not good politics.

Of course, the scenario of this film is unlikely, and much of the satire must have been lost on the average teen viewer who patronized the film because it featured two popular teen television stars. Openly criticizing Nixon, the Watergate scandal, and Stone and Pakula's filmic renderings is a tough sell for an audience predominately born after 1975. Therefore, Fleming's film criticizes the powers that be, and the youth of America who allow the media to manipulate youth culture's role in the democracy, accepting all that is reported without becoming involved in the political process.

Another brand of presidential fiction is found in Mike Nichols's adaptation of *Primary Colors* (1998), based on a comic novel by Joel Klein. Klein was a reporter for *Newsweek* covering Bill Clinton's run for the White House in 1992. For his novel, Klein changed Clinton into Governor Jack Stanton—a natural candidate for office who is able to pull into his orbit young, talented, altruistic workers who believe in him body and soul. However, Klein draws a two-faced politician of the most dangerous kind in his image of the Clintonesque Stanton, as he reveals the man to be a shrewd deal-maker, an abominable husband, and a glutton in both its literal and figurative sense.

Nichols's film adaptation, written by his long-time colleague Elaine May, focuses on the enigma of Stanton (John Travolta), channeled through Henry Burton (Adrian Lester)—a green campaign manager now working with seasoned pros, including the smooth-talking Richard Jemmons (Billy Bob Thorton) and the trash-talking Libby Holden (Kathy Bates). As Burton becomes more embroiled in the day-to-day operations of the campaign, his political ideology becomes sullied, with him finding his only relief in speaking frankly to Staunton's intelligent, though long-suffering, wife, Susan (Emma Thompson). Along the way, Burton finds that the rumors concerning Stanton's infidelities are true, and that even though the governor is a genius at the art of politics, he is a contemptible human being. In light of Bill Clinton's rapid ascent to national fame and his eventual humiliation for indiscretions similar to those portrayed in the movie, the novel and film provide a rather cynical rethinking of the forty-second president.

Whether the performance by an actor as a president is found to be effective or not may not be all that important; what is important is how the film uses the president to tell its story. Each film discussed here or listed in the filmography documents the culture's attitude toward its president. From seeing the president as the cornerstone of democratic order to cynically questioning his ability to govern, Hollywood has reflected America's attitude toward its president.

Notes

1. Motion picture newsreels were one important feature of mass communication from the 1920s until the advent of television news in the 1950s. According to the Library of Congress, by 1930, some eighty-five million Americans attended one of roughly seventeen thousand movie theaters each week. At most screenings, spectators saw newsreels—short subject films, updated twice a week—depicting the news events of the day, often showcasing the then-president and first lady. Five motion picture companies made the bulk of these features: Fox Movietone, News of the Day, Paramount, RKO-Pathé, and Universal. For particulars concerning documentary features focusing on the president, see Bill Nichols's *Representing Reality* (1991).

2. The "debate" is fully documented in *JFK: The Book of the Film* (1992), an annotated screenplay that advertises "340 Research Notes" and "97 Reactions and Commentaries."

References

Caroli, Betty Boyd. *First Ladies*. New York: Oxford University Press, 1995.

Cook, Blanche Wiesen. *Eleanor Roosevelt, 1884–1933*. New York: Penguin, 1993.

Custen, George F. *Bio-Pics: How Hollywood Constructed Public History*. New York: Routledge, 1992.

Goodwin, Doris Kearns. *No Ordinary Time: Franklin and Eleanor Roosevelt: The Home Front in World War II*. New York: Simon and Schuster, 1995.

Klein, Joe. (as Anonymous). *Primary Colors*. New York: Random House, 1998.

Nichols, Bill. *Representing Reality: Issues and Concepts in Documentary*. Bloomington: Indiana University Press, 1991.

Page, Elizabeth. *Tree of Liberty*. New York: Buccaneer Books, 1990.

Rommel-Ruiz, Bryan. "Redeeming Lincoln, Redeeming the South: Representations of Lincoln in D. W. Griffith's *The Birth of a Nation* (1915) and Historical Scholarship," in *Hollywood's White House: The American Presidency in Film and History*, ed. Peter C. Rollins and John E. O'Connor. Lexington: University of Kentucky, 2002.

Shenkman, Richard. "Foreword," in *Hollywood's White House: The American Presidency in Film and History*, ed. Peter C. Rollins and John E. O'Connor. Lexington: University of Kentucky, 2002.

Staples, Donald E. "*Wilson* in Technicolor: An Appreciation," in *Hollywood's White House: The American Presidency in Film and History*, ed. Peter C. Rollins and John E. O'Connor. Lexington: University of Kentucky, 2002.

Stone, Oliver and Zachary Sklar. *JFK: The Book of the Film*. New York: Applause, 1992.

Filmography

1776. Dir. Peter H. Hunt. William Daniels (John Adams), Ken Howard (Thomas Jefferson). Warner Brothers, 1972.

Abraham Lincoln. Dir. D. W. Griffith. Walter Huston (Abraham Lincoln). Feature Productions, 1930.

Abraham Lincoln's Clemency. Dir. Theodore Wharton. Leopold Wharton (Abraham Lincoln). Pathé, 1910.

Alexander Hamilton. Dir. John G. Adolfi. Montagu Love (Thomas Jefferson), Morgan Wallace (James Monroe), Alan Mowbray (George Washington). Warner Brothers, 1931.

All The President's Men. Pakula, 1976.

Amistad. Dir. Steven Speilberg. Nigel Hawthorne (Martin Van Buren), Anthony Hopkins (John Quincy Adams). Dreamworks, 1997.

Annie. Dir. John Houston. Edward Herrmann (Franklin D. Roosevelt). Columbia Pictures, 1982.

Birth of a Nation. Dir. D. W. Griffith. Joseph Henabery (Abraham Lincoln). Epoch Productions, 1915.

Born Again. Dir. Irving Rapper. Harry Spellman (Richard M. Nixon). Embassy Pictures, 1978.

Brave Warrior. Dir. Spencer Gordon Benet. James Seay (William Henry Harrison). Columbia Pictures, 1952.

Buffalo Bill. Dir. William A. Wellman. Sidney Blackmur (Theodore Roosevelt), John Dilson (Rutherford B. Hayes). Twentieth-Century Fox, 1944.

Buffalo Bill and the Indians, or Sitting Bull's History Lesson. Dir. Robert Altman. Pat McCormick (Grover Cleveland). DeLaurentis and Talent Associates, 1976.

Centennial Summer. Dir. Otto Preminger. Reginald Sheffield (U. S. Grant). Twentieth-Century Fox, 1946.

Citizen Kane, Dir. Orson Welles. RKO Radio Pictures, 1941.

The Court Marshall of Billy Mitchell. Dir. Otto Preminger. Ian Wolfe (Calvin Coolidge). Warner Brothers, 1955.

Dick. Dir. Andrew Fleming. Dan Hedaya (Richard M. Nixon). Canal, 1999.

Distant Drums. Dir. Raoul Walsh. Robert Barrat (Zachary Taylor). Warner Brothers, 1951.

The Dramatic Life of Lincoln. Dir. Phil Rosen. George A. Billings (Abraham Lincoln). Rockett–Lincoln, 1924.

Ever the Beginning or *My Girl Tisa*. Dir. Elliot Nugent. Godfrey Tearle (Theodore Roosevelt). United States Pictures, 1948.

Far Horizons. Dir. Rudolph Mate. Herbert Heyes (Thomas Jefferson). Paramount Pictures, 1955.

Give 'em Hell Harry. Dir. Steve Binder. James Whitmore (Harry S. Truman). Theatre Television, 1975.

Gorgeous Hussy. Dir. Clarence Brown. Lionel Barrymore (Andrew Jackson). MGM, 1936.

The Great Victory/Wilson or the Kaiser? The Fall of the Hohenzollers. Dir. Charles Miller (Woodrow Wilson). Screen Classics, 1919.

Guns of Wyoming or *Cattle King*. Dir. Tay Garnett. Larry Gates (Chester A. Arthur). MGM, 1963.

Hearts Divided. Dir. Franz Borzage. George Irving (Thomas Jefferson). Cosmopolitan Productions, 1936.

Hearts in Bondage. Dir. Lew Ayers. Frank McGlyn (Abraham Lincoln). Republic Pictures Corporation, 1936.

How the West Was Won. Dir. John Ford. Raymond Massey (Abraham Lincoln). MGM, 1963.

The Howards of Virginia. Dir. Frank Lloyd. Richard Carlson (Thomas Jefferson), George Houston (George Washington). Columbia Pictures, 1940.

I. Q. Dir. Fred Schepisi. Keene Curtis (Dwight D. Eisenhower). Paramount, 1994. *Iron Horse*. Dir. John Ford. Charles Edward Bull (Abraham Lincoln). Fox Film Corporation, 1924.

JFK. Dir. Oliver Stone. Warner Bros., 1991.

Jefferson in Paris. Dir. James Ivory. Nick Nolte (Thomas Jefferson). Merchant-Ivory, 1995.

Legend of the Lone Ranger. Dir. William Fraker. Jason Robards (U. S. Grant). MCA Universal Pictures, 1981.

The Littlest Rebel. Dir. David Butler. Frank McGlynn (Abraham Lincoln). Twentieth-Century Fox, 1935.

Macarthur. Dir. Joseph Sargent. Ed Flanders (Harry S. Truman), Dan Herilhy (Franklin D. Roosevelt). Universal Pictures, 1977.

Magnificent Doll. Dir. Franz Borzage. Burgess Meredith (James Madison). Universal Pictures, 1946.

New Mexico. Dir. Irving Reis. Hans Conried (Abraham Lincoln). Justman/ United Artists, 1951.

Newsies. Dir. Kenny Ortega. David James Alexander (Theodore Roosevelt). Buena Vista Pictures, 1992.

The Night Riders. Dir. George Sherman. Francis Sayles (James A. Garfield). Republic Pictures, 1939.

Nixon. Dir. Oliver Stone. Anthony Hopkins (Richard M. Nixon). Cinergi Pictures Entertainment, 1995.

No More Excuses. Dir. Robert Downey, Sr. Lawrence Wolf (James A. Garfield). Impact, 1968.

Of Human Hearts. Dir. Clarence Brown. John Carradine (Abraham Lincoln). Loew's/MGM, 1939.

One Man's Hero. Dir. Lance Hool. James Gammon (Zachary Taylor). Arco Films and MGM, 1999.

The President's Lady. Dir. Henry Levin. Charlton Heston (Andrew Jackson). Twentieth-Century Fox, 1953.

Primary Colors. Dir. Mike Nichols. John Travolta (Jack Stanton [Bill Clinton]). Universal, 1998.

Prince of Players. Dir. Phil Dunne. Stanley Hall (Abraham Lincoln). Twentieth-Century Fox, 1955.

Rebellion. Dir. Lynn Shores. Allan Cavan (Zachary Taylor). Cresent Pictures, 1936.

The Remarkable Andrew. Dir. Stuart Heisler. Brian Donleavy (Andrew Jackson), Gilbert Emery (Thomas Jefferson), Montago Love (George Washington). Paramount, 1942.

The Reprieve: An Episode in the Life of Abraham Lincoln. Dir. Van Dyke Brooke. Paul Logan (Abraham Lincoln). Vitagraph Company, 1908.

The Right Stuff. Dir. Philip Kaufman. Robert Beer (Dwight D. Eisenhower) and Donald J. Moffat (Lyndon Johnson). Ladd Company, 1983.

Secret Honor. Dir. Robert Altman. Philip B. Hall (Richard M. Nixon). Sandcastle 5 Productions, 1984.

Silver Dollar. Dir. Alfred E. Green. Emmert Corrigan (Chester A. Arthur). First National Pictures, 1932.

Silver River. Dir. Raoul Walsh. Joe Crehan (U. S. Grant). Warner Brothers, 1948.

Sitting Bull. Dir. Sidney Salkow. John Hamilton (U. S. Grant). United Artists, 1954.

Sunrise at Campobello. Dir. Vincent J. Donehue. Ralph Bellamy (Franklin D. Roosevelt). Warner Brothers, 1960.

Stars and Stripes Forever. Dir. Henry Koster. Roy Gordon (Benjamin Harrison). Twentieth-Century Fox, 1952.

The Story of Will Rogers. Dir. Michael Curtiz. Earl Lee (Woodrow Wilson). Warner Brothers, 1952.

The Tall Target. Dir. Anthony Mann. Leslie Kimmel (Abraham Lincoln). MGM, 1951.

Tennessee Johnson. Dir. William Dieterle. Van Heflin (Andrew Johnson). MGM, 1942.

Thirteen Days. Dir. Roger Donaldson. Bruce Greenwood (John F. Kennedy). Beacon Communications, 2000.

This is My Affair. Dir. William A. Selter. Frank Conroy (William McKinley). Twentieth-Century Fox, 1937.

Wilson. Dir. Henry King. Alexander Knox (Woodrow Wilson). Twentieth-Century Fox, 1944.

The Wind and the Lion. Dir. John Milius. Brian Keith (Theodore Roosevelt). Columbia Pictures, 1975.

Yankee Doodle Dandy. Dir. Michael Curtiz. Captain Jack Young (Franklin D. Roosevelt). Warner Brothers, 1942.

Young Mr. Lincoln. Dir. John Ford. Henry Fonda (Abraham Lincoln). Twentieth-Century Fox, 1939.

CHAPTER 12

RADIO

TIMOTHY W. KNEELAND

Radio has expanded the influence and penetration of the presidential persona in the lives of everyday Americans. Radio has also provided a means to humanize and demystify the presidency through dramatic and comedic serials as well as satire and parody.

KDKA in Pittsburgh, the first commercial radio station in the United States, began the age of radio presidency in November 1920 by dedicating its first broadcast to live coverage of the Harding-Cox election. Since that night, the presidency has become part of the daily life of Americans, who encounter the office and the office-holders in their living rooms, cars, and offices. Candidates and presidents competed with other forms of entertainment for radio airtime as they tried to persuade voters and to project an image of leadership to the public and to gain public or congressional support for general policies and specific legislation. In turn, radio heightened public response to presidential image-making through popular programming, newscasts, and more recently, political talk radio, creating in the public mind images of the presidency that were often at odds with those desired by the residents of the White House.

The new medium brought with it both opportunities and challenges for the chief executive. Presidents after Warren G. Harding were expected to adapt their communication style to the medium of radio to promote their agenda. The most powerful president in the twentieth century in all areas of both foreign and domestic policy was Franklin Delano Roosevelt, who better than his predecessors understood the power of radio as a tool of his administration. Roosevelt was president during the "Golden Age of Radio," the decades of the 1930s and 1940s when census reports indicate that radio was the primary medium of news and entertainment for Americans. Ninety percent of American families owned at least one radio set and listened an average of three to four hours a day. According to historian Gerd Horton, "radio saturated popular culture more quickly and completely than any other medium."[1]

In the 1950s, television pushed radio to the background of American politics and culture. Some were prepared to write radio's obituary, but the postwar youth culture provided a new market for radio, transforming the industry and leading to a growth in the number of radio stations. The vitality of radio continued in the 1970s, when an estimated 97 percent of American homes had one or more radios and individuals were said to spend nearly twenty-five hours a week listening to them.[2] Radio became ubiquitous in the last quarter of the twentieth century: in homes, cars, businesses, over the phone during prolonged "holds," and finally available on the Internet either as an adjunct to an over-the-air broadcast or as a stand-alone station. Rather than decline, the number of radio stations proliferated through the end of the twentieth century when there were approximately twelve thousand AM and FM stations broadcasting daily.

Richard Nixon understood the changes in the popular medium and used them to circumvent the White House press corps and national media, who were critical of his presidency. The Nixon White House developed an audio press release and made it available to thousands of small radio stations that were unable to afford to station reporters in Washington, D.C. By leapfrogging the Washington-based news media, Nixon sent his messages directly to the people. Another radio innovation occurred when President Ronald Reagan initiated the practice of delivering a Saturday Radio Address, which became a staple of all subsequent presidents. George H. W. Bush, Bill Clinton, and George W. Bush continued this practice in one form or another. These Saturday radio addresses, unlike the infrequent prime time Fireside Chats of FDR, allowed presidents a weekly opportunity to shape the Sunday television, radio and newspaper coverage of the presidency, which in turn might set the tone for press coverage of the presidency throughout the week.

As presidents exploited the medium to reach the public, the public through the channel of political talk radio have taken presidents to task for their actions or inactions on critical domestic and foreign policy. On a daily basis, these mostly conservative radio call-in or talk shows hold up presidents for contempt or commendation among listeners estimated to be in the tens of millions.[3]

Presidents on the Radio

From 1920 until 1948, radio played a crucial role in presidential elections. By circumventing the printed press, radio gave candidates direct access to the listeners, uncensored by newspaper editors or publishers. At the same time, radio proved devastating to those candidates whose oratorical skills, vocal characterization, or speaking abilities were not polished. The weakest candidates tended to be those who were predisposed to the oratory of the nineteenth century, when the style of public address had been honed by politicians standing before large crowds, who sought through their often inflammatory speech and physical gestures to appeal to the crowd's emotion. Furthermore, to project their voice across long distances, they often shouted. Radio, in contrast, was suited to candidates who adopted a conversational speech that was devoid of regional dialect and who calmly sought to explain their viewpoint to audiences.[4]

Radio was more than a campaign tool. It allowed sitting presidents to gain public support for their agendas and build political support for their decisions. Radio played a primary role in presidential image making and public opinion formation until 1948. Thereafter, it played a secondary role in providing the public with information via radio newscasts. More recently, its role has been to allow the president to directly address the public via a weekly Saturday radio address.

Calvin Coolidge

Despite the nickname "Silent Cal," Calvin Coolidge was the first president to effectively use the radio. Vice President Coolidge became president in August 1923 following the unexpected death of President Warren G. Harding. On December 10, 1923, Calvin Coolidge delivered a radio eulogy to Harding, and thereafter Coolidge became a monthly presence on radio, tying his addresses to occasions as diverse as Lincoln Day, George Washington's Birthday, the Daughters of the American Revolution convention, an Associated Press meeting, a Better Homes meeting, a Memorial Day Commemoration, and a debating contest.[5] Some of these talks were heard throughout the country, whereas others were aired from stations in key markets such as New York City or Washington, D.C., and could be heard in surrounding states, thus reaching the largest target of potential Republicans and swing voters.[6]

Coolidge's 1925 inauguration was the first inauguration ever broadcast on radio and was heard by an unprecedented fifteen million listeners. Coolidge spoke to more Americans in his radio addresses than all prior presidents had reached in all their years of speechmaking. They gathered in groups in the private offices and homes of those who owned radio receivers or gathered outside storefronts airing them over loudspeakers.[7] So great was his audio recognition by the public that one poll of American radio personalities conducted in the mid 1920s put Coolidge ahead of leading radio star Will Rogers.[7] Coolidge's mastery of the medium was a combination of vocal quality and rhetoric. His speeches were brief and to the point, and like later presidents Franklin Roosevelt and Ronald Reagan, Coolidge preferred simple analogies to explain complex problems and reinforced traditional American values such as optimism, morality, and patriotism.

Because of Coolidge's success, presidential candidates became more radio savvy in the 1928 campaign. They developed the five-minute radio talk and adopted elements of popular culture, vaudeville, and dramatization to their political ads.[5]

Herbert Hoover

Herbert Hoover was elected in 1928. One expert has said, "He was completely bereft of all vocal qualities needed to make his address effective."[8] Unlike Coolidge, Hoover was unable to invoke simple American themes using the language of ordinary Americans. Indeed, during the depth of the Depression he retreated from radio, and his image became associated in popular song and jokes with "Hoovervilles," or shanty towns; "Hoover blankets," newspapers wrapped around people for warmth; and "Hoover flags," empty pockets turned inside out.[9]

Franklin Delano Roosevelt

In 1932 the Democrats nominated the perfect radio candidate, Franklin Delano Roosevelt. Roosevelt captured the public imagination by breaking a long-standing tradition that presidential candidates abstain from attending their party's nomination convention for fear that the public think them ambitious office seekers. Flying to Chicago to accept the nomination in person, Roosevelt's journey captivated radio listeners across the nation. Roosevelt prepared his acceptance speech with radio in mind, crafting it to be heard rather than read. Roosevelt combined both a genial tone and the ability to speak in the language of everyday Americans, which allowed him to outmaneuvered presidential contenders in four elections.[10] Rather than appear eager to serve a third term, Roosevelt stayed away from the Democratic convention in 1940 and broadcast his acceptance speech from the White House.

In the election of 1944, Roosevelt battled Republican nominee Thomas Dewey. Both candidates stooped to verbal mudslinging, with Dewey attacking Roosevelt's health and mental competence and Roosevelt painting Dewey as a liar comparable to Hitler.[8] Roosevelt, relying on his radio prowess, reached out to the nation in a speech delivered September 23, 1944. Speechwriter Samuel Rosenman believed this, the so-called "Fala Speech," was Roosevelt's rhetorical zenith. The Fala Speech came about after press reports that after visiting a naval outpost in the Aluetian Islands, Roosevelt had mistakenly left

behind his beloved dog, Fala. Supposedly, Roosevelt ordered a battleship returned to the island to pick up and taxi his dog to Roosevelt's ship. The story
hinted at an arrogance in and an abuse of power by Roosevelt. His Fala Speech,
however, simultaneously blasted Dewey and other critics as liars while humanizing Roosevelt's image and creating sympathy for the dog-loving president.[11] Roosevelt began by reminding his listeners that the repeated lie as a tool
of politic destruction was first suggested by Hitler in *Mein Kampf*. He then listed
a number of assertions by Republicans which he quickly disqualified. He ended
this pseech by disarmingly claiming that while such "concocted" and "malicious
falsehoods" did not bother him, they did offend his "little dog, Fala." This
verbal slight-of-hand turned aside criticism of FDR and instead moved the
listener to consider the source of allegations against the president.

This campaign also saw more five-minute spots that were both funny and
poignant as they featured politicians, radio and movie celebrities, veterans,
and mothers of soldiers fighting in the war. By airing them at the end of
popular radio shows, they achieved the maximum listening audience.[12]
Roosevelt arranged his traditional election eve extravaganza featuring everyday citizens, soldiers and sailors, and a Who's Who of celebrities from
Hollywood and radio. Whether by design or happy accident, Roosevelt cut
short his own speech near the end, thus leaving an unexpected gap, which
many stations filled with music. Dewey, who was to broadcast in the time
following, at 11 PM, found that many listeners responded to the music as a
signal to turn off their radios! Roosevelt racked up another electoral victory.[8]

In some measure Franklin Roosevelt's election to office an unprecedented four times can be attributed to his radio genius; furthermore, his
success as a president was dependent on his ability to circumvent congress
and hostile newspapers and to reach the public directly through his radio
addresses. Roosevelt made at least three hundred radio addressees as president, including the Fireside Chats.[13,14] The Fireside Chats were the most
finely crafted use of radio by any president and became emblematic of the
rhetorical presidency. These radio broadcasts endeared Roosevelt to the
American public and were critical to his legislative and policy successes. In
dealing with Congress, Roosevelt could point to the large audience and high
volume of positive mail these radio speeches garnered.[15] An estimated 64
percent of Americans heard Roosevelt's his first address "on the Bank
Crisis" on March 12, 1933,[13] and they responded by sending him half a
million letters.[8] (Brown 66). Roosevelt's largest radio audience tuned in to
hear his declaration of war on Japan, December 8, 1941; the address became commonly known as the "Day of Infamy" speech. As much as 73
percent of the population tuned into this address.

Roosevelt understood that his broadcasts had to be timed to reach the
public when they were most likely to tune in. For example, before his State
of the Union Message in 1936, Roosevelt persuaded Congress to hold its
joint session in the evening, ensuring that when he read his annual message

it would secure the peak radio audience available at 9:00 PM.[16] In 1944, recovering from the flu and unable to go to the Capitol in person, Roosevelt sent Congress the printed text of his speech during the day but delivered the same speech on the radio that evening at 9:00 PM.[6]

So popular and powerful were his speeches that Norman Corwin could state: "[i]t is no exaggeration to say that a man could walk around any suburban block during an important presidential address and hardly miss a word of the speech."[17] Local radio stations airing competitive programs against one of Roosevelt's prime time addresses lost their audience. Movie theaters packed in crowds when they played a newsreel showing Roosevelt delivering a radio broadcast but had a vacant theater on those Sunday nights when the president was on the air. Roosevelt became so accustomed to the microphone that he once joked that following his retirement as president he would become a radio commentator.[8]

Harry S. Truman and Dwight D. Eisenhower

After Roosevelt's death, Vice President Harry S. Truman became president. Truman used radio frequently, but he was not the performer that Roosevelt was.[6] Truman's largest radio audience tuned in to hear him announce that meat would be available on the open market again, and his lowest ratings came in a speech spelling out his reasons for vetoing the Taft-Hartley Bill.[18]

Truman was more interested in the possibilities of television than radio. When he ran for election in his own right in 1948, Truman selected the city of Philadelphia for the Democratic Convention because the city had the facilities to broadcast the convention on television. During his campaign, Truman rejected radio addresses and embarked on an old-fashioned whistle-stop campaign that, to the surprise of some, secured his election in 1948.[19]

Truman was the last radio president. Historically, he gave the first presidential telecast from White House, and after 1948 he gave television-radio simulcasts. His successor, Dwight Eisenhower, advanced the use of television over radio, and his "fireside chats" were televised. The success of television as a presidential vehicle was a reflection of the decline of the Golden Age of radio (ca. 1933–1950) and the beginning of the Golden Age of television (ca. 1950–1970). In the 1950s, radio listenership fell dramatically as listeners became viewers, and the most popular radio programs such as *Jack Benny* and *Burns and Allen* became television programs.[20] After 1948, the importance of radio in elections also diminished. Short radio ads in local or regional markets, or customized ads for specific ethnic groups, replaced national radio addresses in presidential campaigns. Candidates, who were more interested in visual rather than audio impact, moved to television.

Kennedy to Ford

Both John F. Kennedy and Lyndon Johnson favored television. Indeed, Kennedy used television as effectively as Roosevelt had used radio. It was not until Richard Nixon that presidents sought new ways to gain political advantage through the radio. With nearly ten thousand radio stations and eighty million radios in homes, cars, and offices, the Nixon administration saw an opportunity to reach this audience through the audio press release. These "Spot Masters" allowed small market radio stations to call a special number and receive prerecorded extracts from speeches made by cabinet level officials in the Nixon administration.[21] These broadcasts reached across race, gender, and age barriers and gained audiences of older and younger Americans, commuters, and housewives who were less likely to be reached via newspaper or television.[22]

Gerald Ford suspended the radio service, but Jimmy Carter revived it in 1978 by making two feeds available every weekday in the morning and afternoon, during the so-called "drive time," when there was a captive radio audience of automobile commuters.[21]

Ronald Reagan

Ronald Reagan instituted a new form of radio presidency by creating the Saturday Radio Address.[23] An analysis of Reagan's speeches reveals that his remarks closely resembled the way most Americans speak: Neither long-winded nor abstruse, Reagan favored a limited vocabulary familiar to most Americans, tied to stories that evoked popular American virtues.[24] Reagan's radio message may have been twofold, providing not only the manifest message for that week but the latent personification of Reagan as a cowboy president. Reagan liked to wisecrack before going on the air, but on more than one occasion his comments were broadcast. One well-known incident included his joking reference to legislation outlawing Russia and the announcement that "we begin bombing in five minutes." To stop the controversial jokes from airing, his staff installed a red light to alert the president that the microphone in from of him was live. Nonetheless, such comments persisted and helped solidify Reagan's image as an outspoken cowboy—an image carefully built into the Reagan presidency through staged photographs at his Santa Barbara ranch and select interviews in print and broadcast, as well as through his rhetorical reference to the West in his speeches.[25]

Bush, Clinton, and Bush

Reagan's immediate successor, George Bush, did not use the Saturday radio address for his first two years in office but returned to this practice in the final years of his presidency.[26] Presidents Bill Clinton and George W. Bush have both continued this practice. Clinton went so far as to include an audience in the Oval Office when he delivered his addresses because he found that it enhanced his delivery.

Radio on the Presidency

Radio created public images of presidents and the presidency through newscasts, presidential speeches, and press conferences, but also through entertainment programs and political parodies of presidents and, more recently, through political talk radio.

Imitations of the president on the radio have been a staple of radio since Will Rogers imitated Calvin Coolidge's speech pattern on a radio show broadcast from Kansas City.[27] Pseudo-presidential voices were initially used as part of the *March of Time*, a radio series that dramatized weekly news events. The October 30, 1938, broadcast of *Mercury Theater*'s "War of the Worlds" included one actor who sounded so much like Franklin Roosevelt that many listeners were fooled into believing it was the president, adding to the belief that Martians really had invaded the United States. As early as 1934, presidential press secretary Steve Early became concerned that Roosevelt's voice might become too familiar to the public, thus losing its effectiveness, so he requested the radio industry stop airing Roosevelt impersonations on popular programming, and they willingly complied.[28]

Comic parodies of the president have been just as notable as the dramatic recreations. Perhaps the most famous example of presidential satire occurred in November 1962, with the release of the comedy album, *First Family*. Selling over six and a half million copies in the first six weeks of release, this comedy album was the fastest-selling record in history at that time. The album was a parody of the Kennedy family, depicting President Kennedy in various familial settings in a satirical way. Typical was the skit in which the Kennedys turned a family conversation into a press conference, or the one in which John turned a bedtime story for Caroline into a recitation of his accomplishments.[29] The impersonation of the president was the work of actor Vaughn Meader and former radio disc jockey Bob Booker. Meader sounded so much like Kennedy that the White House received a steady stream of mail from listeners who thought it was Kennedy they heard on their radio.[30] Meader released a sequel album in the spring of 1963, but the assassination of Kennedy on November 22, 1963, ended public interest in it. The actor, so closely identified with his Kennedy impressions, found his career in a tailspin from which it never recovered. Bob Booker went on to produce the comedy album *The New First Family* (1968), but later attempts to repeat the success of Meader failed.[30]

In 1974, Garrison Keillor launched *Prairie Home Companion*, a radio variety show, on Minnesota Public Radio. The program's popularity grew, and it soon became a staple on Public Broadcasting Stations throughout the nation. *Prairie Home Companion* continued the tradition of vocal caricatures of sitting presidents, including Ronald Reagan, George H. W. Bush, Bill Clinton, and George W. Bush.[31] Typical was an exchange aired on the "Joke Show," April 27, 1996, in which Bill Clinton was featured as too politically correct to tell a good joke, and former president George H. W. Bush was too verbally challenged to tell a funny one.[31]

Other popular sources for the public understanding of the presidency came from radio comedy and drama. Radio star Gracie Allen, following in the footsteps of Will Rogers and Rudy Vallee, "ran" for president. Allen, of the comedy team of Burns and Allen, launched her radio campaign for the presidency in March 1940 by announcing on the air the formation of her third party, the "Surprise" party. Her "campaign" for the presidency included visits to other major popular radio program such as *Texaco Star Theater*, the *Bob Hope* show, *Fibber McGee and Molly*, and *Jack Benny*.[32] Gracie's tongue-in-cheek campaign featured a book on how to run for president and a convention in Omaha, Nebraska, said to have attracted a quarter of million attendees.[33] Thus, the lighter side of the presidency, if not the underside of politics, was showcased to the delight of radio listeners.

Radio news and special programming were not the only means of covering the presidency. In the early Cold War era, a dramatic series called *Mr. President* depicted the lives of various presidents. Actor Edward Arnold portrayed a different president in every episode of the formulaic series. Each week, the president, acting out of his innate sense of justice and desire to help the American people, took an unpopular course of action. He faced opposition from a variety of antagonists—foreign powers in one episode, and politically calculating congressional leaders in another. As Mr. President sought to make America and the world a better place, his faithful and clearly unmarried female secretary attended to him. Her job, each episode, was to fret that the president worked too hard. Clearly, the show reinforced the status and power of the presidency while also humanizing the office.[34]

After the resignation of Richard Nixon in 1973, presidents were more often mistrusted than esteemed. Political talk radio both reflected and shaped this perception. The format began in 1987 after the repeal of the Fairness Doctrine by the Federal Communication Commission (FCC). The Fairness Doctrine, initiated by the FCC in 1949, required broadcast stations airing political opinions to offer airtime to those with competing opinions. With the demise of this doctrine, a host of mostly conservative radio talk shows exploded onto the airwaves, dominating stations on the AM dial.[3] George H. W. Bush felt the wrath of talk show hosts when he broke his "No New Taxes" pledge to the American people in 1990, and Bill Clinton was under constant barrage by talk radio hosts and audiences, leading some pundits to suggest that conservative radio aided in the impeachment of Clinton in 1997.[35–37] In the 1990s, talk radio and satire began to blend in shows offering a mix of presidential parody and a steady diet of presidential commentary. Two nationally syndicated entries include the southern-styled humor of *John Boy and Billy Big Show*, which is broadcast in twenty states as well as on the Internet, with millions of morning listeners, and the New York musings of "shock jock" Howard Stern, who has been an outspoken critic of George W. Bush.[38]

Radio added substantially to the public's ability to identify with the twentieth-century presidents. Potential presidential candidates, particularly from 1924 to 1948, found radio a useful tool for presenting themselves to the public. Presidents Calvin Coolidge, Franklin Roosevelt, and Ronald Reagan enhanced their popular appeal by using radio to tie basic American values to their own administrations. Popular images of the president found in comedic or dramatic programming, especially before the resignation of Richard Nixon in 1973, tended to be lighthearted satire or dramatic but supportive entertainment. Since 1973, the presidency has enjoyed far less reverence and respect on the radio; instead, the presidency is most often the object of satire and ridicule on variety shows, talk radio, and conventional radio programming. The relationship between popular culture and the presidency is mirrored by radio: When the presidency was esteemed by the public, the reverence for the office was reflected through radio, but when public mistrust of the office and its occupants grew, so too did radio's role as an outlet of popular frustration, thus confirming radio's historic role in reflecting popular sentiment toward the office and its occupants.

Notes

1. Gerd Horten, *Radio Goes to War: The Cultural Politics of Propaganda during World War II* (Berkeley: University of California Press, 2002), 2–3.

2. David Manning White and John Pendleton, *Popular Culture: Mirror of American Life* (Del Mar, Calif.: Publisher's, 1977).

3. Sean Paige, Tiffany Danitz, Jennifer G Hickey, and Keith Russel, "Talking the Talk," *Insight on the News* 14 (1998):9–15.

4. Kathleen Hall Jamieson, *Packaging the Presidency: A History and Criticism of Presidential Campaign Advertising* (New York: Oxford University Press).

5. Edward Chester, *Radio, Television and American Politics* (New York: Sheed & Ward, 1969).

6. Elmer E. Cornwell, *Presidential Leadership of Public Opinion* (Bloomington: Indiana University Press, 1965).

7. Malcolm Lee Cross, "Calvin Coolidge," in *Popular Images of American Presidents*, ed. William C. Spragens (Westport, Conn.: Greenwood, 1988), 297–324.

8. Robert J. Brown, *Manipulating the Ether: The Power of Broadcast Radio in Thirties America* (Jefferson, N.C.: McFarland, 1998), 26.

9. Arthur M. Schlesinger, *The Crisis of the Old Order, 1919–1933* (Boston: Houghton Mifflin, 1957), 245.

10. Gil Troy, *See How They Ran: The Changing Role of the Presidential Candidate* (Cambridge, Mass.: Harvard University Press, 1996).

11. Samuel I. Rosenman, *Working With Roosevelt* (New York: Decapo Press Reprint, 1972; 1952).

12. Steven Fraser, "1944," in *Running for President: The Candidates and Their Images 1900–1992*, vol. II, ed. Arthur Schlesinger Jr. (New York: Simon and Schuster, 1994), 217–236.

13. Franklin D. Roosevelt Presidential Library and Museum, "Fire Side Chats of Franklin Roosevelt," http://www.fdrlibrary.marist.edu/firesi90 .html (accessed June 1, 2003).

14. Franklin D. Roosevelt, *FDR's Fireside Chats*, ed. Russel Buhite and David Levy (Norman: University of Oklahoma Press, 1992).

15. Ryan Halford, *Franklin D. Roosevelt's Rhetorical Presidency* (New York: Greenwood, 1988).

16. Newton N. Minow, John Bartlow Martin, and Lee M Mitchell, *Presidential Television* (New York: Basic Books, 1973).

17. Norman Corwin, "The Radio," in *While You Were Gone: A Report on Wartime Life in the United States*, ed. Jack Goodman (New York: Simon and Schuster, 1946), 375.

18. Richard, E Neustadt, *Presidential Power and the Modern Presidents: The Politics of Leadership from Roosevelt to Reagan* (New York: Free Press, 1990).

19. J. Leonard Reinsch, *Getting Elected: From Radio and Roosevelt to Television and Reagan* (New York: Hippocene Books, 1988).

20. David Halberstam, *The Fifties* (New York: Villard Books, 1993).

21. John Anthony Maltese, *Spin Control: The White House Office of Communications and the Management of Presidential News* (Chapel Hill: University of North Carolina, 1992).

22. Murray Edelman, "The Politics of Persuasion," in *Choosing the President*, ed. James David Barber (Englewood Cliffs, N.J.: Prentice Hall, 1974), 149–173.

23. Robert C. Rowland and John Jones, " 'Until Next Week': The Saturday Radio Addresses of Ronald Reagan," *Presidential Studies Quarterly* 32 (2002):84–111.

24. Lee Sigelman and Cynthia Whissel, " 'The Great Communicator' and the 'Great Talker' On the Radio: Projecting Presidential Personas," *Presidential Studies Quarterly* 32 (2002):137–146.

25. David Gergen, *Eyewitness to Power: The Essence of Leadership, Nixon to Clinton* (New York: Simon and Schuster, 2001).

26. Lee Sigelman and Cynthia Whissel, "Projecting Presidential Personas on the Radio: An Addendum on the Bushes," *Presidential Studies Quarterly* 32 (2002):572–576.

27. Erik Barnouw, *A Tower of Babel: A History of Broadcasting in the United States to 1933* (New York: Oxford University Press, 1966).

28. Robert E. Gilbert, "Franklin Delano Roosevelt," in *Popular Images of the Presidents*, ed. William C. Spragen (New York: Greenwood, 1988), 347–386.

29. Bob Booker and Earle Doud, *The First Family*, Cadence Records, 1962.

30. Nicholas Cull, "No Laughing Matter: Vaughn Meader, the Kennedy Administration and Presidential Impersonations on the Radio," *Historical Journal of Film, Radio and Television* 17 (1997):383–400.

31. *Prairie Home Companion*, http:www.prairiehome.org (accessed June 1, 2003).

32. *Burns and Allen*, Ralph Levy (producer/director). The Burns and Allen Show, 1940.

33. Gary W. Coville, "Gracie Allen's 1940 Presidential Campaign," *American History Illustrated* (1990):62–65, 74.

34. *Mr. President*, ABC Radio, 1947–1953.

35. Haynes Johnson, *The Best of Times: America in the Clinton Years* (New York: Harcourt, 2001).

36. Diana Owen, "Talk Radio and Evaluations of President Clinton," *Political Communication* 14 (1997):333–353.

37. David C. Barker, "Rushed Decisions: Political Talk Radio and Vote Choice, 1994–1996," *Journal of Politics* 61 (1999):527–539.

38. Donna Petrozello, "Exanding Horizons," *Broadcasting and Cable*, 127 (1997):26.

CHAPTER 13

TELEVISION

MELISSA CRAWLEY

The relationship between television and the president began on April 30, 1939, at the New York World's Fair. President Franklin Roosevelt broadcast a brief address to a small television audience in the New York area, using a signal relayed from the top of the Empire State Building. The first presidential appearance on the new medium, Roosevelt's television debut would forever change both politics and the presidency.

Since Roosevelt's inaugural broadcast, television has become an "eye-witness" to the nation's highest office, affecting how citizens understand and experience their leaders. Through television's cameras, the public has watched presidents in celebration and in defeat, in triumph and in scandal, in life and in death. Presidents have used television to persuade, encourage, confess, and repent. Some of the nation's most significant experiences of presidents are collectively shared and remembered because television's cameras were there to record them. Television, however, is more than a broadcast record of presidential history. Although news cameras have captured presidential assassinations, resignations, and confessions, television's entertainment formats serve an equally important role in bringing the president to the people.

Although news is a significant component of broadcast television, drama and entertainment formats are central to its programming schedule. Paterson suggests that these formats "offer a mirror and a window to the culture of the audience they seek to serve."[1] Drama and entertainment on television both reflect society and challenge it to see beyond itself. When the president is represented through these formats, television is reflecting the nation's history and challenging it to understand the future by allowing the public to experience the president in ways that inspire, educate, entertain, and amuse. This chapter explores the president in popular programming to understand how these television formats may influence the public's perception of their leader.

President Harry S. Truman leads Walter Cronkite of CBS on the first television tour of the White House. (AP/Wide World Photos)

Touring the White House

When the CBS network broadcast *The President of the United States at Home: White House Tour with President Harry S. Truman* in May 1952, the television audience was already accustomed to seeing the president on their screens. Throughout the early years of the decade, Truman spoke to the nation via television on various political issues. It was his personal tour of the White House with three CBS reporters, however, that gave television viewers a new perspective on the president. Not just the subject of news, the president now became entertainment. Guiding Walter Cronkite, Bryson Rosh, and Frank Bourgholtzer through the White House, President Truman played host to the nation by explaining the historical significance of various rooms and pieces of furniture. The audience was then treated to a special musical performance by the president, who played Mozart on the piano. The performance was significant because it redefined the president's public image. Before the White House tour, the public saw a matter-of-fact President Truman—a decisive leader who only appeared on their television screens to announce domestic policy issues and important foreign policy discussions like the decision to drop the atomic bomb. The broadcast of the White House tour gave the public a glimpse of the private, dynamic Truman who, in 1952, was preparing to leave office. The timing of the broadcast was perhaps Truman's way of making a more intimate connection with a nation that he had lead through a challenging period of history.

Presidential invitations to the White House would be extended to the television audience by future administrations. The CBS network repeated the tour with Jacqueline Kennedy in 1962 in a broadcast entitled *Tour of the White House with Mrs. John F. Kennedy*. A young and glamorous first lady, Jacqueline Kennedy's solo tour of the White House promoted the vitality of the Kennedy administration. As Truman did, she guided a reporter through various rooms, describing paintings and antique furniture. President Kennedy appeared in a brief interview with his wife at the conclusion of the program, where he discussed her contributions to making the White House "a stronger panorama" of the country's "great history." Kennedy's minor role in the broadcast was effective because it created a scene of domestic harmony while casting the spotlight on the popular first lady.

Almost three decades later, another president welcomed the nation into the executive mansion. President George H. W. Bush gave a tour to ABC *Primetime Live* reporters Sam Donaldson and Diane Sawyer in 1989. Along with First Lady Barbara Bush, the president took the television audience into the residential part of the White House, including his private office. Accompanied by the family dog, Millie, the Bush's tour included a screening of home movies shot during an extended family holiday in Maine. In 2000, President Bill Clinton gave a tour of the White House as his "gift" to the nation during the holiday season. In *First Family's Holiday Gift to America: A Tour of the White House*, President Clinton guided cameras into rarely seen rooms of the White House in addition to parts of the building's private residence. President George W. Bush took a different approach two years later, offering NBC news anchor Tom Brokaw access to a day in the life of the president in *The Bush White House: Inside the Real West Wing*. Although the domestic angle of Bush and Clinton's White House tours strengthened the paternal image of the presidency by creating a metaphorical link between the president's family and the "family" of Americans, George W. Bush's invitation to the White House focused on the president's work life. The "day in the life" tour included the president presiding over meetings, interacting with his advisors, and even exercising in the White House weight room. The program was both a clever attempt at cross promotion (it was broadcast as a lead-in to a repeat episode of the network's successful drama *The West Wing*) and an attempt to show Bush as an active and engaged leader.[2]

Opening the White House to television cameras creates a more accessible presidency by dissolving the boundary between public and private spaces. These productions offer an intimate yet controlled view of the presidency that often satisfies the public's desire for both the ordinary and the extraordinary in their national leader.

Drama

If, as Paterson suggests, television drama production "offers viewers national images and myths,"[3] then its relationship with the presidency would seem to be a natural one. The president is both an image that symbolizes the country and a mythic representation of the nation's history. Television's dramatic stories often communicate these aspects of the presidency by recreating the heroic deeds of the country's founding fathers.

As one of the nation's most revered leaders, George Washington's image endures across decades of television drama. Despite being "one of the most misunderstood and elusive men in history,"[4] Washington is most often portrayed as a heroic military leader whose inspirational character forged a nation. This focus suggests that television drama reflects the most common traits assigned to Washington's "mythic" status.

Dramas that portray Washington include *George Washington and The Whiskey Rebellion* (1974), a recreation of his first domestic challenge as president, as well as *The Rebels* (1979), one in a trilogy of made-for-television movies adapted from John Jakes's books on the American Revolution (Marill 1996, 42). In *George Washington* (1984) and *George Washington II: The Forging of a Nation* (1986), Barry Bostwick plays the first president, with Patty Duke as Martha Washington. *The Crossing* (2000) reinforces Washington's reputation as a courageous and fierce general in its story of the Battle of Trenton. In the drama, Jeff Daniels, as Washington, leads his weary and defeated soldiers across the Delaware River into one of the most significant episodes of the American Revolution. The made-for-television movie portrays the "fortitude and strength of character" that inspired Washington's men "to accomplish the seemingly impossible."[5]

The presidency of Thomas Jefferson is also treated reverentially in television drama. *The Patriots*, which appeared in two versions, (1963 and 1976) traces Jefferson's rise to the office and focuses on his early conflicts with Alexander Hamilton. In one of the more ironic debates between the two, the slave-owning future president is depicted as valiantly fighting for the inclusion of equal rights and a no-slave clause in the Constitution. Jefferson is also portrayed in *The Rebels* (1979), *The Adams Chronicles* (1976), and *George Washington II* (1986). In 2000, television drama explored a more intimate side to Jefferson's life, detailing his possible romantic relationship with his slave Sally Hemings in *Sally Hemings: An American Scandal*. Perhaps a reflection of the time, the production's focus on the controversial love affair coincided with similar scandals happening in the Clinton administration.

In addition to Washington and Jefferson, Abraham Lincoln appears frequently in television drama. A popular subject, Lincoln was first depicted in television's early "prestige dramas," or theatrical plays. These live plays were original works transmitted weekly from New York that often featured relatively unknown actors and directors.[6] In 1950 and again in 1951, actor Raymond Massey played Lincoln in an adaptation of Robert Sherwood's Pulitzer Prize–winning play, *Abe Lincoln in Illinois*. A year later, Studio One adapted *Abraham Lincoln* from a 1919 play that portrayed important events in the life of the president. When plays were replaced by other drama formats, Lincoln continued to be a popular choice. The president was depicted in Hallmark Hall of Fame's *Abe Lincoln in Illinois* (1964), the 1975 miniseries *Lincoln*, *Captains and the Kings* (1976), and *Mister Lincoln* (1981), a one-man show for PBS. During the 1980s and 1990s, Lincoln was a character in ten additional television productions.

In his work on Abraham Lincoln and the formation of national memory, Schwartz argues that "images of President Lincoln embody our nation's mixed historical memory about the meaning of the Civil War."[7] Although the events of Lincoln's presidency offer numerous opportunities for television drama to tap into this association, Lincoln's popularity may also be a result of how he is characterized in these dramas. Historically, Lincoln's relationship to the tumultuous events of the Civil War and Reconstruction reveal a complex man, yet his image is often simplified in television depictions. Whether they deal with his role in the Civil War or with more personal aspects of his life, most television drama portrays Lincoln as an honest, wise, and humble president, whose talented oratory skills and paternal leadership freed the slaves and saved the Union. Lincoln's endurance on the small screen is perhaps a testimony to the appeal of this ideal representation of presidential character.

Later presidents of the nineteenth century, including Polk, Jackson, Cleveland, McKinley, and Grant, also appeared in television drama. Whereas Polk is portrayed in *Dream West* (1986), Jackson is depicted in *Davy Crockett: King of the Wild Frontier*, a three-episode series of Disneyland broadcast, which ran in 1955. President Jackson also appears in *War of 1812* (1999). Grover Cleveland is portrayed in *The Wild, Wild West Revisited* (1979), and William McKinley is depicted in *Captains and the Kings* (1976). President Grant appears in *Lincoln* (1988), *Emma: Queen of the South Seas* (1988) and the weekly series of *The Wild, Wild West* broadcast from 1965–1969. Lesser known and perhaps not as interesting to modern audiences, these leaders were most often portrayed in supporting roles.

Television drama's treatment of twentieth-century presidents similarly follows the Lincoln and Washington representations. They, too, are depicted in dramas that focus on the defining moments of their administrations as well as those that illustrate their personal triumphs and struggles while in office.

Although Theodore Roosevelt's cinematic portrayals are numerous, television depictions of the president are limited to *Eleanor and Franklin* (1976), *Captains and the Kings* (1976) and *Eleanor and Franklin: The White House Years* (1977). Theodore Roosevelt first captured the nation's attention during the Spanish-American War, when images of his volunteer cavalry, the Rough Riders, rode across cinematic newsreels. The films made Roosevelt a war hero, in part because they "featured what the public wanted to see—action and speed."[8] The films also showcased Roosevelt's larger-than-life persona. Although this image was popular, it limited the future president's television appearances because it was not easily translated to the intimate nature of the small screen.

Many of the portrayals of Franklin Roosevelt in television drama focus on his role in the Second World War. These include *Enola Gay* (1980), *The Winds of War* (1983), *War and Remembrance* (1988) and *World War II: When Lions Roared* (1994). The productions explore Roosevelt's complex and cautious approach to WWII as he struggles to support the Allies while maintaining America's neutrality. In more personal treatments of his life, the president's stormy yet loving relationship with his wife, Eleanor, is examined. In these productions, Roosevelt is also portrayed as bravely fighting the crippling effects of polio while working for national change [*Eleanor and Franklin* (1977); *Eleanor and Franklin: The White House Years* (1977); *FDR: The Last Year* (1980)].

President Truman's appearances in television drama are also framed in relation to the world events that defined his term. Often, equal attention is given to his personal style, with several early depictions focusing on the president's down-to-earth manner. Many of these dramas were broadcast in the 1970s. They often contrasted Truman's "plain speaking" image with then President Nixon's less candid style. In 1975, *Give 'Em Hell Harry*, portrayed President Truman in a one-man show by James Whitmore. A year later, another one-man drama, *Harry S. Truman: Plain Speaking*, won an Emmy award for its chronicle of the life and political career of the thirty-third president. Based on Truman's writings, the drama focuses on the president's life from childhood to his tenure in the White House. Also in 1976, ABC Theatre broadcast *Collision Course: Truman vs MacArthur*, a teleplay concerning the working relationship between the president and the general. That same year, Truman is the subject of *Meeting at Potsdam*, this time played by Ed Flanders. Other portrayals of the president include *Tail Gunner Joe* (1977), *Day One* (1989) and *Hiroshima* (1995). For many critics, the most successful depiction of Truman is by actor Gary Sinese in 1995's *Truman*.[9] In each of these productions, "the man from Missouri" is portrayed as an honest, humble, and sincere leader.

Perhaps the only modern president to achieve a mythic status similar to Lincoln and the founding fathers is John Kennedy. Assassinated in 1963,

Kennedy was a young, engaging president whose death was deeply mourned by the American people. For some, the loss of his presidency became a symbol of unfulfilled promise. However, Kennedy also had a controversial personal life, and television's dramatic recreations often focus on both the private and public side of the president. On the political side, *The Missiles of October* is a 1974 drama that focuses on Kennedy's handling of the Cuban missile crisis. The production depicts the president's fear and resolve as he struggles to prevent war without sacrificing national security. Several dramas combine elements of Kennedy's personal and political life, including the miniseries *Kennedy* (1983), *Hoover vs. Kennedy: The Second Civil War* (1987), *The Kennedys of Massachusetts* (1990), and *JFK: Reckless Youth* (1993), which depicts the first thirty years of the president's life. These intimate depictions of the president often focus on his charm, romantic affairs, and turbulent personal relationships.

Other presidents of the modern era appear with less frequency in dramatic television productions. President Eisenhower is in both *Tail Gunner Joe* (1987) and *J. Edgar Hoover* (1987). Lyndon Johnson is the focus of *LBJ: The Early Years* (1987) and also appears in *J. Edgar Hoover* (1987) and *Hoover vs. Kennedy* (1987). In *Backstairs at the White House* (1979), a miniseries focusing on a family who served the presidency over fifty-two years, many presidents appear including Taft, Wilson, Harding, Coolidge, Hoover, Franklin Roosevelt, Truman, and Eisenhower.

For the most part, the television dramas exploring Richard Nixon's presidency focus on the scandal of Watergate and the president's resignation. Emphasizing Nixon's deceit, they offer a picture of a suspicious and paranoid leader who was corrupted by power. *Blind Ambition* (1979) is a four-part drama about the Watergate affair that includes scenes recreated from transcripts of White House tapes. In 1989, *The Final Days* depicts those troubled times, and *Kissinger and Nixon* (1995) focuses on the president's relationship with his aide.[10]

In general, the depictions of Ronald Reagan in television drama support his image as an amiable president who often favored stories over facts. In productions including *Guts and Glory: The Rise and Fall of Oliver North* (1989), *Without Warning: The James Brady Story* (1991), and *The Day Reagan was Shot* (2001), this characterization of Reagan frames the president as somewhat disengaged from politics and makes his aides and advisors the central subjects.

Documentary

Because it is concerned with depicting real events, the television documentary may be considered distinct from the medium's dramatic forms. Whereas documentaries, like drama, are organized around the idea of narrative, their storytelling function is often educational in nature. Although the documentary is widely found on television channels such as The History Channel and Discovery, television's more popular commercial networks have merged the documentary with traditional drama to form docudramas— a blurring of fact and fiction and entertainment and information.

As with drama, television documentary treatments of the presidency often focus on the early founders and presidents whose administrations are marked by significant events. President Lincoln is the subject of a 1992 documentary entitled *Lincoln* that examines the president's personal and political life through letters, speeches, and diaries. Almost a decade later, Lincoln is again the subject of a documentary in *The American Experience: Abraham and Mary Lincoln: A House Divided* (2001). This six-part series uses archival photographs, interviews with experts, and the written words of both the president and his wife to construct their dual biographies.

Popular PBS filmmaker Ken Burns directed a two-part documentary on Thomas Jefferson for PBS in 1997. Simply entitled *Thomas Jefferson*, it examines the political and family life of the president. Burns constructs the plot around the three most recognized ideas in the Declaration of Independence: "life," "liberty," and the "pursuit of happiness."

In an earlier PBS documentary, John Quincy Adams and John Adams were the subjects of *The Adams Chronicles* (1976), a thirteen-part series that focused on the personal triumphs and tragedies of the Adams family. Several early presidents were also the focus of *Founding Fathers* (2000), a production for The History Channel. Also in 2000, directors Phillip and Peter Kunhardt explored the presidency in a ten-hour documentary series called *The American President*. More recent presidents, including Kennedy, Truman, Nixon, Bush, and Clinton, have also been the subjects of documentaries. Althoughsome productions trace the candidates' rise to office, other documentaries focus on the major events that marked a particular presidency, including the Gulf War and the terrorist attacks of September 11.

Comedy/Variety

Presidents have been the subjects of television variety programming since the early days of broadcasting, and the appearance of presidential candidates may be traced to the early 1960s. Although television's drama formats recreate the presidency's triumphs and tragedies, its comedy formats provide benign outlets for criticism and dissent. Experiencing the president in this way allows the television audience to find humor in both the institution and the men who occupy it.

As television's comedy/variety formats made their debut, so too did the genre's irreverent treatment of the president. In 1964 the NBC network premiered *That Was The Week That Was*, a show that presented topical satire in the form of one-liners, songs, and skits. Originally a BBC program, the American version of *TW3* (as it was popularly known) featured David Frost as a principle performer. The show offered satirical sketches of presidential candidates that often combined comments from studio performers with footage of the candidates. In one skit, the show's performers suggest that the answer to the Republican Party's 1965 attempt to change its image is to put on a topical humor television show with Barry Goldwater and Richard Nixon as hosts.[11] Eventually, the sharp political satire of *TW3* pushed the show into numerous battles with network censors that ultimately resulted in a forced hiatus in the weeks before the 1964 presidential election.[12] Canceled after one season, *TW3* returned in 1985 and continued its satirical look at the presidency, this time with skits on Ronald Reagan. In one sketch mocking the president's intellect and childlike demeanor, Nancy suggests that the couple get some sleep because Reagan is meeting "one of the most important men in Latin America tomorrow," to which the president replies: "Oh! Ricardo Montalban. I hope he brings Tatoo!"—a reference to the lead actor from *Fantasy Island*, a popular television series of the time. (Broadcast April 21, 1985, on NBC).

The topical, political satire of *TW3* would be repeated by two other shows during the 1960s: *Rowan and Martin's Laugh-In* and *The Smothers Brothers Comedy Hour*. *Laugh-In* was fast sight gags, minisketches, and one-liners, whereas *The Smothers Brothers* focused on developed sketches and musical numbers. Both programs reflected the growing antiestablishment feeling of the decade. *Laugh-In* would occasionally direct its one-liners to presidential politics. In perhaps the most ironic statement by a future president, Richard Nixon, then a candidate, made a cameo appearance and said the show's popular catchphrase "Sock it to me?" The hosts of *The Smothers Brothers*, more caustic in their satire than the creators of *Laugh-In*, would engage in many fights with the CBS network over their social commentary. In one controversy, blacklisted folk singer Pete Seeger performed a song entitled "Waist Deep in the Big Muddy," whose political undertones were clearly intended as a criticism of President Johnson and the Vietnam War.[13] The political process also came under comic attack from show regular Pat Paulsen, who ran the fictitious "Pat Paulsen for President Campaign."

With the cancellation of *The Smothers Brothers*, presidential satire on television declined until NBC debuted *Saturday Night Live* (*SNL*) in the fall of 1975. Featuring live sketches, *SNL* reintroduced television audiences to presidential comedy with skits focusing on the clumsiness of President Ford. As played by comedian Chevy Chase, Ford would "appear" throughout the show's first two seasons as bumbling and accident-prone. Ron Nessen, Ford's press secretary, quickly became aware of the show's growing popularity and saw the skits as a good public relations opportunity. He commented later that "you win by showing you can laugh at yourself."[14] Nessen eventually appeared as guest host, with President Ford taping a few lines for the broadcast, including the show's signature opening, "live from

New York, it's Saturday Night."[15] The impact of *SNL* on Ford's defeat during the 1976 election is unclear, but for those involved, including Dick Cheney, Ford's chief of staff; Nessen; and many of the show's cast members, the impressions were believed to be a significant contributing factor.[16]

Presidential satire, specifically the impersonation of presidents, became a fixture on *SNL* that still exists today. Throughout the years, comedians have played presidents from Nixon to George W. Bush.[17] Whereas the Ford impersonations were based on slapstick, the later impersonations were more authentic in terms of voice and mannerisms. Dana Carvey's impression of George Bush for *SNL* was popular with both viewers and the president, who even asked Carvey to perform the impersonation at the White House shortly after he lost reelection.[18] In 2000, the impersonations of George W. Bush and Al Gore by Will Ferrell and Daryl Hammond, respectively, prompted the real-life candidates to join the show and poke fun at themselves. Perhaps Bush and Gore recognized what Ron Nessen had understood years earlier: Presidents (and candidates) who were seen to embrace *SNL*'s satire could deflect some of its effect, demonstrate their sense of humor, and (more strategically) reach a large segment of potential voters.

In 2001, the first situation comedy featuring a standing president as its central character premiered on the cable channel Comedy Central. Canceled after eight episodes, *That's My Bush*, created by Matt Stone and Trey Parker, was a satirical take on the Bush presidency. While the Associated Press suggested that the series was "juvenile, coarse, and impishly determined to offend," critics at the *Washington Post* called it "tasteless, appalling and funny as hell."[19] The show's claim to humor aside, most commentators agree that it was more a parody of the situation comedy form rather than a parody of the president. Although *That's My Bush* did satirize the president personally and politically (various episodes spoofed Bush's position on abortion and the death penalty), the humor derived more from the idea of the president as the bumbling head of a household rather than the incompetent leader of the nation.

Talk Shows

Television talk shows have become a powerful way for presidential candidates to reach voters. Whereas early talk shows relied on presidential impersonators as guests, later programs welcomed real candidates who recognized the potential offered by the format.

The earliest version of the talk show began in September 1954 with the NBC network broadcast of *Tonight*, a 90-minute program hosted by Steve Allen. A combination of talk, jokes, sketches, and guests, the series was taken over by Jack Paar in 1957 and broadcast as *The Jack Paar Program* on NBC from 1962 to 1965. In a 1962 broadcast, impressionist Vaughn Meader plays

John Kennedy. In one skit, Meader answers random questions from the studio audience as if he were Kennedy at a press conference. The joke is replayed in a similar sketch during which Meader is seated at the Kennedy family dinner table. During the course of the meal, the "president" takes mundane questions from his family, including wife Jackie and brother Bobby, and answers them with the same tone and formality he would use with the press. The scene's humor comes from a gentle mocking of the president's distinctive accent rather than an attempt at biting political or personal commentary.

Since the debut of *The Jack Paar Program*, the talk show has become a popular addition to the broadcast schedule. Talk shows offer presidential candidates a chance to show their personal side, as well as their sense of humor. One of the first candidates to take advantage of the more intimate nature of talk shows was Bill Clinton. His 1992 appearance on *The Arsenio Hall Show* gave him the opportunity to personally reflect on the effect of the Los Angeles riots and to discuss his plans for "reconnecting people to the American dream."(Broadcast on Fox on June 3, 1992). In a memorable moment, he joined the studio band and played the saxophone, a performance that was consistent with his attempts to court young voters.[20] Eight years later, presidential candidates Al Gore and George Bush made separate appearances on *Oprah*, *The Tonight Show*, and *Late Night with David Letterman*. They shared good-natured jokes and their campaign messages, hoping to increase their appeal to the programs' diverse audiences.

Television coverage has made the president accessible on both personal and political levels. Although this coverage most often takes the form of news broadcasts, television drama and entertainment programs also make a significant contribution to our experience of the president. Unlike the news, these formats connect us to the humanity of the presidency by sharing the personal stories of our leaders. In television's drama formats, presidents are shown as husbands, fathers, and friends, and entertainment programs allow us to criticize and find humor in our government. Both formats offer a shared sense of our national leader that moves beyond understanding the presidential image as a strictly "factual" broadcast, ultimately providing insights into our nation's history and ourselves.

Notes

1. Richard Paterson, "Drama and Entertainment," in *Television: An International History*, ed. Anthony Smith with Richard Paterson (Oxford University Press, 1998), 57.

2. Throughout the coverage of the 2000 presidential campaign, George W. Bush's inexperience was often an issue. Choosing to show Bush actively

running the government was perhaps a response to those critics who suggested that he could not. The episode, however, did not silence all of Bush's critics. Aaron Sorkin, creator and executive producer of *The West Wing*, claimed in an interview with Tad Friend of *The New Yorker* that the White House had purposely inflated Bush's schedule so that he appeared busier than normal and that the show was "a valentine to Bush." (Tad Friend, 2002, "*West Wing* Watch: Snookered by Bush," *The New Yorker* 78 (March 4):30–2) Sorkin's controversial accusations were widely reported.

3. Paterson, "Drama and Entertainment," 62.

4. Stuart Leibiger, "George Washington, The Crossing, and Revolutionary Leadership" in *Hollywood's White House: The American Presidency in Film and History*, ed. Peter Rollins and John O'Connor (Lexington: University Press of Kentucky, 2003), 20.

5. Leibiger, "George Washington," 19.

6. Paterson, "Drama and Entertainment," 58.

7. Bryan Rommel-Ruiz, "Redeeming Lincoln, Redeeming the South: Representations of Abraham Lincoln in D.W. Griffith's *The Birth of a Nation* and Historical Scholarship," in *Hollywood's White House: The American Presidency in Film and History*, ed. Peter Rollins and John O'Connor (Lexington: University Press of Kentucky, 2003), 77.

8. J. Tillapaugh, "Theodore Roosevelt and the Rough Riders: A Century of Leadership in Film," in *Hollywood's White House: The American Presidency in Film and History*, ed. Peter Rollins and John O'Connor (Lexington: University Press of Kentucky, 2003), 98.

9. Alvin Marill, "Hail to the Chiefs," *Films in Review* 47 (1996):43.

10. During 1995, the relationship between a president and his aides was also a feature of cinematic representations of the presidency. A central focus of *The American President* is the interaction of fictional president Andrew Shephard (Michael Douglas) with various aides. The film lead to the development of *The West Wing*, a television series that heavily features a president's relationship with his aides.

11. This episode was broadcast on April 20, 1965.

12. David Marc, *Comic Visions: Television Comedy and American Culture*, 2nd edition (Malden, Mass: Blackwell, 1997), 102.

13. Bert Spector, "A Clash of Cultures: The Smothers Brothers vs. CBS Television," in *American History/American Television: Interpreting the Video Past*, ed. John O'Connor (NY: Frederick Ungar, 1985), 160.

14. Doug Hill and Jeff Weingrad, *Saturday Night Live: A Backstage History of Saturday Night Live* (New York: Vintage Books, 1986), 180.

15. Ibid., 182.

16. For a more detailed discussion on the potential effects of Chase's impersonation on the 1976 election, see Hill and Weingrad (1986).

17. A compilation of these impersonations is available on the video, *Saturday Night Live Presidential Bash* (1992).

18. Elizabeth Bland and Lina Lofaro, "Impersonating the President: A Ha-Ha Away from Power," *Time* March 19, 2001, 72.

19. Mark Armstrong, "Comedy Central's Boffo Bush!" *Eonline*, April 5, 2001, http://www.eonline.com/News/Items/0,1,8072,00.html (accessed February 21, 2003).

20. A significant part of Bill Clinton's presidential campaign strategy was to appeal to young voters. In addition to The Arsenio Hall Show (where the goal was also to appeal to African-American voters), he went on MTV, where he played the saxophone and answered both political and personal questions—including one on what type of underwear he preferred. Clinton later credited his appearance on the "Choose or Loose" forum with energizing young people's interest in politics. ("Choose or Loose" was a town-hall style meeting on MTV where presidential candidates discussed political issues and answered questions from an audience of young adults.) This one was broadcast on June 16, 1992, and hosted by former VJ Tabitha Soren and former CNN anchor Catherine Crier. The fact that after his appearance America had the highest voter turnout for 18- to 24-year-olds since 18-year-olds were given the vote indicates that he was right.

Television Show Bibliography

A large part of the research for this chapter was conducted at The Museum of Television and Radio (Los Angeles and New York). Open to both the public and researchers, the museum offers facilities to search and screen its television and radio archives.

Abe Lincoln in Illinois, The Pulitzer Prize Playhouse, ABC Television, Robert Sherwood (play), October 20, 1950.

Abe Lincoln in Illinois, The Lux Video Theatre, CBS Television, Richard Goode (director), February 12, 1951.

Abe Lincoln in Illinois, Hallmark Hall of Fame, NBC Television, George Schaefer (director), Robert Hautung (writer), Robert Sherwood (play), February 5, 1964.

Abraham Lincoln, Westinghouse Studio One, CBS Television, Paul Nickell (director), David Shaw (writer), John Drinkwater (story), May 26, 1952.

The Adams Chronicles, PBS Television, Virginia Kassel (director), Sherman Yellan, Millard Lampell, Anne Howard Bailey, Corinne Jacker, Sam Hall, Roger Hirson, Ian Hunter, Tad Mosel, Philip Reisman Jr. (writers), 1976.

The American Experience: Abraham and Mary Lincoln: A House Divided, PBS Television, David Grubin (director), David Grubin, Geoffrey Ward (writers), 2001.

The American President, PBS Television, Philip Kunhardt Jr., Peter Kunhardt (directors), April 9–13, 2000.

Backstairs at the White House, NBC Television, Michael O'Herlihy (director), Lillian Rogers Parks (book), Frances Spatz Leighton (book), Gwen Bagni, Paul Dubov (writers), 1979.

Blind Ambition, NBC Television, George Schaefer (director), Taylor Branch (book), John Dean (book), Maureen Dean (book), Stanley Greenberg (writer), May 20-23, 1979.

The Bush White House: Inside the Real West Wing, NBC Television, January 23, 2002.

Captains and the Kings, NBC Television, Douglas Heyes, Allen Reisner (directors), Taylor Caldwell (novel), Douglas Heyes, Elinor Karpf, Steven Karpf (adaptation), September 30, 1976.

Collision Course: Truman vs. MacArthur, Anthony Page (director), Ernest Kinoy (story, teleplay), 1976.

The Crossing, A&E, Rober Harmon (director), Howard Fast (writer), January 10, 2000.

Davy Crockett: King of the Wild Frontier, Three episode compilation of *Disneyland*, ABC Television, (*Davy Crockett: Indian Fighter*, December 15, 1954; *Davy Crockett Goes to Congress*, January 26, 1955; *Davy Crockett at the Alamo*, February 23, 1955), Theatrical release, June 1955, Norman Foster (director).

Day One, CBS Television, Joseph Sargent (director), Peter Wyden (book), David Rintels (teleplay), 1989.

The Day Reagan was Shot, Showtime, Cyrus Nowrasteh (director, writer), December 9, 2001.

Dream West, CBS Television, Dick Lowry (director), Evan Hunter (writer), David Nevin (novel), April 13–15, 1986.

Eleanor & Franklin, ABC Television, Daniel Petrie (director), James Costigan (writer), Joseph Lash (book), January 11, 1976.

Eleanor & Franklin: The White House Years, ABC Television, Daniel Petrie (director), James Costigan (writer), Joseph Lash (book), 1977.

Emma: Queen of the South Seas, Fox Television, John Banas (director), Geoffrey Dutton (novel), Ann Chapman, Rob Chapman, Petru Popescu (teleplay), 1988.

Enola Gay: The Men, the Mission and the Atomic Bomb, David Lowell Rich (director), Millard Kaufman, James Poe (writers), Gordon Thomas (book), Max Morgan Witts (book), 1980.

FDR: The Last Year, NBC Television, Anthony Page (director), Jim Bishop (book), Stanley Greenberg (writer), 1980.

The Final Days, ABC Television, Richard Pearce (director), Bob Woodward (book), Carl Bernstein (book), Hugh Whitemore (teleplay), 1989.

First Family's Holiday Gift to America: A Tour of the White House, Fox Television, Jeff Margolis (director), Dave Boone, Stephen Pouliot (writers), December 15, 2000.

Founding Fathers, History Channel, Mark Hufnail, Melissa Peltier (directors), Max Fletcher, Melissa Peltier (writers), 2000.

George Washington, CBS Television, Buzz Kulik (director), John Boothe, Richard Fielder (writers), James Flexner (biography), April 8, 10, 11, 1984.

George Washington II: The Forging of a Nation, CBS Television, William Graham (director), Richard Fielder (writer), James Flexner (biography), September 21–22, 1986.

George Washington and the Whisky Rebellion, William Francisco (director), 1974.

Give 'Em Hell Harry, CBS Television, Steve Binder (director), Samuel Gallu (writer), 1975.

Guts and Glory: The Rise and Fall of Oliver North, CBS Television, Mike Robe (director), Ben Bradlee Jr. (book), Mike Robe (teleplay), 1989.

Harry S. Truman: Plain Speaking, PBS Television, Daniel Petrie (director), Merle Miller (book), 1976.

Hiroshima, Showtime, Koreyoshi Kurahara, Roger Spottiswoode (directors), John Hopkins, Toshiro Ishido (writers), August 6, 1995.

Hoover vs. the Kennedys: The Second Civil War, Syndicate Movie, CTV Television, Michael O'Herlihy (director), 1987.

J. Edgar Hoover, Showtime, Robert Collins (director), 1987.

JFK: Reckless Youth, ABC Television, Harry Winer (director), Nigel Hamilton (book), William Broyles Jr. (teleplay), November 21, 23, 1993.

Kennedy, NBC Television, Jim Goddard (director), Reg Gadney (writer), 1983.

The Kennedys of Massachusettes, ABC Television, Lamont Johnson (director), Doris Kearns Goodwin (book), William Hanley (teleplay), 1990.

Kissinger & Nixon, TNT, Daniel Petrie (director), Walter Isaacson (book), Lionel Chetwynd (teleplay), December 10, 1995.

LBJ: The Early Years, NBC Television, Peter Werner (director), February 1, 1987.

Lincoln, NBC Television, George Schaefer (director), Loring Mandel (writer), Carl Sandburg (book), 1975.

Lincoln, NBC Television, Lamont Johnson (director), Gore Vidal (novel), Ernest Kinoy (teleplay), 1988.

Lincoln, ABC Television, Peter Kunhardt (director), Philip Kunhardt III, Philip Kunhardt Jr. (writers) 1992.

Meeting at Potsdam (AKA *Truman at Potsdam*), PBS Television, NBC Television, George Schaefer (director), Sidney Carroll (writer), Charles Mee Jr. (book), 1976.

The Missiles of October, ABC Television, Anthony Page (director), Stanley Greenberg (writer), December 18, 1974.

Mister Lincoln, PBS Television, Gordon Rigsby (director), Herbert Mitgang (writer), February 9, 1981.

The Patriots, NBC Television, George Schaefer (director), Robert Hartung (adaptation), Sidney Kingsley (play), 1963.

The Patriots (AKA: *The Hollywood Television Theatre: Patriots*), PBS Television, Bob Hankal, Robert Strane (directors), Sidney Kingsley (play), 1976.

The President of the United States at Home: White House Tour with President Harry S. Truman, CBS Television, May 3, 1952.

Primetime Live, ABC Television, Roger Goodman (director), September 21, 1989.

The Rebels, ABC Television, Russ Mayberry (director), Sean Bain, Robert Cinader (writers), John Jakes (novel), 1979.

Sally Hemings: An American Scandal, CBS Television, Charles Haid (director), Tina Andrews (writer), February 13, 16, 2000.

Tail Gunner Joe, ABC Television, Jud Taylor (director), Lane Slate (writer), 1977.

That Was the Week That Was, NBC Television, Marshall Jamison, Hal Gurnee (directors 1963), James Elson (director 1965), Bruce Gower (director 1985), 1963–1965, 1985.

Thomas Jefferson, PBS Television, Ken Burns (director), Geoffrey Ward (writer), February 18–19, 1997.

Tour of the White House with Mrs. John F. Kennedy, CBS Television, NBC Television, Franklin Schaffner (director), February 14, 1962.

Truman, HBO Television, Frank Pierson (director), David McCullough (book), Thomas Rickman (teleplay), 1995.

War and Remembrance, ABC Television, Dan Curtis (director), Earl Wallace, Dan Curtis, Herman Wouk (teleplay), 1988.

War of 1812, Brian McKenna (director, writer), Terence McKenna (writer), 1999.

The Wild, Wild West, CBS Television, "The Night of the Inferno," Episode 1.1, Richard Sarafian (director), Gilbert Ralston (writer), September 17, 1965.

The Wild, Wild West Revisited, CBS Television, Burt Kennedy (director), William Bowers (writer), 1979.

The Winds of War, ABC Television, Dan Curtis (director), Herman Wouk (writer), 1983.

Without Warning: The James Brady Story, HBO, Michael Toshiyuki Uno (director), Mollie Dickenson (book), Robert Bolt (teleplay), 1991.

World War II: When Lions Roared, ABC Television, Joseph Sargent (director), David Rintels (writer), 1994.

INDEX

About the Editor and the Contributors

John Matviko teaches communication and popular culture courses at West Liberty State College. He holds a master's degree in speech—public address and rhetoric from the University of Pittsburgh. John has long been active in popular culture organizations; he was a founding member of the Mid-Atlantic Popular/American Culture Association and for eight years he produced the American Culture Association's newsletter and served on their executive board. John's research interests include popular culture, media ethics, television studies, and rock and roll.

Melissa Crawley teaches in the cultural studies department of Macquarie University in Sydney, Australia. She received her Ph.D. from Northwestern University in radio/television/film; her dissertation examined the representation of the president in the television series *The West Wing*. Her research interests include television studies, representation and identity, and presidential politics and the media.

Sandra Czernek teaches history at West Liberty State College. She holds a master's degree in history from West Virginia University. Her research interests include the Gilded Age, art history, and Appalachian culture.

Juilee Decker teaches art history at Georgetown College (Georgetown, Ky.). She received her Ph.D. from the joint program in art history and museum studies at Case Western Reserve University and the Cleveland Museum of Art in 2003. She has published essays on Victorian popular culture, American public sculpture, and English prints.

Tony Giffone teaches in the Department of English and Humanities at Farmingdale State University of New York. He received his Ph.D. from

New York University and has long been interested in the uses of the historical past in popular culture. In 2002, he coedited a special edition of the *Mid-Atlantic Almanack* on aspects of Victorian culture in contemporary popular culture.

Arthur Holst is Legislative and Regulatory Affairs Manager for the Philadelphia Water Department. He earned his Ph.D. in political science at Temple University. Arthur has contributed to a number of reference works on various subjects related to political science, history, and the environment. He is also an adjunct faculty member at Widener University in the Master of Public Administration Program.

Benjamin Hufbauer teaches American art and architectural history in the Department of Fine Arts at the University of Louisville. He received his Ph.D. from the University of California at Santa Barbara. Benjamin is currently completing a book for the University Press of Kansas on presidential commemoration dating from 1900.

Elliot King teaches courses in journalism, Web development, advertising and public relations, and popular culture at Loyola College in Maryland, where he is the founder of the Digital Media Lab. He holds a Ph.D. in media sociology from the University of California, San Diego. Elliot has written six books including *The Online Journalist* (with Randy Reddick).

Timothy W. Kneeland teaches political and intellectual history at Nazareth College of Rochester. He earned his Ph.D. in history from the University of Oklahoma. Timothy is the author of *PushButton Psychiatry: History of Electroshock* and various encyclopedia entries and book reviews on political history and the history of science.

Hanna Miller is a freelance exhibition developer based in Asheville, North Carolina. She received her Master of Arts in American history museum studies from the State University of New York's Cooperstown Graduate Program. She is currently at work on a style guide for exhibit-label writers.

Laura G. Pattillo teaches English and is Co-Artistic Director of Cap & Bells Dramatic Society at Saint Joseph's University in Philadelphia. She received her Ph.D. in English from Louisiana State University. Her research interests are dramatic literature and Southern literature, and she plans to turn her dissertation, *Appalachia on Stage: The Southern Mountaineer in American Drama*, into a book.

Jerry Rodnitzky teaches American cultural history at the University of Texas at Arlington. He holds a Ph.D. in history from the University of

Illinois. Jerry has authored four books, including *Minstrels of the Dawn: The Folk-Protest Signer As a Cultural Hero* and, more recently, *Jazz Age Boomtown* and *Feminist Phoenix: The Rise and Fall of a Feminist Counterculture.* He is a founding and continuing advisory editor of the journal *Popular Music and Sciety.*

Katina R. Stapleton currently teaches political science and is a Senior Research Associate in the Campbell Institute for Public Affairs at Syracuse University. She received her doctorate in American politics from Duke University with a concentration in political communication. Katina's research interest is the intersections of popular culture, the media, politics, and public policy.

Scott F. Stoddart is the Executive Director of Special Programs and the Director of Academic Advancement at Marymount Manhattan College. He has published articles on the fiction of Henry James, E. M. Forster, Stephen Crane, and F. Scott Fitzgerald and on the musical plays of Stephen Sondheim. He is currently at work on a book about popular culture in the 1980s for Greenwood Press.